11, 96

Tom,

To great windy
memories

Rob

ALSO BY C. L. RAWLINS

A Ceremony on Bare Ground

SKY'S WITNESS

A Year in the Wind River Range

C. L. Rawlins

Illustrations by Hannah Hinchman

A John Macrae Book
Henry Holt and Company New York

Henry Holt and Company, Inc.
Publishers since 1866
115 West 18th Street
New York, New York 10011

Henry Holt® is a registered trademark
of Henry Holt and Company, Inc.

Library of Congress Cataloging-in-Publication Data
Rawlins, Clem Lewis.
Sky's witness : a year in the wind river range / C. L.
Rawlins.—1st ed.   p.   cm.
"A John Macrae book."
1. Natural history—Wyoming—Wind River Range. 2. Air—
Pollution—Environmental aspects—Wyoming—Wind River Range.
3. Acid deposition—Environmental aspects—Wyoming—
Wind River Range. I. Title.
QH105.W8R38   1992   92-8698
508.787′6—dc20   CIP

ISBN 0-8050-1597-3

First Edition—1993

Designed by Paula R. Szafranski

Printed in the United States of America
All first editions are printed on acid-free paper. ∞
10 9 8 7 6 5 4 3 2

Contents

To Thomas Jefferson Lyon

The moon is where it belongs—in the sky.
And though I sing this one little song,
In the song there is no Zen.

Han Shan, *Cold Mountain Poems*

Part I: Dark of the Year

1

The landscape was there, and more than ever he felt he could not reach it. The rocks and the sky were everywhere, ready to absolve him, but as always he carried the obstacle within him.

Paul Bowles, *The Sheltering Sky*

Wind tears through sage. Frozen to each shaggy twig are chunks of snow that bob with every gust. Higher up, under a long cloud that hides the peaks, there is new snow gleaming, blank white against the mountain blue. Above us the whole sky moves. Clouds, light, great streams of air all rush over our heads in silence.

The air takes voice from what it touches: our bodies, the sage, the bare aspen fringing the hills. It roars, groans, threatens. John slams the door of the pickup and yells a question, but the wind rattles the hood of my parka and I have to yell back "What?"

In December, snowstorms give way to wind, a hard, blue wind that scours the new snow from the Wyoming desert and blasts it for miles. It looks like a white flood, faster than any river. At first, the flakes bounce along the surface, dislodging others. As the wind grows stronger they fly again, miles from where they first came to rest. At last they drift into the lee of a bank or a boulder or a sage. Shorn of their complex, fragile dendrites, they sinter into a hard crust.

Damned wind, it slaps the door out of my grip, bang against the hinge. John yells his question again, and I shake my head and point at

1

the sky. As I hump my big, red pack from the truckbed to the sledge, grains of snow hiss around my boots, parting like stream current.

"Batteries," John yells next to my ear, red nose poking from the burrow of his hood, "did we change the ones in the boombox?"

"Yeah. I did." I'm worried about the clouds still roaring around the peaks, about the condition of the snow up there. John is worried about theme music for the adventure. We have a battered cassette player to cheer up the nights in basecamp, though I would just as soon read. He replies, turning back to the truck. The wind snatches his words. I nod agreement. It's too cold to argue.

The clouds seem lower and thicker, but that may be my imagination. The wind is definitely stronger on this bare ridge, a boulder-strewn moraine that marks the end of a glacial advance. It gusts and shoves us sideways as we circle from truck to sledge, forcing its hands up under our coats, stroking cold fingers along our wrists between glove and sleeve.

Some kinds of cold can be measured: the gust of an arctic front, the change from sunlight to shadow, the fluid ache that slips up the bones of your hands when you touch metal. Gloved, hatted, and layered as we load the sledge, we're prepared for those. Yet as I look up at the long, streaming cap of cloud that hides the summits of the Continental Divide, I feel a private chill. Right now it scares me to look up at these mountains.

I've been loyal, going into them year after year. Without pretending to own them, I've made them the pivot on which my life turns. Today they look sullen and beautiful, cloaked in storm. As the clouds run, the sky's light shifts in huge, soft planes, stealing the depth from snow-covered faces. It's impossible to judge distance and slope. The snow burns blue and white, dimensionless, a vertical curtain hung in the air. This is a light and a weather that raise my fears, though never enough to make me turn and go.

I love the winter mountains, but dread them too, as any sane person should. In a city it's easy to think of the earth as fragile. Out here it feels otherwise. This place doesn't seem weak. This earth won't shatter at our touch.

What seems fragile is how we think of ourselves. Out here I feel the immensity that lies beyond thought. In our minds, we make a small, safe place in which to live. But the world is a presence beyond our acts and dreams. There are blue mountains and white storms. We can prepare, but not predict.

There's a point on each trip when the rules change. In that moment—a white-out crossing a pass or the boom as a weak layer of snow releases—I realize that everything matters except good intentions. The mountains are big and thoughtless, awake without eyes, asleep without dreams.

We finish loading the sledge, cover the gear with a white canvas tarp, and dog it down. The two black snowmobiles squat on the frozen dirt of the road, snow drifting around them into the season's last tiretracks. Their blunt noses point at the peaks. Ugly beasts, but they'll get us to where the skiing begins, twenty miles on. We hitch the sledge to John's machine. I'll break the trail. In the west, the sky has opened, but the Divide is still hidden by wind-driven cloud. I tie my skis and poles to the rear rack while John paws through his daypack.

"Ready?"

John locks the truck and we pull the starter cords. A dome of noise slams down around us. We'll head up the snow-covered road to Big Sandy Opening where it ends at about nine thousand feet. Using a tiny cabin as base, we'll continue on skis to Black Joe Lake where a snow collector waits. Starting up the windswept road, we dodge rocks and scoured patches of earth above the fenceline of Big Sandy Ranch, log buildings huddled above a frozen creek, deserted in winter. The road loops around the haymeadows and fences, and we bear left near Grass Creek to follow the air's way up from wind-stunted sage through outcrops of reddish granite. The wind has exposed rocks and gravel, so we swerve to follow tongues of snow, hearing an occasional scrape or screech from the runners. The road climbs in wild curves around the rocky reefs, through leafless aspen into the shelter of lodgepole pine, where we gain deeper snow.

This is perhaps my fortieth ski trip into the Wind River Range. John and I are going up to collect snow samples near the Continental Divide. Our purpose is to monitor air pollution. Even in this range, far from large cities, there is concern about acid rain and snow. To the southwest, upwind, is the Overthrust Belt, perhaps the largest remaining deposit of oil and natural gas in the lower forty-eight states. In 1981, oil companies formed a consortium to drill a deposit of sour gas—so-called because of its high sulfur content—and process over a billion cubic feet per day, releasing unsalable gases and by-products into the air. When sulfur goes into the air, it forms sulfuric acid.

The Forest Service asked for an environmental impact statement, and the state of Wyoming placed terms in the permit that required field studies in the wilderness areas—Bridger, Fitzpatrick, and Popo Agie—downwind. Cooperative agreements were signed to start the process. Money would come from the companies, the state, and the Forest Service. Monitoring for airborne acids would begin on the rain and snow as well as on sensitive alpine lakes, with the Forest Service doing most of the actual work.

One force behind the effort was Al Galbraith, a genial hydrologist from Jackson, who saw a chance to start a pilot study of air pollution in the high mountains of the West. Though computer models had issued from universities and consulting companies, there was little field data. Galbraith and his helper, Bo Stuart, located designs for rain and snow collectors, wrote a ream of guidelines, and then hired some of the rougher elements to set things up in the mountains.

One problem was that the Forest Service had to play by the rules of the Wilderness Act. It forbade the use of motorized transport and permanent installations, even to protect wilderness values. This was bad news for bureaucrats: no scenic helicopter flights or well-heated research stations overlooking alpine lakes. The monitoring effort would have to depend on the means the act allowed—horses, hiking boots, and skis—which is how we barbarians got into the game.

I look back at John, and he waves his gloved hand forward and down. We creep under the skirts of the storm, pellets of snow pecking at us, then into a patch of clear air. The pines look black. It will be dark in an hour. We reach a height where we can see out to the west, over the dark spine of Muddy Ridge, mostly rock with a fringe of battered pine. Beyond that, the high desert rolls like a sea. There are ranches hidden, a few roads, but nothing marks them for the eye. There is a river, the Seeds-ke-dee Agie, the Prairie Hen River, the one we call the Green, but it tucks into the folded land. From here, the most apparent features are the scale of the country and the sweep of the oncoming clouds.

Like a huge arrowhead, the valley of the upper Green points

north, hemmed by mountains. To the west are the Wyoming and Salt River ranges, and to the north is the Gros Ventre Range, which stretches up to form the east rampart of Jackson Hole, all layered of sedimentary rock, limestone, sandstone, and shale. On the other flank, running southeast to northwest, is the highest and most geologically massive range, the Wind Rivers.

Crossing cold desert at about seven thousand feet, the prevailing southwesterlies must clear the wall of summits that marks the Continental Divide. For a hundred miles, peaks rise above thirteen thousand feet, less a barrier to the prevailing wind than they have long been to human travel. Between Union Pass, at the north end, where the granite-hearted Wind Rivers join a sedimentary plateau that links them to the Absarokas, and South Pass, where they descend to the topographic puzzle of the Sweetwater River and the Great Divide Basin, no paved road crosses the crest. There are trails, but most traverse high passes and are not easy routes even on foot.

It's cold country, with the yearly average temperature around three degrees F above freezing in the basin and ten degrees lower in the mountains above. The Shoshoni walked it as a summering ground, hunting and gathering in the valleys, and climbed into the mountains for bighorn hunts, ceremonials, or simply for the beauty. They have a tradition that the souls of the dead go up into these mountains to spend eternity. In fall the bands moved south to the desert or east to the relative warmth of the Wind River Valley. As temperatures edged toward the precipice of winter, sometimes eighty degrees F below freezing, the great herds, buffalo, elk, and antelope, moved out, too, leaving the upper basin to wind and snow.

The country is defined as much by weather as by rock. Summer storms gather over the desert to the southwest, then break on the granite reefs of the range in howling, brief rains punctuated by lightning or, high up, pellet snow. Rising air is cooled as its pressure decreases, shedding about 3.5 degrees F for every thousand feet. The colder this air becomes, the less water it can hold, and the excess moisture condenses. Above freezing, this condensation becomes droplets of fog or rainwater; below freezing, it emerges as ice, of which snow is a fine and airy form.

In winter the storm track shifts to the northwest, bringing down arctic air. Then, the difference between clarity and snowstorm may be just a few degrees, or a thousand feet. On days like this, the Wind Rivers wear a muffler of icy cloud, a stationary snow flurry that starts below ten thousand feet and ends on the lee side of the range, where the air has lost water and gained heat in its descent.

The snowcloud looms over our heads, dusting us. We stop and shut off the engines to stretch and warm our hands. The road winds through glacial features, threading meadows of sandy outwash, climbing the rubble of moraines. After twenty roundabout miles, we reach Big Sandy Opening, a glacial meadow that undulates along the base of high peaks like the dragon at St. George's feet. The cabin is hidden in the pines on the dragon's right shoulder. There are no fresh machine or ski tracks in the meadow. The wind has been at work. In this year of drought, the December snow is thin— about two feet on the level—and the heavy machines sink within a few inches of the dirt but grind on nevertheless, each carrying a bushel of snow on its hood.

The Opening is a two-mile gouge in bedrock filled with water-sorted sand, the outwash of a receding glacier. Big Sandy Creek meanders through it, joined by tributaries. There are low, curving hillocks and kettle ponds in the expanse between ranks of dark pine, all covered in snow. We are close to the cloud's belly. The winds buffet us as we head out into the open. I try to follow blown-in tracks, aiming for the culvert bridge over Temple Creek. Marty, my previous partner, once put his machine nose down in the black water. He was driving into a snowstorm and made up for not being able to see by going fast. The snow was deep that year, overhanging the banks of the stream. He survived, but it took hours to wrestle the snowmobile out. His recounting of it made me shudder every time.

The tail of my machine sideslips off a frozen track, and I spin out in loose snow, getting stuck. John stops his engine and wallows up to help me heave the machine back onto the track. Underway, I kneel on the seat, stretching up to see over the spindrift, trying to sense the contours and the hidden traps—stumps, boulders, and ponds not quite frozen hard.

So far, this is not bad. On other trips, we've been flipped, stuck, whited-out, and thoroughly pummeled by the rigors of mechanical transport. Before I got this job I had never driven a snowmobile. By necessity, I've learned how, but my greatest satisfaction is to get where I'm going and to shut it off. Our time on snowmobiles is filled with trouble. Marty, my partner for three winters of acid-rangering, got furious at their mechanical orneriness. I'd round a curve in the pines to see him kicking and cursing his balky mount as it wallowed, half rolled over in loose snow. Bad luck seems to hover around snowmobiles. So, to cut the racketing engines and clip into skis came as a relief.

We cross Temple Creek, the water showing black. The Opening is about a half-mile wide, rippled like a sea under the wind. In some spots, willows or the heads of wild grass rise from the white surface. They help me to recall the course of the road, to avoid sudden drops and boulder patches hidden by drift. We head to the turnoff for the cabin, a mile farther along, nicely hidden by the forest's edge. John waits while I pack a turnaround loop and take down the wire gate. Digging out a rolled machine in the dark is something I've done more than once. I circle to build my nerve. Then comes a full-throttle run to break trail up the hill. The black machine raises a plume of snow, trying to roll off the hill's shoulder into a thicket of willows. I heave my weight hard left. I steer in half-controlled swoops up through the pines toward the little shack, the jointed track spinning out in sugary snow, and pull the hill with the last gasp of momentum.

I circle the cabin, glad to see the board walls under their dark red paint. This was my home for several of the finer summers of my life. I smile at the white screen door and drop down the hill to pack a wider track for John and the sledge. At the turnaround I stop and wave him on. He idles up to the straightaway before the gate, then screws the throttle down, almost losing it where I did. I hear his boot whack the side of the machine as he throws his weight. He goes out of sight. Then the engine noise falls to an idle and stops. I follow him up to unload.

The inside of the cabin is white, with a saddle rack, a wooden table, and two bunks on the west wall. On the north, next to the bunks is a small propane stove, which can be turned on from the bed for morning coffee. Beside the stove is a propane refrigerator, old, with rounded corners, superfluous at the moment. This cabin is as much home to me as any place. The east wall holds an ingenious cupboard, covered by a tabletop that hinges out like a studio bed to be supported by a single leg. Next to it is a sink with a tap for cold water from the spring, which I never hooked up, preferring instead to carry a bucket. In the east corner by the door is a boxy coal stove, white enameled with a black iron top. The floor, of tongue-and-groove fir, is painted the same chocolate red as the exterior. The door is paned with glass and looks as if it should issue on flowerbeds rather than on ragged lodgepole and a garden of shadows.

At sunset, I step out. The sun descends from a layer of cloud and sends wild light into the lodgepoles for a moment before it dips into more cloud at the horizon. The air is colder now. I can hear draft roar up the stovepipe and the top plate's muffled clang as John

stokes the stove. Bright sparks scatter from the chimney's mouth. The west holds a faint, porcelain blue above low-ridged moraine hills. To the east, a waxing moon rises through a spear-garden of lodgepoles. The white trim on the cabin has gone blue, the walls violet. Through frost, the windows are a pale gold.

I look at the little house that was my home for—how many seasons? I started riding the range up here in 1981. I went out with two horses, ten days at a time, to check the grazing allotments. I spoke improvised Spanish to the shepherds, making friends with them. I loved the work. The rancher who became my nemesis—this is what I suppose—influenced the Forest Service to pull the money from my job the year after I caught him spreading strychnine. After we investigated, collected the stomachs of dead animals for analysis, and raised general hell, he got off with a timid lecture from the district ranger.

A letter came, informing me my riding job was no more. I called up and got stonewalled, but then heard about another job in the Winds, helping a hydrologist on a study of acid rain. They needed a horsepacker and wild man, someone who could get in and out of the mountains with grace. The swap, from grazing cop to acid ranger, appealed to me. After I changed jobs, the money for a range rider appeared again. My successor was an easy-going guy. He called this place the Cowboy Cabin. I call it *La Casita Perdida*. The Little Lost House.

I can hear the thump of the boombox. John is relaxing, which takes a lot of decibels. Is it the Screaming Blue Messiahs? Alpha Blondie? The Pixies? The walls absorb the words and only the bass escapes.

When I lived in this cabin I used to watch the sunset from one of the great boulders the glacier dropped along the slope. I walk south and west, ducking through the willows below the little spring, looking for moose tracks. There are two sets, partly filled with snow. In the gathering dark, I follow the route I walked when catching horses, through the willows into the pines and then into a small clearing.

A few sets of squirrel tracks converge on a cone cache under the biggest pine of all. A faint light clings to the horizon. To the west, across the Opening, is a round pond concealed by pines. In late summer its surface is rich with green pads and lilies that bloom clear yellow. With a cold night hovering, it's good to recall those water lilies of August. I picture the pond now, frozen around the dead, brown pads, the life gone down into the roots. I think of the life in those flowers as a liquid spark, waiting out the frozen months. Over the ice lies two feet of snow.

The light drains from the west as the cloudcap thins and the temperature plunges. The wind shifts to the northwest, bringing cold air off the North Pacific. The wind dies and a deeper cold grips the range along with night. When a polar air mass settles in, the last trace of moisture condenses in minute crystals that don't fall from any cloud: they blink out of the air itself. Close to the ground, the crystals don't have time to form elegant rosettes. They melt the instant they touch my face, feeling less like weather than like a prickling of imagination.

Away from the cabin it's quiet. The only things moving are the moon, the falling ice crystals, and me. My pacs make soft chuffs as I wade the snow. Frozen twigs issue muffled crunches from underneath. Not long until the solstice. What Frost called "the darkest evening of the year." In December, night comes early. I stand and try to feel the night around me as if I were standing silent with another person. I'm trying to feel like a part of this, beyond the threat of the cold, the barrier of the snow, but the night is too big, too open.

I take off my right mitten and pinch needles from a fir and crush them. I breathe in the resinous odor, incense without burning. Full dark, now. I stoop and take up some snow. The cold is like a white star in my mouth. Then, it changes to water and trickles familiar down the back of my tongue. My fingers hurt. I put my mitten back on. The cold tracks my limbs. I've been standing for a while. Too long. Too cold. I want to go back.

I wind around boulders and brush through bare willows until I see the lighted windows. In the glow, I check the snowmobiles, dented and scratched with their brown Forest Service emblems. No new damage. Suddenly, in spite of my dislike for them as things, I feel a stab of affection. They carried us up here. I bounce the rear ends to clear ice from the tracks. My hands ache. Frost slips from the metal like white dust.

• • •

As I step inside, my glasses fog. On the woodstove, snow seasoned with pine needles is melting in a galvanized pail, and a pot of water boils unheeded for tea. From the tape-player hung on the wall, the Pixies shriek. John is gorging happily on tortilla chips, scooping red salsa and humming into a bottle of Bass Ale which he raises, trumpetlike, toward heaven. He nods and sings a phrase along with the tape, something with the words "molest" and "parking lot."

In December, when each day has a lot more dark than light, there is much to be said for walls that don't flap when the wind blows. For a cabin in which you can stand and stretch, for light enough to read, and for windows, even plated with frost. I let the bliss of our situation sink into me with the heat.

Tomorrow, twelve days before the solstice, John and I will head out with light loads to pack trail. Our route lies up the long, gla-ciated drainage to Big Sandy Lake, where it is likely that no one has skied this year. Given the sugary texture of the snow, the trailbreak-ing may be difficult. We'll push a ski-trail as far as we can and then return to the cabin. Marty and I used to carry full packs and make a camp at the end of the first day. We often camped about six miles in, near Big Sandy Lake. Too near. Cold air sinks to the lowest point in the landscape, in this case the lake.

After some grim nights in camp, with late starts owing to the cold, we decided to try the entire trip in a day, about eighteen miles. Without full winter camping gear, our packs would be light. Skiing out, the added weight of the snow sample would be less punishing. But without camping gear, we'd have to move quickly.

Our first attempt ended six miles in. The snow thawed as we climbed, and by afternoon our skis plunged deeply with each step and then caught under a buried crust. Marty and I fumed, and at three o'clock admitted defeat. We cached the sampling gear and skied back down our tracks to the cabin in the dark, grunting frus-tration with each swing of arm or leg.

Using headlamps, Marty and I started again before dawn. We raced up our hard-frozen tracks and made Big Sandy Lake by mid-morning. At the outlet of Black Joe Lake, about two miles beyond, was our goal: a bulk snow collector, in essence a nine-foot-high trashcan lined with six-foot plastic bags to collect snowfall.

Above Big Sandy Lake, we found better snow and made a quick climb up a ridge to the collector. There, we bagged the sample and raced out, returning to the cabin an hour after dark, completely drained. By spending the first day breaking track, then making a quick round-trip on the second we avoided two miseries: breaking trail with massive packs and enduring a night in camp by the frozen lake. John and I carry on with the same tactic: two lightweight trips rather than one heavily laden camp-out.

If we came here for fun we would camp high simply to be up there. The bitter cold would be part of the pleasure, the *out-thereness*. But we wouldn't be dragging a sledge full of snow-coring tubes, plastic bags, sample bottles, data sheets, pliers, wrenches, and similar aggravations. Instead of unbolting collector tubes and sticking a coring tool into the snowpack, we would be cutting fast tracks up to Temple Pass and carving sweet turns down, burdened only with sunscreen, rum, and chocolate. Any suffering would be the fruit of liberty.

And, too, we wouldn't have to haul a seventy-pound bag of snow back out along with all the aforementioned tools and camping gear. Work is work.

Marty began these monitoring trips by picking different partners from his roster of unemployed climber friends in Jackson Hole. They had some fair-sized epics and got only fragmentary data. The gear wasn't adequate to the task. Snow collectors fell over and were buried by drifts. I started the third winter, 1986, after a fellowship at Stanford, where, in winter, the hills turn to mud.

Long before, I started out skiing at resorts, working toward an instructor's pin. After a couple of years, I got bored with the yo-yo rhythm of lift skiing and the social scene that clings to it. I began skiing the backcountry about '71, with a used pair of hickory skis from Norway. Since then, I've ridden a ski lift about twice.

I scratch a hole in the frost and peer through the pane. My pocket thermometer, hung on a nail outside the door, is pegged at − 20°F. It goes no lower. Snowmelt steams in the pail. John is perched on the upper bunk, reading. I ask him how he thinks Marty and Susan are faring in Asia, where they have gone to climb and to traverse the Baltoro Glacier on skis. Susan is John's ex-girlfriend. He grimaces. Under loose bangs his eyebrows arch, and he rolls his eyes to the ceiling. "Probably fine," he says. "They deserve each other."

I ask him about his last trip, bicycling in Central America with a woman named Shana. He grins. "It's hard to believe it's on the same planet as this. There are a thousand greens. Even the heat seems green there."

Next he tells me about Rio, then about almost being robbed while climbing the granite domes there. "The poverty and the sense of want is incredible. It hangs in the air like fog." He talks again about Susan, about the trip they made through Asia two years ago. Then he goes silent, returning to his book.

I rearrange objects—first-aid kit, longjohns, wax bag, head-lamp—in an order minutely better for an early start. This is a nomad's ritual, the comfort of handling a few possessions, tokens against the expanse. Having zipped some small items into a pocket of my pack, I unzip it to check precisely what I put there: deep-powder baskets, spare ski cable, notebook, avalanche beacon. Just as I thought.

Mountaineers can be obsessive about checking gear, since so much else in the mountains is beyond control. Our route to the snow collector is easy and relatively safe, yet we are very much on our own. The critical factor is extreme cold. A skiing accident up near the collector site could immobilize one of us. The other would pack a shelter pit and stack enough deadwood for a fire, then care-fully ski down the drainage to a point where radio contact might be possible. If the Forest Service or county sheriff answered the call, it would still be hours before a flight could be arranged, and, in December, it would be dark. Most helicopter pilots sensibly refuse to fly the high mountains at night. The uninjured skier might try to return with a snowmobile, but would more likely get it stuck in the complex woods and moraines, and become exhausted heaving the heavy machine out of snowpits. Then there would be two persons in distress, instead of one. Skiing back to the cabin for emergency camping gear and skiing back up would be smarter but more stren-uous, a twenty-seven-mile day on top of anxiety.

We don't talk about this, preserving our outer confidence, nor about the fact that neither of us is here as a "self-appointed inspec-tor of snow-storms and rainstorms" as Thoreau joked in *Walden*. This is 1989. Walden Pond is a dirt-lined swimming pool for met-ropolitan Boston with condominiums closing in. We're up here to inspect snowstorms for their content of sulfates, nitrates, heavy metals, and other airborne dividends. It's a world that we have a hard time believing. One of our best reasons for being here is to be away from all the bad news. The mountains, to the eye and ear, still make the same sense they have always made.

The lantern gutters. John and I both leap up. A few strokes of the pump and a twist of the cleaning needle restores the light. The shadows retreat.

I write in my notebook. John glances, but doesn't ask. Thrown constantly into close quarters, snowcaves and tents, one learns to respect fragile barriers: lowered eyelids, a layer of cloth. He slides from the bunk and rummages the food. "There are some cookies here," he says. I say nothing. "They're chocolate chip," he says, raising one like a lens to the light. "Real chocolate." He takes a tiny nip and makes his face grave, like a Frenchman tasting wine. "Excellent," he says. He holds one out to me. "We should have some."

John is affable, with a reticence that manages to be polite without being prickly. He wants to talk, so I stop writing. We muse on what to pack for lunch, whether to eat all the chocolate-chip cookies now—which John favors—or save them for the trail, whether one more cup of tea will interrupt the night's sleep, what tape to play. His banter is as soft-spoken as the cassette player is raucous. Between bouts with employment, he's a thorough nomad, unsettled, perhaps a little numb. Given something to eat, a bottle of dark beer, and music, he'd sit out the apocalypse with a slow grin.

After two cookies, I shuffle gear, scrape skis and rewax them, drink a nut-brown bottle of Watney's, worry about snow conditions, and then try to read. John plays a tape and samples the foodstock. "Cashews. Amazing. Very good." At last he climbs up to the top bunk and his breathing slows. I go to sleep as the fire dies and frost thickens on the windows. Cooling, the wood in the cabin walls makes a ticking sound.

2

But wild ambition loves to slide, not stand,
And Fortune's ice prefers, to Virtue's land.

John Dryden

The coal stove in the cabin dates from the invasion of American kitchens first by gas, then by electricity, chancy sources of heat. A kitchen heater, it has a small, narrow firebox mounted high in a cabinet of white porcelained steel made to circulate air without growing hot to the touch. Stoves like this were sold to complement the new gas or electric, offering the familiarity and reliability of coal and sitting like a good aunt beside the risky, newfangled appliance. It's not a woodstove nor a heating stove either, though we use it as both. The firebox is small and too high. At $-35°F$ it takes hours to warm the cabin above freezing.

The cabin, too, is a relic. It was lost to official memory except for the occasional use of the horse pasture. My friend Mitch, the previous rider, suggested it as a place for a nap. The first thing I noticed coming up the hill was a pine flagpole, white paint almost entirely peeled, outgrown by the lodgepoles around it, a dead trunk hidden among live trees.

As a range rider, I needed a place to stay while patrolling the upper Big Sandy country. I found a screen door in the shed at Dutch Joe Guard Station, seven miles down the dirt road, and mat-

15

tresses to replace the mousy ones. On a sharp September morning, I fired the stove-in-residence, a squatty, cheap, sheepcamp range, and noticed flames licking out the oven door toward the woodbox. The firebox was gone, burnt through. I found the present stove in the kitchen at Dutch Joe. It had been hauled there but never attached to a chimney, being used as a counter to hold pots and pans.

I got a few sections of new stovepipe and wrestled the stove into a pickup with my friend Grant's lugubrious help. He whined that we would get into trouble if anyone found out. I knew we wouldn't. The professionals, seeking inner harmony, made a practice of not noticing anything that wasn't typed on official letterhead.

I roll from my bag and add more wood, bolts of dead lodgepole. The stove radiates a modest warmth. I know the history of these things: the stove, the big cast-iron fry pan that has stayed with the cabin for ten years—evidence that the place is seldom used—and the screen door, which slaps the boards at each exit or entrance. I care for them in a slight yet fierce way.

Though I can still see my breath inside, John emerges from his bag and makes tracks for the outhouse, a gripping ritual on subzero mornings. He steps back in as the water boils, mumbling *"schatzo muy frio."* This is High Skid, our tribal tongue, a grab-bag lexicon that has evolved to deal with life in the peaks. It works partly by faulty grasp of a foreign language and partly by mad association.

Skid is—roughly—what skis do. It also connotes poverty: Skid Row. Backcountry skiers usually have more pride than money, so we've made up a dialect to set us apart, gibberish to the flatlander and the infidel, a code, like Latin for priests.

"The *nieve? Barbaridad.* Cal shred. *Trés schatzomente."* (trans: The snow? Ugh. Sierra Cement. Really shitty.)

Lift skiing is an industrial amusement, parking in a crowded lot, paying exorbitant ticket prices, posing in lift lines, being hauled up mountains on steel cables by diesel engines, skidding down clear-cuts: it's a symptom more than a sport. Backcountry skiing is for anarchists and coyote angels. Your feet get cold and no one admires your new outfit. The weather and snow might be unspeakable. You can get lost or avalanched. It can be miles to the nearest amenity. Ski mountaineering, with overnight camps, is even more deeply eccentric. It's for those who will suffer for days in return for a few seconds of grace.

Backcountry skiers tend to dress like Pathans, swill beer, and wolf tamales at the bar, muttering like conspirators behind chapped hands. Toward closing time they argue over the bar tab and then sleep illegally in old vans behind the dumpsters. They also lie to pilgrims: "Ginger Twist? Who told you about that one? Hmmmmm." The eyes stop down to f16 as the forefinger polishes the sunburnt chin. "I think it's that one where you follow the snaky ridge up from the place where the snowplow slid off two years ago. There's a road sign I think: AVALANCHE DANGER. DO NOT STOP OR PARK. Park there. The first part's a thrash. You go up toward these little scraggly trees, or maybe it's a rock face. Anyhow, way up. You can see the cornice. And then you contour left . . . or is it right?"

Winter mountaineers confront all kinds of difficulties, their own bodies not least. Crapping is one of the most memorable aspects of winter alpinism, though it is seldom written about. In the Skid-Boy tongue, *schatzo*—a latinized word from the German for "treasure," chosen for its sound—is a noun for both action and result. It is modified by traditional Spanish adjectives of number and kind: *perfecto, tremendo, peligroso* (on a narrow ridge), *doble, horroroso*. The grammar is flexible.

Once, in a great hurry, I attempted a *schatzo urgente* without removing my skis. It was a hasty act, but seemed to be going all right until the frost on my ski bases melted loose. The next second, I took a spectacular, squatting flip, almost doing a cannonball into my own scratchpit. Evasive maneuvers in free-fall saved my honor, but I ended bare-assed and face down in fresh powder, my handful of tissue bravely extended to still greater depths.

It was very early, very cold. *Schatzo atroz.*

This is not the sort of subject one finds in most nature tales, where adjectives tend to be loftier than the peaks. After the superlatives, the epiphanies, and *Götterdämmerung* sunsets, one longs for an honest thump or a stumble. Truth is slippery, but there is value in aiming for it. A story is also a sort of map: it should bear some real landmarks.

John, dressed in navy blue long underwear above old wool pants,

is eating instant oatmeal with butter and walnuts, then drinking his coffee as if it were the spring of his blood. Under toffee-colored bangs his eyes close at each tip of the mug and are hidden by steam. He does not look heroic, nor would he wish to. He is hungry. I nurse my black mug, full of black coffee. Each sip fogs my glasses. The stove rumbles with fire, yet the air in the cabin is not much above freezing. The windows are galvanized with frost that melts only in the top corner of the highest panes. The daypacks are ready. Our long skis rest, waxed, against the outside wall. Soon we will be gone.

The air gave up its water last night. On the snow, fallen stars of frost make tiny, piercing rainbows at the first touch of light. We glide out from cold shade into the long opening. Two moose, motionless except for the twitch of ears, watch us from the willows by the frozen creek. Young bulls, they share an ice-age strangeness, a dark unpredictability.

Of the large ungulates, only moose can winter in deep snow. Their long legs and loose shoulders allow them to travel where elk and deer founder. A moose can lift its front hoof to eye level while standing flatfooted, essential for breaking trail. Moose can live on coarse, woody forage, like the leafless willows that rise plum brown above the snow. In deep snow, moose seem to swim, arrayed in line, the strongest breast-stroking a trail for the rest. When they reach fresh forage, they beat out a yard that gets bigger as they browse. When they've munched the shrubs down to thick stems, they strike out across the sea of snow for the next willow island. The two moose watch us intently. As we pass, their heads drop and they return to chewing willow tips.

The stream is frozen, covered in snow and hoarfrost. The tracks of snowshoe hare and coyote braid along the streambed, blue holes in a diamond field. In the forest flanks are squirrel and marten tracks, but smaller creatures are holed up, waiting out the deep cold in torpor. If they move, they move under the snow, burrowing through the fragile hoar crystals along the ground. After the moose, we see nothing moving, nothing live except trees. The meadows narrow and we top a hill, then drop to the creek. The snow is soft and heavy, so we switch breaking trail, the leader sinking about eight inches, churning a wake of crystals into the sun.

We follow the iced-up creek, making a bend east through lodgepoles and crossing a snow-bridged tributary where we hear the hollow warble of water through boulders. The trail then climbs abruptly in switchbacks to a rocky bench, the scored, granite surface on which the glacier rode ten thousand years ago. The bench dips and rises near one level, carved in resistant bedrock. On both sides the mountains rise in jointed outcrops and rubble, cut by talus-filled stream gorges, to a ridgeline of cirques and twelve-thousand-foot peaks, each nick and slash precise in the dry, cold air.

Setting out on skis is a relief. My anxiety rises during the hours of preparation, sorting gear, figuring the weights, tightening the bindings. Out here, the strong, repeated pump of my thighs, the grip of the cold, the familiar aches and resistances all blend into comfort. I feel like I was born to be up here on skis; every stride, every breath is a confirmation.

About an hour into the trip, we break out into another long meadow, the largest since we left Big Sandy Opening. At its upper end, the creek is open as it cascades down a boulder-strewn channel, vapor lifting from black riffles. Around it the pines hold shadow, with snowcaps shining in the crowns above. Feeling the heat of effort, we stop to shed parkas despite the temperature's being still below zero. Through this meadow runs the wilderness boundary. We might legally ride the snowmobiles this far if we chose to get them bogged down, to heave them out, and to fetch them up at crazy angles against pines.

Wilderness buffs have been about as welcome in the ranks of the Forest Service as Nader-trained populists are in the boardroom of General Motors. There is some devout lip service, since public pressure is intense, but wilderness doesn't bring in hard cash like timber or grazing, a weakness in a budget-driven organization.

The entrenched, bureaucratic part of the Forest Service is ambivalent about the Wilderness Act, since it means such places are to be left mostly alone. Leaving places alone doesn't crank big budgets or generate jobs. The prohibition on motors is galling to persons for whom a pickup is a kind of second soul. Any wilderness, even the tame, designated sort, is a threat to the commissars who brighten at the word *management*.

Manage what? Manage not to screw it up? I've been to conferences at which wilderness managers pump each other up for the task of convincing the rest of the Forest Service that wilderness is something besides a legal roadblock. Behind the determined brightness of such affairs lurks a certain amount of despair. You can almost see the careerists wondering if it's too late to switch tracks. As seasonal employees, we stand somewhat apart from the bureaucracy, or at least we do in our own minds. We also love the mountains more than we love the law.

There are good points to the law. Without the wilderness boundary, we wouldn't have this work: the managers would call in a helicopter and fly to the collectors in green snowmobile suits, each clutching a steel-clad thermos. The mid-to-upper echelons of the Forest Service are filled with ex-soldiers who got into the Civil Service on veteran's preferences, men who like heavy hardware, four-wheel-drive trucks, helicopters, chainsaws, and bulldozers. Wilderness designations, like demilitarized zones, make little sense to them, and they chafe at the restraint.

What good is a wilderness, said one, if you can't get in there and manage it; if you can't build drift fences and pipelines and sheep troughs? It's all one mountain range, but we have to play by too many different sets of rules.

Laws forcing the Forest Service to hire women, combined with the present lack of a militarized generation, have changed the agency at the root. Having absorbed environmental ethics from subversive professors, new members aren't as quick to follow orders. When official policy is contrary to biological common sense, some are likely to object or resign, choosing integrity over security. It's an uneasy time.

The human struggle in the Forest Service tracks a deeper question: having reached a fuller knowledge of how nature works, can we change our collective life to accord with the natural systems on which we depend? Congress, aptly representing the public, passes wilderness bills and then bellows "Get the Cut Out!" Congress is two faced, like a hog with a mouth at both ends.

I'm not sure why we believe Congress can help us out of our predicament. There is a limit to the rule of law, as any student of Indian treaties will testify. Belief and habit shape our days; laws passed contrary to these—like the fifty-five-mile-per-hour speed limit—are simply disobeyed. This is the weakness in wilderness-by-legislation.

When logic fails, faith prevails. Or, said the venerable Francis Bacon, "Man prefers to believe what he prefers to be true." Is there a human right to foul these places, whether temples or leftovers? My life in these mountains tells me it's wrong. I believe it's wrong. This is only a first step, but without it the whole journey fails. Science is a worthy tool, often misused, but it is faith or fear that moves us to act. Logical reasons are never enough to leave a thing alone.

If we are foolish in treating the wilderness as a church, might we be equally so in treating the rest of our public land like a brothel? If we had good rules, there would be only one set, dependable as gravity. As it is, we have a hodgepodge of laws and imaginary lines, scribbled across the continent. The imaginary line at our feet—the wilderness boundary—has power, so John and I travel under our own. We stare at the sign. "Feel anything?" I ask.

"Hungry," says John.

The sun heats us up, so we shed another layer. Steam rises from our shoulders as we eat a mix of peanuts and chocolate drops and take big gulps of water. Changing places, I mush along the meadow and climb a slant into thick pines above the cascade, looking down into black water sliding over lips and fangs of anchor ice: fast water freezes from the bottom up. We traverse the slope, pushing the pace to stay warm in the shade, slowing for the patches of sun.

Emerging from the trees, we get the first good view of where we are going, east to an amphitheater defined by rock walls that plunge sheer and naked from sky to timberline, into glacial basins filled by lakes that spill over in cascades, waters converging like the ribs of a palm leaf toward the stem. Where stem meets leaf is Big Sandy Lake, in which five streams pool and mix to fill the muscular creek that loops under ice to our right. The left-hand ridgeline rises from the fractured dome of Laturio Mountain, dipping to Fish Creek Pass, lifting at Bunion Mountain, and sharpening to the broad point of Warbonnet before dropping in a prismatic wall to the notch of Big Sandy Pass. Dead ahead, on the far side of Big Sandy Lake, are the shattered pyramids of Mitchell, Dogtooth, and Big Sandy peaks; to the right, hiding further summits, is the ridge of Schiestler, shaped like a newspaper hat, and then the great south-slanting ramp of Temple, 12,972 feet, with a complex north wall that shadows large alpine lakes. A west-running spur of Temple ends in a granite flat-iron, which broods over timbered ridges and the expanse of Big Sandy Opening. At our backs, southwest, is the low, coniferous line of Muddy Ridge and the vastness of the cold-desert plateau that hides the upper Green River.

The topography is dramatic, the result of forces in free play. The eldest rock in the Wind Rivers is a mix of granite and metamorphic gneiss, called migmatite. Around Medina Mountain in the center of the range the migmatite cooled about 3.4 billion years ago. Nearby

Hall's Lake reflects rock that may be even older, close to the 3.8 billion years claimed for exposures in Greenland.

Geologists say that these bodies of rock originated deep in the earth's crust, more than five miles down where it rides on the mantle and swirls like red sauce. Mixed in like chopped onion are bits of rock that don't quite liquefy. Around the liquid zone, the crust softens and is buckled by waves of pressure, the layers of sedimentary grains welding together in light streaks of quartz and feldspar and dark ones of hornblende and biotite. Under our skis, under the thin snow and frozen soil, under the bedrock, about as far straight down as we have come from the cabin, rock is melting and flowing.

The older rocks solidified, rose into the light, and were weathered, then were reburied around 3.4 billion turns ago, when some of the migmatite completed its change into gneiss. The cycle repeated between 2.9 and 2.6 billion years ago, when the older rocks were surrounded and infiltrated by a flood of magma from below. This cooled slowly, crystallizing into the present fine, silvery, monolithic granite that forms the walls around us.

The Wind Rivers, young mountains composed of old rock, rose about sixty-five million years ago, as a crustal disturbance called the Laramide Revolution heaved up fresh mountain ranges like mushrooms all over the western part of the continent. A thick mantle of softer sedimentary rock was shed during the uplift, sliced off by glacial ice, dissolved by floods, and carried off by streams. Immense stress cracked the body of the rock west of the present range in a great, slanting thrust-fault, the eastern side rising above the western and eventually riding over it. The rapid uplift continued for twenty million years, while erosion removed rock from the rising plane and deposited it in the valleys of the Wind River to the east and the Green River to the west. After the orogeny—this is what geologists call the rise of mountains—slowed, the eastern block continued to ride over the sinking block to the west until the igneous layer that was once a single body had been separated vertically about forty thousand feet, with the western block buried under thirty-two thousand feet of sediments and the eastern one rearing almost seven thousand feet above the surface. The new range had—still has—a broken, precipitous southwest face and a gentler slope to the northeast, like a huge wave breaking toward the Great Basin.

Several major glaciations chopped peaks and ridges, scooping troughs down the flanks of the range like great, dull claws. The last retreat started about ten thousand years ago, leaving the terrain in its present shape: a southwest scarp that juts up from the wide valley, then levels into a glaciated plateau at about ten thousand feet before rising again to a crest of rock peaks that mark the Divide like the upthrust, bony plates along the spine of a fossil stegosaurus, shading remnant glaciers that are the largest in the lower forty-eight states.

Since then, vegetation has bearded the slopes, and thin soils have developed. A few shallow lakes have filled with silt and sedges, while most are still deep and clear: over a thousand of them. The rock doesn't weather fast. Chemically, it resembles glass in the way that sedimentary rocks like limestone resemble chalk, so rain, even acid rain, doesn't dissolve it.

Yet when water seeps into surface joints and freezes, it acts as a wedge, forcing cracks open. Ice can glue shattered blocks in place until meltwater lubricates them, and a rectilinear chunk slips out to spark and shatter down the talus slopes. This melt-freeze cycle is a yearly, and at times daily, phenomenon. Mountaineers learn the danger of being under a rock wall when the sun thaws the ice in cracks and rockfall begins to buzz like buckshot. Last summer, a student in an outdoor leadership school died when a rock skipped down a glacier and caught him under the rim of his climbing helmet.

Glacial ice is a more intense medium for gravity than flowing water. In resistant rock, the head of a glacier plucks out blocks loosened by melt-freeze erosion, cutting and polishing sheer cirque walls, like those above us, and faceted peaks. The weight and inexorable flow of the ice fractures rock frozen in it and grinds boulders together like molars, bedding itself on an abrasive layer of stone that scrapes at the bedrock. Large glaciers show currents of broken rock on their surfaces. After being tumbled and milled, the rock melts out in heaps along the edges, leaving parallel ridges called lateral moraines. At the snout of the glacier, boulders too heavy to be washed away stack up in a terminal moraine, while smaller fractions roll and float away in the meltwater, forming lakebeds or outwash plains like Big Sandy Opening. The finest sediments make

it far downstream, into the valley of the Green, where they moved
with the river for millions of years and now settle out behind Flam-
ing Gorge Dam.

The height of the range is owed to vigorous uplift, but the steep-
ness and elegance are glacial work. It is the abrupt, heavily glaciated
southwest face of the range—our side—that combs rain and snow
from the air and sluices it down cleanly like a rank of Pyrex funnels.
These mountains get five times the precipitation of the valley, most
of it coming as snow. Cupped in granite, snowmelt is the treasure
of these mountains and the wealth of all the ranches and towns
below.

From the boundary meadow, we climb through pines to succes-
sively smaller meadows that mark points where the glacier rested
for a while on its retreat, filling its U-shaped gouge with coarsely
ground granite. The creek meanders through these depositions, then
cuts steeply down gorges between them. In the meadows, where the
water slows, ice forms at the edges and covers the surface; in the
gorges, where the flow is turbulent, anchor ice freezes from the bottom up, and the stream leaps and pirouettes through a translucent
obstacle course of its own making.

The gorges are postglacial, water following the easiest course
along a fault crack or along blackish, intrusive veins of softer and
more brittle diabase that snake through bedrock. Frost-wedging
shoves blocks from the gorge walls for the stream to trundle in its
descent. These boulders, edges still sharp compared to the rounded
shapes of glacially deposited stone, are assorted by size where the
stream enters the gentler gradient of a meadow and loses force; the
finest sediments are found at the tail of a meadow. This alternation
of vigorous downcutting with deposition is usual in mountain
streams, which cut canyons in a V or a notch shape, depending
on the bedrock. When the glacier grows down the canyon again, it
will follow the notch of the streamcourse and spoon out another
broad U-shaped track; then, the Big Sandy River will carry tons of
these peaks, finely ground, and spread them like meal on the desert
below.

We are down to shirtsleeves, John's plaid wool and my polypro-
pylene. He wears green wool officer's slacks tucked into his gaiters,
and I wear climbing bibs gotten cheaply when I worked at an out-

door shop. The temperature has come up to about 10°F, so we're comfortable, even a little hot, in the sun. At ten thousand feet, lightly filtered by atmosphere, the sun heats our bodies and we sweat, while in the shadow of the pines, the moist hair at my nape freezes and the chill bores in. The day is brilliant, yet clouds are building at our backs. A wind pushes up the slope and then abates.

Our skis are built for mountain touring, one finger wider than cross-country racing skis, metal edged, with broader tips and tails to help them turn. They are double cambered, with a gentle arc from tip to tail and a shorter arc—the wax pocket—superimposed under the foot. This lets the wax engage the snow when the ski is weighted, allowing the skier to climb or push off into a smooth glide in which the spring of the unweighted ski disengages the wax. Friction melts the snow against the ski base to a skin of water, allowing the finest boogie of all.

John's skis are near new, while mine are secondhand, Canadian relics, absurdly long with little skiing bears on the tips. The bases, after three years of marginal-condition skiing, look like scratching posts for lions. I used to fill the rips and holes after each trip, but now I've slipped back to once a season.

Our leather boots rise above the ankle, stiff, like mountaineering boots with square-toed soles that mate with ski bindings. The best backcountry ski boots can double as snow-climbing boots, serving to crampon or to kickstep up steep snow. John has three-pin bindings. After ripping the toe off a boot while cartwheeling with an eighty-pound pack down a slope of boilerplate crust, I am resigned to less elegant but more bombproof cable bindings.

While our chosen gear is heavier than a racer or a day skier would have, it allows us to travel fast in a variety of snow conditions and gives us enough heft and control to descend steep slopes. We carry large packs and need to make abrupt turns to slow down, miss boulders, and avoid cliffs. Still, we sacrifice control for lightness. You can't torque a pair of long backcountry skis around; you have to finesse them. Alpine touring gear, similar to that used at resorts, with stiff plastic boots, short, broad skis, and release bindings, is too heavy: good for the downs but bad for the up-and-over. Ultralight racing gear would be fun in the meadows, but hell on the heights.

We stop for lunch at the Diamond Lake Trail, sitting on a dead-fall pine, gnawing onion bagels, cheese, and apples kept from freezing by being packed close to the back and next to an insulated bottle of hot tea. Near the downed trunk are two sets of tracks, coyote and hare. There is a melted-out area with brown spots—blood. Around are puffs of fur and a rabbit's foot. I pick it up. The pads are completely hidden in fur: a snowshoe hare. The coyote jumped it and caught it, then ate it in the sun. We eat quickly and start again, before our feet begin to ache. To travel light and fast in the cold, one has to move continuously. We get up as one, the lack of words somehow a comfort.

The clouds are closer and the wind harsher, with three hours until sunset. The snowcloud looms up, then over us. We wind through ragged forest, climbing continuously. Tiny frost-flakes appear in the air, spinning down slowly. We're inside the cloud. The light changes as it builds and thins, rolling like surf against the Divide. On the move, we talk little and ski fifty or a hundred feet apart, the leader slowing and the follower closing when the snow deepens or the slope rears up. The trick is to find a pace at which we can stay in constant motion yet keep from perspiring, never pushing hard enough to need a full stop.

Winter survival consists in no small way of knowing how to conserve the body's heat and how to use the muscles to make it. Movement should be deliberate, and this rhythm carries into a slow persistence of thought. The rhythm of modern life, with stop lights and half-hour dramas, is a jerky stop-start. Winter's enforced steadiness makes the lapses sweet: cutting an improbable chain of telemarks down a steep pitch is like love and whiskey to the senses, sweet because it can't last.

Our scheme is to break a good trail to the lake, check the soundness of the ice, and then race back to the cabin for a full night's rest. A good start tomorrow will bring us to the lake early, with full packs, but with only two miles of breaking to the collector instead of nine. No one has come this way—no one ever does—so we break new trail every trip.

The snow is thin this year. On last week's ski into the northern part of the range, we found a bit over two feet near a lake that usually has twice that. The snow was sugary and loose, low in moisture, so we sank, hitting rocks and deadfall with our skis. Thin snow also meant the creeks were thinly bridged, and an unusually warm November kept them running instead of frozen hard. Starting across Hobbs Lake, on uniform snowcover that usually means solid ice, I punched a ski pole into liquid slush and made a catfooted retreat. Water sponging up through the inch of porous ice froze like iron to my skis, taking twenty minutes of chipping and profanity to clear. We detoured the lake to reach the collector.

The day after, scouting the larger, deeper Seneca Lake from a pass, we saw the blue shadings of slush pools on the two-mile ice crossing. A dry summer after drought had lowered alpine lakes and dried many inlet streams. After the first ice-up, the snowpack melted against the earth and started the streams running again. Water overflowed onto the lake ice, forming multiple layers separated by slush. Sometimes, the lake ice cracks and water surges up from below. Whatever the reason, looking down at the weak ice changed our plans. We talked about going around, but to ski the granite domes and sharp talus bordering the lake requires a deeper snowpack, so we postponed our climb to the highest collector.

The previous winter, 1988–89, was unusually cold with little snow. Skiing with Marty, I found Seneca Lake solid, gunmetal ice blown glassy in spots by high winds which batted us around as we skated across on our skis, seeing a few thin spots—evocatively black—on the three-hundred-foot-deep lake. Since large lakes are like thermometers for regional climate, the present winter's warmth makes me uneasy, quite apart from having been, literally, on thin ice.

Since I began these trips, I've sensed a warming trend. The high lakes freeze weeks later in the fall and thaw the first week of July instead of midmonth. The snowline hovers higher in fall and recedes faster each spring. But the most palpable sign of warming to me is our choice of ski waxes. They come in a spectrum ranging from white polar wax—the hardest, for cold snow—through light green, green, blue, purple, red, and yellow—soft wax, the consistency of peanut butter—for melting snow.

For midwinter, I once carried only hard waxes: white, light green, green, blue, extra blue, nothing softer than purple. But recently, I've often used purple wax and even red wax in December and

January. While this isn't something I'd write up for a journal, it is a fairly unequivocal sign of a warmer snowpack.

"Do you want to break trail?" John says. I uncouple the train of thought and go to work, as Marty put it, doing the push-push in the bush. Lift the knees, shove the skis. The bushes are thinning out, though. Diverging from the creek, we meander up through rocky knobs and dales, following a rising contour across the side-slope, as the summits lift and lean toward us. The clouds thicken and spit pellet snow. Breaking trail uses the same muscles as climbing stairs, with the skis weighted under snow like shoes with lead soles. We grow tired more quickly. The sky opens to a blue hole ringed by clouds, like white coral in tropical sea. John takes over the breaking again, and we reach the gentle notch where Big Sandy Lake opens at our feet, iced and glittering in its ring of peaks, cloud shadows dodging across it to join the deeper blues growing from Schiestler and Temple.

The sun is low. We ski down to the lake. I go out and probe the surface with a ski pole. The ice feels weird, slushy and uncertain under a deceptively blank mantle of snow. Slushy ice usually looks different under snow, but this all looks the same. Is it all slush? I make a careful loop and come back. Farther east, John does the same. The ice is even worse there. From the shore, I can see a slight rise and fall of the surface as he skis. Thin ice or imagination? "Iced up my bases," he shouts. "Way slushy out here." I shudder and picture him breaking through, but he skis back without incident.

We talk it over between mouthfuls of nuts and chocolate, chipping blobs of ice from our ski bases. The ice is no good. Tomorrow we'll have to ski around the lake, adding distance in return for safety. We stare moodily at the ice, wetness sponging up into our tentative tracks, turning them a deep blue. Even though this was our plan, the state of the ice has left us uneasy, feeling thwarted. The sun deserts the lake basin. It's suddenly cold as we turn back. The cloud layer gathers at face-level. The momentum we had coming up deserts me on the climb out. We stop again at the top to add a layer, then ski away down the long slope, savoring the whoops and runs, suffering the brief uphill slogs.

The cloud opens. Schiestler and Warbonnet, to left and right, stand like huge gateposts, dark on their east faces, still bright on the west. Then the cloud closes in. The woods are all shadow as we descend, pines darkening, their trunks growing heavy, the cold pooling almost visibly at their bases. We gain speed in our track, then cut out of it, making long turns, ducking tree limbs and sliding out from under the cloudcap to a clear sky and a radiant chill in the highest meadow.

The sun is half above the horizon, falling into deeper hues. The brush of low-angled alpine light on snow is soft, yet so absolutely distinct that each snow crystal insists on its own wavelength. Light scales down the spectrum and strikes the earth—lodgepoles, cliffs, and snow—without the diffuse glow seen on the coasts, where the humid air itself is the medium for color. Up here, in thinner air, white sunlight gathers red and gold from its long slant through our atmosphere and burns them into every object in its path: light gray boulders become live coals. Green pines turn to complex strokes of ink, and each shadow spreads like a fresh bruise. The east holds all the named blues—cobalt, turquoise, Delft, lapis, Mediterranean, sapphire, navy, indigo. And then, as the light descends to its lowest note, come the blues without names.

Someone—Goethe?—said that colors are the suffering of light. A pretty thought. Is mind the suffering of matter? Is art the suffering of will?

The light goes wherever it goes: away. We unravel the last miles beside the creek in full darkness, over snowbridges, edging around rocks. The snow gets colder until the surface freezes hard. Our track is an icy runnel. Outside it, we skitter on hard crust. We ski past the trail register, the outhouse, the signboard, the empty parking lot, then onto the snow-filled road, up the hill. Running down the south side, the cold stiffens the skin of my cheeks. Then, we run out of speed. My face feels like a mask. It's an effort to move my legs. Our skis clatter on hard crust as we slip out into Big Sandy Opening with the moon coming through a snowcloud over our left shoulders, fuzzy and muffled as a spider's nest in a fur hat.

3

Were they [the Indians] driven from their forests, the peltry trade would decrease and it is not impossible that worse savages would take refuge in them.

Lords Commissioners for Trade and Plantations, *Report to His Majesty George III,* 1772

*T*he cabin is a frozen skull. We pump the gas lamp, stoke the fire, and begin to eat what comes to hand, boiling a pot of water on the propane stove for chocolate. We don't shed any layers yet; I add a pile coat to keep from shivering until the stove makes a difference. John rips open a bottle of ale. When the boombox loses its coat of frost, he slots in a tape and the Screaming Blue Messiahs emerge, chanting "Smash the Market."

We clog our ski boots on the hollow fir floor and let out mating-cat yowls. "Bloated Pleasure Beasts!" exclaims John with a radiant smile beneath his mustache of beerfoam. The spaghetti and Chilean wine we were saving for a celebration meal after bagging the sample become—at John's urging—tonight's menu. "Tomorrow night we may be too thrashed to enjoy it," he says with a Medici grin.

We're still full of blind impetus. We can't stay seated. We pace, shiver, devour handfuls of peanuts, and stomp to the music. Eventually, as the cabin grows warm enough to sit still, our tiredness takes over. I slump in the single chair while John slouches on a bench.

We eat to the snarl of Sonic Youth, which reminds me of lying awake one night in October in the Gramercy Park Hotel, listening to New York City: street howls, metallic whangs, subway tremors, and the hoot of auto alarms. I was there on a poetry-reading tour and didn't sleep—though I tried—for several nights on end. The area around the hotel was reputed to be one of the quieter parts of Manhattan, in decibels if not in a social sense. This cabin, surrounded by quiet and dark, is a long way from town, farther from any city.

John puts on a Brian Eno tape, which puts me in a bad mood. I scowl. John grins. I sit and brood. In the city, my friends ask me in hushed voices about acid rain. *Is it bad? Will the fish die?* Not soon, I say, maybe not for a long while. The lakes are holding their alkalinity, buffering what acids arrive in rain and snow, but we're not sure why. In the streams the insects—stoneflies, mayflies, caddises—seem to be holding up okay. The drought makes things hard to define. The trees up high aren't growing properly, but that could be the drought or global climate change. We should have the precipitation data analyzed by spring, I say, but my faith grows thin sometimes.

The field collection is hard work for two, so the printouts tend to stack up along the walls. There's a hydrologist who has been working on the data, but she had a long battle to get the right computer to start the job and is a year behind. The software is still incomplete, with a team in Colorado working to get the bugs out and to write programs for resources besides air quality. The hydrologist—Cheryl, my boss and friend—thinks of air quality work as both onerous and risky, a brief detour in a long hydrological career: straight-line career tracks are more respectable.

When she might be analyzing the data, she gets saddled with reports on application of total quality management principles for accelerated implementation of best management practices in the forest planning process. TQM for AI of BMPs in FORPLAN. There are endless committees and ad hoc teams, each with meetings that may require a few hundred miles of driving. For every action, a numbered form must be submitted, reviewed, and filed. Another friend, the rare ironic bureaucrat, calls this "feeding the beast."

Cheryl longs for those rare days in the field when she actually gets to see the watersheds she is supposed to manage.

The upper-level scientists who could interpret the data spend most of their days worrying budgets together and flying to conferences. The administrators—people managers—scheme ways to grab more of the budget for administration. They regard actual trees and mountains as impediments to the proper flow of concepts and money. None of us is at fault. All of us work too hard. We all have good intentions. Still, my friends lower their voices in corners at parties and ask, *What are you finding out? Is it bad?*

Sulfate's down, I say—*Good*, they answer—but not as much as precipitation is. The drought. *Bad*, they say. Same for nitrate. *Same what?* Same trend . . . we think. *Don't you know?* Not enough to carve it in marble. We still don't have all the numbers in the goddamn database. *Why not?* Too busy collecting more numbers. I'm the field hand, the dog that fetches the bone. Too many bones out there. A regular bone pile. *You sound like Bush*, they say—*more studies, blah, blah, blah*. I ball up my fists.

We know that the deposition of sulfuric and nitric acids is about ten times the preindustrial baseline, I say. It's obvious that's not good for the mountains. Anyone can look at the air in Salt Lake City and smell it and tell that it's bad. It stinks, it burns your nose, you can't see through it. What evidence do you need? Don't you have any senses left? How can you ignore the *air*?

But most of us ignore it and wait for Congress to act. We just don't know what to do about it. How do we cease most of the activities that we like to think constitute our lives?

We're an adjustable species. Things get really bad before most of us get upset—the way they are in the mountains downwind of Los Angeles, where ozone kills pines and airborne lead has eliminated the last wild condor. In the southern Sierras, vigorous hiking can be hazardous to human health. But those mountains, even hammered and poisoned, still look a lot better than the city. People still go up there to get away.

The changes are in small increments at first, hard to notice if anybody was to track them, which mostly no one does. We don't have a good eye for natural detail. That's why the chemistry is important, the measurement of miniscule change, parts-per-billion, trends in concentration. The big stuff comes later, probably all at once. No prophetic ashes and no runes, unless ice itself is a rune. Reductively speaking, a sign is what we came for. To bag our weighty evidence and struggle out with it, to the world where analyses are made, accounts are rendered, laws are passed, citizens are born and die. But I don't think of this work as my knightly duty. John is even less committed to an ideal. At times, I think we come up here so as not to be there.

Hallelujah. The tape ends. Before John can react to the quiet, I manage to sneak out a Paco de Lucía guitar tape and slot it into the box. John asks me how I liked the Eno tape. I shrug, but not too deeply. "I'd have to hear it again."

One of the ways we get along on these trips is by muting our differences. To live and work together in tight quarters and travel under stress, we have to cultivate our likenesses. "I liked the one I heard at your place—the morbid-sounding Brits."

"Yeah," he says, "The Sundays. S'good." Seated in the lantern light, John looks vaguely noble, like a photograph I saw of a young officer in the Polish cavalry on the eve of the Blitzkrieg. He gives off an air of fatalism—I tag it as European, but maybe it's from growing up in the urban east. It's a heaviness, an almost genetic remorse. He sighs and looks at the frosted window. He's thinking but not saying much.

When John is uneasy, he draws in. Marty would erupt. Any irritation, whether a sore elbow or a rotten snowpack, could provoke an outburst. I'm outspoken, too, so we'd rub on each other's nerves. On a long trip with Marty, things could get tense. John grows more distant until he almost disappears. What leads John to sorrow would spark Marty to rage. But John and Marty are friends in a way I'll never be with either of them. I'm a generation ahead of them, with more responsibility for the results of the study. On these trips, each of them asks me about the other. The bond we share is these mountains.

About eight-thirty, the thermometer outside pegs again at $-20°F$, and frost makes hard faces on the windows despite the roar of the little stove. The cold pervades our senses: it can be felt, like the constant roar of surf, pressing on the walls around us. I stoke the stove and adjust the damper to hold more heat. John's head dips to the bunk, jerks up, and then dips again. He is half in his sleeping bag. The wall behind him glistens with melted frost. The same wall, on the level of the bottom bunk, holds frost unmelted, patches of ground glass on the gloss white enamel. I shut down the lantern and John murmurs and rolls over. The bunk bumps the hollow wall. The zipper of his bag makes a tiny snarl. With my headlamp I slide into my bag to read. *The Course of Empire* rests heavily in my hands.

But I think instead. There are aspects of ourselves that we show on these trips that seldom see light elsewhere. I recall coming back from a rough trip, three days of suffering, Marty ripped on Guinness and whiskey, dancing around the A-frame cabin in his polypro longjohns and singing "Venus in Furs."

The mountains in winter have an austere beauty; words like *purity* and *dignity* leap up in response. Yet we seem, in our little tribe, to revel in the opposite. Marty makes jokes about toilets and listens to Iggy Pop on his Walkman, John tells me of white-trash adventures overseas, and I come up with bondage scenarios involving foresters, clerks, and Doberman pinschers. It all seems right at the time.

But I have a Thoreau doll in my head, strolling the inner woods. We argue. He tells me what to leave out.

My friends tell me that they envy my time in the mountains, that it must do good things for the soul. It has. It does. My mind encompasses these contradictions, but there is a corresponding pressure not to betray the ideal: that wilderness makes us pure. I can admire the severe wonders of a corniced ridge for only so long; then I want to eat. Then I want to laugh.

The cold wakes me, which is so rare as to be almost unimaginable: I'm one of those human furnaces whose heart pumps fire through each capillary. Public buildings are to me like tremendous ovens. I sweat out parties in normally heated houses like a fat man in a steamroom. In my imagination, Hell is like the college I attended, a yellow brick building with windows painted shut in which elderly Mormon ladies control the thermostats.

Since we're sleeping inside the cabin, I brought my summer bag, innocently expecting the inside temperature to stay above 20°F or so. Fool. I stab my feet into down booties and relight the stove, cramming it with every possible stick. My watch reads 12:36. John moans and rattles the army-surplus bunk, trying to cut telemark turns in the confines of his down bag. Or chasing dusky beauties with pockets full of chocolate and a bottle of rum in each fist. I dive into my bag. I try to adjust the pile coat I'm using for a pillow. It's frozen to the north wall.

The cycle repeats at three, and I notice that the pail on the stove has a half-inch of ice in it. I slip into longjohns and wear my down booties inside the bag, which helps. The wheek-wheek-wheek of my digital devil-box summons me to the boilers at five. All is frozen. John mutters a curse in Old Norse. The new day gapes.

The cabin never warms up. We shuffle about half-hunched, protecting our vitals. My calves are sore to the touch, and my Achilles tendons have rusted in their sheaths. At such times it occurs to me how large and cold the world is, but neither of us is quite daunted enough to shrug back into the sleeping bags. Instead, we slurp coffee in clouds of steam and labor at our instant oatmeal, which congeals in seconds. We jam gear into our big packs, arguing mildly about who carries the hated snow-coring tubes. These are sections of aluminum that are just long enough to catch the occasional low limb.

Later, after we have fed and flown, green wax squeaks and grips on a fast track and we hasten, despite large packs lumped with sampling gear. We gripe as we go, of cold feet, low pay, corruption in high places. The icy ski tracks are unforgiving; it takes effort to stay upright. The bark of the lodgepoles is rough black and brown, like burnt skin. We push on, from duty or madness, who knows, and gradually begin to feel better, to feel that good warmth in our thighs, that first moisture under our arms. Alive, Alive-O! We catch first sun in a big meadow and shuck layers. The ring of peaks glistens as the light begins to polish the blue bowls and hone the long arêtes. Hard country. Sharp country. Warbonnet, Wolf's Head, the Warriors, Watchtower, Lizard Head, Shark's Nose. These are good mountains. No permits. No rescue squad. You can still die in peace up here.

Snow changes with the sun's touch. Surface crystals lose their cutting edges, and the skis glide farther with each stride, no longer scraping and clattering in the track. The sky opens like a columbine, delicate blue and white, the bloom of light in space, giving us back

a world made strange by cold and dark. I can feel the sun's hand on my brow, the light's weight resting there.

We move as the shadows draw up behind us, and we ski fast, conscious of the passing light. We will be skiing back in the dark, but the less night travel the better. Exhaustion and deep cold are a touchy combination, and the coming of the winter dark far from camp can set fear in the most hardened soul. So we move as fast as we can, pushing higher with only the briefest halts, following our own tracks, no decisions to make yet.

The sky clears until it's a single blue. There is no cloud, no wind, nothing but a high dome of color between us and space. I look straight up into that darkening blue: thin air and then vacuum. Space. If we could ski straight up, it would take only two or three days. But we aim northeast, toward four peaks white as Whitman's beard, shouldered above the low forest wainscot. Under sky, the snow is vibrating white, the sunlight like a great, spiked mace, swung at the mountains. We strike out across the highest meadow, skis rasping against a remnant crust.

On winter trips where there's a definite objective and a long approach, it's wise to agree on a break-point. John and I talk it over as we ski. If we aren't at the lake by two o'clock, we double back and try tomorrow. Skiing around the lake's weak ice will put on a half hour each way. It usually takes an hour to break track up the ridge beyond the lake and at least an hour and a half, maybe two, at the collector. There are unexpected delays: loosened or iced-up bindings, a need to rewax, adjusting the thickness of our clothes. A two o'clock arrival at the lake means not leaving the high point until five. In December, this is full dark. We revise our break-time to one-thirty so as to ski down the steep ridge in twilight at least. Given our pace, I think we'll beat the margin by an hour or more.

Which proves out. Nothing goes wrong. We reach the lake an hour before noon, and I cut a track along the northern shoreline, using the solid ice at the edge and climbing up onto the shore to cross the braid of Lost Creek on snowbridges. The country opens to the south, with the slick wall—no snow, too steep—of Haystack Peak leading to the steeper wall of East Temple, which ramps down to a pass, and then the looming, icy bulk of Temple's north face, a vertical township, the City of Falling Rock.

In late summer, the view from this point resembles Albert Bierstadt's painting *The Rocky Mountains,* which it may have inspired. Bierstadt is the most loved of the early landscape artists who traveled the West, his paintings full of the Olympian grandeur that the East fantasized as the *primum materium* of the West. So it is, but not quite in the manner of Bierstadt. The shoreline in the foreground is identical to that in the painting, though lacking the gnarled oaks and tipis of his German Romantic imagination, even in high summer. The cascade is here, though not as thunderingly dramatic, and the grand theater of summits, but there is a raw, choppy look, a broken rhythm that he couldn't catch.

In the painting there's also a hint of another perspective, east-northeast from above the old Rendezvous ground about fifty miles away on a bench above the Green River, looking up the cataract of Pine and Frémont creeks to the Divide's dragon spine along Frémont Peak. That view has a broader sweep, a geographic immensity missing from the present one, though it is an aspect Bierstadt lends through his romancing of the alpine light, more painter than geologist.

What he accomplished, with such painters as Thomas Moran who went to Yellowstone with the Hayden Survey in 1871, was to idealize the western landscape, to offer it as a potential shrine. Bierstadt's paintings helped to establish the Rockies as the equal of the Alps in grandeur. Moran's painting *Grand Canyon of the Yellowstone* was bought by Congress and hung in the Senate lobby. The romantic imagination, which by then invested grand landscapes with moral virtue, has been a powerful motive for conservation in America, from the national park movement up to Earth First! But the mountains don't know this.

Today, the light is a razor, slicing each rock edge from the one above with unholy precision, as if to say there's nothing here that can't be seen. Filtered through thin air, striking the rock and ice and snow, it becomes comprehensible, our light. Bierstadt's light was that of the European forest and the American east coast, carried out here in his inner eye, glowing on a grove of oaks that never grew. Every age has its conventions. Though Bierstadt tried, he couldn't rise to timberline and the clarity of this light. But there is a presence in his work, as if he had seen something beyond expression. He loved. He tried. We all do.

We stop for breath. We have been traveling fast, racing the light. We pass a water bottle and chew some nuts. "Heard of Bierstadt?" I ask John.

"Beer What?" he asks. I explain. He knows the painting but doesn't like it. "It's too . . ." He falters. "It's like one of those publicity photos, lots of fuzzy highlights. You wonder what the person really looks like."

We chance the north inlet and quickstep the slushy ice to safety, climbing onto snow with earth underneath, not water. The snowpack above the lake is complicated by springs and then by the many mouths of Black Joe Creek, which we cross on snowbridges, chaste arches, shaded blue. Beneath them, the water is not deep, but flows black in contrast to the snow. Perhaps there are refugee brook trout, rare as we two here, gathered for a spot of sunlight after the jeweled green gloom of the lake. For seven months of every year, this lake is under ice.

Choosing a snowbridge is more complex than choosing a hat: the reward is that nothing happens, while the consequence of error happens fast. Wading or swimming is difficult with skis, especially when large blocks of broken snowbridge accompany you down. Where the stream is fast or deep, there is a chance of getting sucked under the ice, which is usually fatal. When you choose the wrong hat, the floor doesn't open and swallow you whole, an effect that would quickly depopulate major cities. We take turns leading out and have our reward: nothing happens.

The outlet creek from Black Joe Lake is so steep and the target of so many avalanche paths that it tumbles a lot of rock in its cascading channel. Nearing Big Sandy Lake, the gradient eases, and the water isn't strong enough to shove its burden farther, so the rubble has formed a shield-shaped delta. As the stream shoots out of its gorge, it braids across the rising pile of stones. We cross it seven times, on seven bridges of snow.

We round the lake and stop to eat at the point of the steep ridge between the drainages of Black Joe and Clear lakes. We look north to Sundance Pinnacle and the steep east face of Warbonnet. Karl Bollinger, who in 1953 climbed the nearby peak bearing his name, fell and died the next day on Warbonnet. A few years ago, a solo climber plunged from the face, his body discovered by friends camped below. On a narrow spur of Bollinger Peak, called Wolf's Head, a woman from Pennsylvania named Tersis Ross was killed by lightning in the late seventies—out of several deaths, these are the ones I remember. When someone dies, they are bagged up and flown out, hauled away from that last glimpse of beauty. If I die up here—this is not flippant—I would rather be left alone. Hidden in the rocks where my bones won't bother anyone. Who in his right mind aspires to formalin and a concrete vault? Up here, that seems like an abomination. There is a pause in the wind. The sun glares on the fields of snow. We eat the same bagel and cheese lunch as the day before, dependable as whale blubber, and skin up for the climb.

Once made of sealskin though now woven of mohair or nylon, climbing skins are adhesive strips that stick to the bottoms of skis. Our skins are set up with a metal loop for the tip and a tailhook, which helps keep them on when cold lessens the grip of the glue. The glue sticks even to ski wax and demonstrates marvelous bonding properties when touched to wool hats or long hair. The shrieks of a neophyte being detached from a climbing skin are awful. With practice, one can skin up in a couple of minutes and remove them in less, with both skis on, popping the tailhook with a ballet step, zipping the skin free, and folding the sticky inner surface against itself without mishap. Ski-Chi. The Back-Bowl Way. John does it with a perfect grace, master of this unrecognized art.

Then we start the steepest climb of the trip. Marty would charge up this ridge like a Cossack, seldom stopping for breath let alone speech. If I managed to get the lead, through the sneaky tactic of starting while he was wolfing his second bagel, he never failed to catch and pass me with a sniff, taking a steeper line to demonstrate his superiority. For Marty, life seemed to have a scorecard. John is more companion than contender: he has the endearing habit of breaking lots of trail without making it an issue.

We zag up between short rock faces and old whitebark pines, never rushing, but seldom stopping except to squint out the route. The summer trail—gone under snow—slips north off the ridge and switches up the north-facing slope in heavy spruces above the gorge of Black Joe Creek. We've taken that line when the snowpack is stable. Given the slightest chance of avalanche, the north side becomes a trap. Any slide, even a small one, could slam a skier hard into a tree. In the steepest spots, the slide would swoop down a shovel-shaped glade and fly off the cliff above the creek. There are slide-tracks down the slope, openings in thick woods where no tree survives. We stay above, on the whale's back, looping higher with each traverse until we reach a level spot. From the ridge, there are views of such indifferent splendor that any decent philosopher would shut up and blush.

Mountains. Rough. A herd of them. I realize that I think of them as huge, deliberate beasts. Or maybe as visible parts of an even greater beast. The north buttress of Haystack is a cracked tusk, streaked black with water, red with lichen, harder and closer than the sky, so forceful that it seems a fist punched out from the magma, barely contained by the crust. Some mountains watch you; this one does. Across the creek, the snagglepatch ridge of Mitchell, Dogtooth, and Big Sandy peaks carries the Divide south, a long flank of onion-skin slabs under blocky pinnacles, coursed by falls of talus. Past Big Sandy Peak, the ridge broadens into a remnant plateau above the head of Black Joe Lake, then humps up into Wind River Peak, the highest summit in the range's south end, all but invisible from the west, seldom visited.

We follow the spine of the ridge, high above two frozen lakes, traversing snow-covered ledges and slipping into narrow, cupped glades. The sun is passing its height, south of us, coasting down a low arc to the west. We cut left off the ridge and drop, turn, turn, turn, through whitebarks to the creek to look for a crossing. The snow, though denser and more skiable than the snow farther north, is still thin. The boulders are imperfectly cushioned and snow-bridges are fragile. I find a dubious-looking one and weigh across, hearing the water's black chuckle below. I hang onto a breath. Nothing happens.

We're there. The collector, a galvanized tube of thin steel like a vertical culvert without the wiggles, is covered only to the first of three joints, about three feet deep. Without the glamor of scientific usage, which proclaims this a "Turk-type Wilderness Bulk Snow Collector," it's an expensive trashcan aimed at heaven. We drop our packs and lay out the tools. With a wrench and driver, we unbolt the top two sections, tip them to a slant, and extract a thick poly bag. It holds rain and wet, fall snows frozen in an eighteen-inch plug, then succeeding layers of unmelted snow, the government's reason for turning us loose up here.

This constitutes a bulk snow sample, a frozen lump to be carried out, melted, weighed, mixed, tested for pH and conductivity, split into one-liter bottles, and shipped to the National Atmospheric Deposition Program lab in Illinois for detailed assay. The gnomes of Champaign, Illinois, will take this hard-won water and run it through a bunch of machinery that cost more than the mortal existences of John and me and most of our friends. After a year, they will send back a hideous wad of computer printout, columns of figures headed by chemical signs: Ca, Mg, K, Na, NH_4, NO_3, Cl, SO_4, PO_4, H+, followed by the centimeters of water that carried all this stuff to earth.

It would be quicker if I could just scoop up snow, taste it, roll it around in one cheek, spit it out, and then yell into the radio "Salt Lake City—Shut It Off—NOW!" But such brute simplifications will not do. We struggle out with great gifts of snow and get numbers in return. So far, the columns of figures don't mean much to me. Part of my assignment is to "assist in the analysis and interpretation of data," but none of my bosses seem eager to tangle with it either. Who wants to be the bearer of bad news? It's been stacking up for five or six years, growing like a puffball. When I look at the pile of printout, about the size of a six-year-old boy, my vision blurs and my mouth gets dry. Somebody should bear down and analyze. I'm not ashamed to say it won't be me. I'm willing to risk life and limb—at a lower rate of pay—to collect the raw material, but not willing to spend my life in an analytical crouch. Mountains, not chemistries, are my passion. If I loved money, computers, and paper, I wouldn't be up here.

John and I are beasts of the field, Temporary Technicians, the golden retrievers of science. This is our stick, thrown by the cities and their supporting cast of power plants and petrochemicals. Taken aloft by the sky. Brought back by snowfall. This sample is not as heavy as some, a queen-size pillow of ice and snow, thirty-five pounds at most. We punch it to a smaller size and compress it into my pack. This is—to all appearances—the object of our trip. But it always disappoints me, this mute, frozen bundle. Having it means we have to turn back. That's what one of my climbing partners said about summits, which he claimed were the worst part of a mountain. Worthless. All you do is stand around getting frostbite, and then you have to go back.

Out of a green canvas case comes the detested snow-coring kit— three-foot threaded sections of wrist-size aluminum tube marked in inches, a spring scale, a notebook, and a two-liter bottle, the necessities for self-torture. Snow coring is worse than rappelling. You can tell amateurs because they love rappels. Climbers *hate* rappels. No edge. Nothing but a rope and a few pissant scraps of alloy between you and the big Yahooooo. Everyone who has ever come on one of these trips has loathed taking snow cores. The Bondage Kit, we call it. The Whip. After thirty or forty of these gigs, you'd sooner pack a bundle of live cobras. Good thing there aren't any glaciers at hand. "Coring kit? Oh, um, well, we had this, ummm, minor epic with a crevasse and, yup. S'history."

John asks me what I'm mumbling about. "Heat," I declare. "Women," I affirm. "Food," I say, and he nods. Probably thinks I'm getting hypothermic. Hallucinating. Irrational. On second thought, he knows I'm irrational even when warm. One of my qualifications for this job. So, a sudden attack of logic would mean that danger lurks. *Logic—Killer of the Unprepared.*

The sun banks southwest and the air cools fast. Handling the aluminum tubes is like pushing frozen pins into my fingers. Wearing the scale on a cord around my neck, I plunge the coring tube into the snow while John notes the depth. Then, I hang the tube from the scale while he reads the weight. If the wind is blowing, which, fortunately, it isn't now, the tubes spin and bounce, making this a jolly interlude. Then comes the worst part. He opens the bottle and I whack the tube, causing the core to drop into the bottle. Or at least most of it. The remainder freezes fast to the metal. I beat on the tube—which hurts when your hands are on the verge of frostbite. If you bang on the tubes with something hard, they will dent. I slap and swear. The last kiss of sun slides up my face and over the ridge. Cold. Colder. More of the plug breaks loose. I dig at it with the little chrome dagger that came in the kit, for *hara-kiri.* Honorable exit after failure to collect sample for Empire. This sinister item, which looks like a medieval poignard, is actually a GSA letter opener. Standard issue in snow-coring kits. The last of the core comes free and slides into the bottle. The sequence is bemoaned—I am Chief Bemoaner—and repeated until the bottle is full, four cores this time.

This accomplished, we stuff scattered gear into our packs and hasten to leave. We switch our feet back and forth to scrub the ice from our skis, then run down the slope to the creek. Part of the snowbridge has collapsed, leaving barely enough to trust. John makes his owl-eyes, first at the creek and then at me. Neither of us wants to break more trail to find another crossing. So I trust it first. Nothing happens, so he follows and we force ourselves up the short, steep slope to the ridge.

We regain our high point, looking west this time at the circle of peaks. The sun is leaving, and dreadlocked summits already cast ragged shade across the lake ice. Given good snow, and this is nearly good, the ridge we descend is a superb run, steep enough for flashy turns, a slalom course of rocks and conifers set between nice drop-offs. With a heavy load, I telemark most of the turns, throwing in some narrow parallels where there's room between spruce and whitebark.

The telemark turn is one of those minor miracles in the otherwise discouraging progress of Western civilization: you scrooch a ski out front, weight it, and it flexes into a simple applied-physics arc, which your body follows. Or so you hope. The advantage of the telemark is that, once learned, it almost always works. What's awkward is convincing one's lower brain to shove that foot out and lean forward on it at speed, when normal primate behavior would be to screech and sit down hard. Parallel turns are simpler in concept—the skis initiate the turn together—but more difficult on touring gear, with its flexible and somewhat tentative connection between skier and ski. The advantage of parallel turns is that they're quicker, since one doesn't need to switch feet when starting the turn. Mastered to the level of reflex, both sorts are pure, nerve-whipping fun. What took us forty minutes to climb takes a sweet ten to go down, gravity willing. Gravity always is.

Big Sandy Lake, in its toothy blue hole, is hellish cold, gusts bashing over the ice as cold air drains from the peaks. We raise our hoods and cinch them tight, pull on overmitts, and set forth. The lake ice is featureless, except for the marks of the wind, and I have the fantasy of being blown back faster than I can ski forward. This is lonely, this isolation by wind and fatigue. I feel like writing in my little notebook, but it's too cold. Staring down at my ski tips, I drift into thought.

Exchanging poems with a woman whose writing about nature is widely admired, I was told that my work lacked selfhood. "I want to see more of you in there," she said. An editor sent back my work with a note: "too calm and remote." The teacher who first touched the spark to my writing, still a friend, noticed the same thing—there is a patch of darkness in what I do, a lack of whatever this century calls "self."

My description is praised, but to some editors it is "mere description." We have a strong need for recognition, the reason that photo editors ask for human figures in scenic photos. In my work, this remoteness or absence or shadow, call it what you like, is in the part where we expect to see a face, the assurance of a being held in common. Reading their words, I was angry and hurt. But now I see it differently.

I've lived as much as I could in the mountains or in the desert, at times alone but often with a lover or a few companions. Solitude, the daily process of living with myself and the physical world, is an accustomed state for me. This is not how most of us want to live, yet this is my life: long walks, expeditions on skis, a handful of friends gathered in big, echoing country, passing food· and tales across a fire.

The land has changed me, disarranged the strata of desire like a fault line in my heart. All the real things that make up this place, even the threatening wind, slowly have become part of what I call my self. I don't contain them, since they go on without me, but they have become the vital organs of my thought. It's hard for me to form an idea without a landscape to hold it. I've lost my sense of nature as an ideal, yet found it in a series of places.

I'm not sure whether this change comes from lifelong intent or from my presence, day to day, in a place that demands to be noticed. I think the same process can take place in unspectacular country, out of a will to know something besides oneself. However it happens, a wall has been breached, a window left open. Wind passes the gate. There are pines and snow inside me as well as out. I no longer know exactly what I am, which makes me hard to see.

I'm tired of thoughts in place of things. I want to escape, by whatever means, the fabric of ideas we have woven to contain the world. This fabric is the work of masses of persons, each individuality a single thread. In our time, the artist is one who snatches a piece of this fabric and trails it like a flag, a great, flapping swatch of self. The cloth may be bloody red or heaven blue. It may dance with stars or tools or mythical beasts. There may be a motto: I Am

Beautiful, God Loves Me, Life Is Suffering, Heaven Is Empty, Ever Onward. Each flag calls us to follow.

Each artist works to improve this personal banner, edging the lion's mane with gold thread, adding a star to the blue field, stitching an appliqué of brighter yellow over the faded sun. A successful career is like an avenue of flags.

I have the sky. It arches, such clear blue, such deep black, holding such perfect and numberless stars, that I look up and neglect to embroider my poor flag. It's nearly worn out. There are too many holes, torn by rock, by broken limbs, opened by the wind. You can almost see right through it. The cloth is too thin to bear another word of wisdom, another hammer, another star. So, standing out here on the edge of what is known, I wave it only long enough to draw your gaze. You stop: Who's that idiot out there on the rimrock, flapping that old blue rag? He looks like a question mark.

And then I hide, rolling my tattered cloth as I duck between the boulders. The flag is nothing. It's the rock I want you to see. And beyond it, the sky.

After a century we reach the west side of the lake, climbing to a saddle where we stop out of the wind and gaze red-eyed at each other, then laugh. "You look like shit," says John. "You look like John," I call back.

Frozen chocolate breaks to a sharp edge: if you bite down before it begins to melt, it can cut your tongue. We melt shards of chocolate and gnaw hard candies, stretching the pleasure until our feet begin to ache. Then we begin the slog that will carry us home, the snow samples radiating their heavy chill inside my pack. Only on the steepest pitches will we veer from our trail. The twin slots of our track are like inverse rails down which we aim and shoot. The short climbs between glides seem like purgatory as we lose the light and the cold settles. I stow my sunglasses and add a down vest to the parka and overmitts, trudging to the next downslope.

There is a slight current of air as the cold begins to drain downhill. The cloud of my exhalations floats on it, staying barely ahead of me, a breath-shadow. When I stop to watch, each breath slips ahead and then disappears.

John and I ski close together, then apart, as our rhythms vary. John is younger, and stronger this late in the day. The sun is out of sight, lost in a bank of iridescent, rippled cloud that looks like a school of god-trout, shimmering off to the south.

I try to watch the sunset but totter with fatigue each time my attention leaves the immediate problem of balance and motion. So I stop while John pushes on. The sunset is irresistible. I see it as an act of love: labial pinks flushing into crimson, building to climactic rose, then relaxing to sleepy china blues, the earth and sky parted only by brushstroke pines.

John is out of sight. I strain to catch him, pumping up the knolls, then whipping out of balance down boulder-dappled moraines quilled with pines. He stops to unwrap a candy and I close in. It gets dark. Always does. I can no longer see detail in the bark of the pines; they look like pillars of coal against the blue backlight. We peer ahead, skiing as quickly as we can, cursing the weight of the packs and saving our headlamps for calamities. Skiing in the dark is an act of faith. Taking steep drops down sidehills after sunset is not something I would recommend to friends, but it's a welcome change after groping along an indistinct track through black pines. Each plunge has a drunken irrevocability. Under my feet the land drops away and my skis race. I'm never quite ready, never quite in balance. There are moments when things happen too fast for the brain. Trunks and limbs whoosh by, and changes in angle punch at my knees and pelvis. The pack's inertia wrenches my hips and neck. To level off still standing is a release.

We must be letting out bat squeaks in our distress, because we manage to duck the low limbs and miss the largest rocks, though not all of them. Snaking through a tilted jungle of boulders and outcrops with quick telemarks to kill my speed, I hear my steel ski edges grind. John hoots. I glance back to see yard-long sparks spraying from the radius of every turn. Looking down to watch the fireworks, I ramp off a bigger rock and catch unwanted air. A deadfall leaps up, roots reaching at my face. My skis thread their own way between black bars of pine while twigs snap on my shoulders. Fighting for lost balance, I squirt out intact into the big meadow. Wincing for my abused skis, I yell into the dark: PLEA-

SURE BEASTS!!! John yells his approval. We don't stop. No help for it. To get down you got to go down, as someone said to me in a wildly different context.

As Venus winks above the sun's bed, we follow the blue ruts we punched coming in. With increasing dark they change from shadows to faint streaks of light. They have a strange radiance, these holes in the snow. I go on, go on, a phrase rewinding in my head, *Aim for the light that splits the earth.* To change from setting my skis in shadow to pointing them along barely perceptible tracks of light takes conscious effort, a sign that my body is close to the limit. My body is not responding; I'm at the edge of comfort, if not endurance. The limit of endurance is farther along. I could slog and slide like this all night, hating it, hating everything, taking the occasional, clumsy fall, if that was what it took to regain warmth and light.

It's a trance. I can move, but I'm detached, steering my body from above. It's a trance that can carry over into hypothermic delirium, so I keep a self-check on the strangeness. Two squared is four, four squared sixteen, all existence is suffering, *Aim for the light that splits the earth*, two pale trails, tracks of flame, Adam and Eve fleeing the garden, bodies branching into a fiery tree, across the moon the wild duck leaves no track or trace, *Amen.* Warmth talks back to the dark, the cold, laughing out of tune like a stream guttering under thick ice. Water. Water. Stay liquid. Christ. *Move.*

John is just ahead, a black shape, scuffling into the dark. I've stopped talking, preferring silence to the indignity of a stutter through stiffened lips, needing to stay with the task at hand, balance the pack, raise the knees, kick the skis, stay on top, steady on, *get down.* We get closer, but each move grows longer, stretching out like a field at the edge of sleep. At the next switchback hill my glasses are so fogged that the kerchief only clears them for the frost of the next breath. My fingers are stiff. I drop the cloth. I bend to pick it up and get dizzy as I straighten. John doesn't stop. He slips away and doesn't look back. A good day to die, no doubt. A good night, not gentle.

I watch his black blur swerving down the slope, fading out. My glasses freeze. I drop my pack, find my headlamp, and give the glasses another futile wipe before starting the final turns of the trip, reeling, top-heavy with cold, following the fuzzy beam of my lamp like a locomotive through fog.

By grace, by whatever lurks in my bones, I make it without biting down on a tree. John is waiting before the tributary creek. The ice cracks but carries our weight. Black and cold. The age of ice. We zombie out across the level meadow where the trail register rests unused all winter in its little box, except for the aliases we sign. Our skis crunch as we break ribbons of ice and scrape as we fight for balance, the tracks frozen hard, the wax worn off. Through the deserted campground onto the snow-covered road, we herringbone down the gullet of the drainage, suffer up the hill, and then take a delirious zero-control headache slide through the flinty darkness down.

At last. We ski at last into Big Sandy Opening, the snowfield shimmering south under a clean seven-eighths moon and one last, blue, frozen moon-mile to Zion. Food and fire and sleep.

Part II: Shadows on the Snow

4

*In the infinitely difficult act of thinking nothing is more difficult
than to separate what is known from what is not known—
unless it be to understand that the separation must be made.*

Bernard De Voto, *The Course of Empire*

*T*he snow has deepened, like memory. I woke up to the February
moon, one day into her last quarter. I started the stove with the
first section of the newspaper I bought in town, crumpling the front
page and its bold headline: *Mandela Freed.* I watched the fire eat the
words, watched the flames grow up through the splits of pine. Then
I went back to my bag while the room warmed.

We left the cabin and made our first two miles in the dark. Now,
in half light, John and I are moving up through ghost-forest, to the
east. Our ski tips dip and surface like dolphins in new snow. The
green wax grips hard and then eases into long glides. Around us,
the lodgepole pines are a cool black, yet to claim their rust and gray
and green from the rising light.

There is no wind; the air is still as mountain air can ever be.
Motionless, the trees have nothing to say. They have no opinions.
They demand no rights. They stand and grow where they can. John
and I ski past them—so many that I only remember a few—the one
thrown down by wind across the path, the one split by lightning
into identical, tortured halves, the one scarred by a deep ax blaze
where the trail bends left.

51

No one lives this high, this far into the mountains. The trees are the residents of the winter country. Collectively, they are the forest, which hems the trail with shadow. I think of walls. Log walls, then concrete and cinderblock, flat and abrasive, the explicit means of confinement. Nelson Mandela is out of jail. Last week in South Africa he walked out of Victor Verster Prison to a tumult of welcome. He was taken as an earnest young man, locked away for saying what he felt—if certain feelings are shared they are known as conspiracies. He emerged, twenty-seven years later, as a gray effigy, a specter of conscience. While I rejoice in his week of freedom, I still grieve for the twenty-seven years in prison.

Up here, all is cold and still, the snow between pines a dimensionless blue, a blue you could fall through and keep falling. The snow creaks under my weight, then sighs with each long forward stride. Out here a thought can last all day. It's like a stream that keeps running under the ice; you can break through the hard surface and find the dark flow at points that are miles apart. Today we will ski sixteen miles. I breathe a white mist. It is still too cold to talk. There is nothing to say. We move like animals in half dark, free in our silence, prehistoric, frost whitening the tips of our hair where it escapes from knit caps.

In the city, there are walls within walls. The only unbounded gaze is up, into the smoky sky. The city sky is blue only straight overhead, a blue hole ringed by heavier shades, rust and bark and mustard, industrial air, America's breath. In the city of night, the electrical glare is a rising dome that blots up white streams of starlight and dims the phases of the moon to rumors. In New York, the jeweled towers were beautiful and terrible. From the night street, there seemed to be no sky above. It was hard to look up, a tightness at the back of my neck. Between buildings there was a void, no stars, nothing but an end to light.

The lodgepoles grow close on either side, in ranks. Lower in this range, hunters cut down the narrow trees and spike them or wire them to those still living, to build horse corrals. In the suburbs, neighbors put up walls of cinderblock, redwood slats, cedar staves, chainlink overgrown by hedge, anything to stop the curious eye. America, the civilized part, is a maze of walls groping toward final connection.

There is a fence of one sort or other around much of the National Forest boundary, stranded barbs, sheep net, or elk fence, an eight-foot wire mesh that looks like an East European frontier, to keep the herds from moving down onto the ranch haymeadows. Where land is counted a possession, something to divide, there must always be fences.

The forest is a permeable barrier, a wall you can slip into and hide. Sometimes the forest looks sullen, on heavy days when clouds cover the peaks, guarded by its own presence. In rain or snow, the forest is an obstacle, latticed with dead limbs, hedged by slick dead trunks. But when the clouds break and sun reaches under low limbs, the woods look more like sanctuary, a haunt for the rebellious.

But these woods are also something like a heart, a dark pulse at the center of what we are. Every country has borders, and we think of them as being the outer limit of the nation, but there are also inner boundaries. I've tried to walk those inner boundaries, to patrol the unknown center, to trust my senses more than words. No matter how set in its power, a country needs watchers who face inward to the heart, who gaze upward to the sky.

I read the paper last night, the first in weeks. Ten days ago, Mikhail Gorbachev forced the Soviet Central Committee to vote the surrender of its own supremacy, seventy-two years after the Bolsheviks dissolved the Assembly and renamed themselves the All-Russian Communist Party. One wall, across Berlin, has been breached. Germany, it seems, will become one again. All these histories unfolding in the same world as this. Prisons, central committees, walls, lodgepoles, snow: a version for every place and every need. Sometimes I wish our history would melt and flow into oceanic memory, mixing like the world's water.

Watching the paper burn, I wondered what events—news, hearsay, people I've never seen—should lay down in my memory along with the smell of smoke, the creak of leather, the look of snow at dawn? Like the snowpack, memory builds in layers, some hard, some soft, some solid ice.

We change places. John's pack floats like an odd-shaped cloud above his legs, his skis alternating below. When I stop I can hear the snow give under his weight, a faint crunch; then his other ski drives forward, like a violin bow rosined with wax. The snow crystals sing in high transients like tiny steel Es. As the ski stops, his weight shifts with the rustle of cloth, a squeak, and a crunch. I listen until he is almost out of hearing. When I move again, the sound of my skis covers the sound from his, and my breath hisses out like blue smoke, frosting my glasses.

The trees go on, lodgepole, Engelmann spruce, mostly tall and straight, crowns reaching for the light. There is no horizon. The sky is blue patchwork. I can feel the weight of all this growth, the captured light and water thrust up from the root and sustained, heart and sap and bark, the needles, resinous and sharp. I sense the life of trees, the multiple selves, the dark magnetism of a single being.

At first you're a stranger to the forest. It's too quiet. You feel as if your every move is seen and judged. Then, without noticing a difference, you feel more at home here than anywhere else. It's as if your heart skips a beat and then begins on an older pulse. After that it's the city that's strange, the commonplaces, catching a train, driving a car, lights that change from green to red. It happens, not quickly or simply; it can't be learned or picked up from a book. It happens in your bones, a promise that can't be taken back.

To what exists, there can be no contradiction. You recognize all things as real—paved streets as well as leafy paths, concrete dams as well as canyons—but your allegiance shifts. You begin to sense what lives outside your thoughts. Your loyalty fixes on wild things and will not rest inside walls or in words. Your new awareness is revolutionary, but not in a transient, political way. Your sense of balance shifts, massively, like a' plate of rock in the earth's crust. You may live quietly, smiling at neighbors, trying to stay unnoticed. But you'll never feel as you did. It's as if you've gained another sense; you belong to something larger than a church or a town or a job, to something like gravity. Things you valued—money, clothes, cars—seem like idle notions, bits of torn paper surrendering to flame.

We stop. In John's gaze, I stand mute. We pass a jug of tea, the fragrant steam touching our faces as we drink. All quiet, we breathe and look around. There is a band of light across the east, barred with trees. We stretch and shift our weight under our packs. The snow squeaks under our skis. We go on.

• • •

An old ski track, barely visible under fresh snow, ends at sunrise, four miles in. We cross Miller Park, a broad, sloping meadow that lies like a white quilt dropped in haste, assorted by gravity into slow undulations and soft peninsulas. The snow is improving with elevation: good, fresh, dry. It rode in on a polar front, with five-degree air, when we were forty miles south, climbing toward Black Joe Lake and complaining of the cold, only to get a blast of wind that let us know how much worse things might be.

We ski north across a rolling highland that stretches north and east to the wall of Divide peaks, their summits three thousand feet above us, their bases at about eleven thousand feet. This broad bench is a distinctive feature of the west side of the range; convoluted into rocky knuckles and trellised gorges, jeweled with lakes, it still averages to a gentle incline compared to the steep western front of the range, thickly timbered slopes, shaggy with deadfalls, that level off at about ninety-five hundred feet. The streams come down this front, often in a series of falls and cascades, too steep for fish to climb. In winter, the cascades turn to staircases of white ice.

It's strange to realize we're grooving along about four feet above sandy soil and thin grass, taking smooth glides over rockpiles and deadfall, suspended by the grace of winter. In fact, we are walking mostly on air. Ice provides the structure, but air makes up most of the volume. At Black Joe Lake, the snowpack was only about 15 percent water. Closer to the sea, snow tends to be heavier, and the pack will have a greater proportion of water to air.

The character of the snowpack changes by region: the dense, icy armor of the Northeast, the slush and crust of the upper Midwest, the wet wool blankets of the Sierra Nevada. Here, in the mountains of the interior, the snow is dry, falling from air masses that have been wrung repeatedly by passage over the Great Basin ranges to the west. By the time a storm gets here, most of the moisture is gone; what's left has a lot of space and cold in which to condense, forming airy, sharp-featured hexes: in skier's jargon, powder.

The largest crystals are those that have plenty of time before reaching the earth. As they fall they grow, water freezing to a pattern, pointing and lacing the dendrites with fine detail, each crystal shivering down a current of air to rest on a granite spire, a pine needle, lake ice, a meadow, a coyote's back.

The shape of crystals is determined by the amount of water available in the air and by its temperature. Above freezing, water vapor forms clouds. Just below freezing, in moist air, it forms soft pellets of graupel, or becomes the icy rime that beards trees in mountains near the coasts. As it gets colder, the graupel stays in pellets but keeps more of its original crystal form. In drier air, rime becomes columns, then heavy plates, then spatial dendrites as the temperature drops.

Lower temperatures form needles, sheaths, then hollow columns. At about 15°F, plates are formed, or in moister air, stellar dendrites—our image for the word *snowflake*. Below 0°F, plates change to hollow crystals or columns. As it gets colder, the forms get simpler, solid crystals shaped like bullets and columns. A polar storm here can leave tiny, solid crystals fine as stardust.

Wind may scour snow crystals from an exposed spot, tumbling them over high passes and depositing them on lee slopes to form slabs and cornices, layered like sand dunes, likely to avalanche. Much of the ice in glaciers on the east face of the Wind Rivers fell as dry snow on the west face and was blown over the ridge.

I love snow. Born in Wyoming, I grew up in the deserts of the Great Basin and the Southwest with snow far above, capping the ranges above each broad valley. Snow was heavenly, exotic, a delicacy. It could be eaten, sculpted, slid upon, rolled in, or simply admired. Like a coat of white wool, it transformed the rocky, scratchy, sunburnt earth into a furry harmony of curve, hollow, cup, breast, and shoulder. It graced the slightest flux of light with pure color, an endless succession of blues, making each coincidence of sun, cloud, and pine a study in perfect composure. It allowed the length of sunrise to lie full and cool along the land. Sunset meant a more fervent glow, sunflower, saffron, gold, mustard, flesh, carnation, lavender, murex, each tone unalloyed, flawless and then completely gone. Whatever good light the sky gave, the snow matched it, beauty for beauty.

As we reenter the trees, we hear a complex warbling punctuated by chirps and yips. A flock of small birds peer down at us from hiding in the dark foliage; they have reddish bibs. John thinks they

are pine grosbeaks, but they look too small; finches, I say, uncertain
of the species. Cassin's? Whatever, he says. They spook at our conversation and leap out as one, setting loose snow from the twigs.
The crystals spin in the diffused light, light and cold on my face. I
brush the snow from my shoulders and blow it from my sleeve.

Once a crystal comes to rest, it joins the society of the snowpack.
Within a short time, it begins to change. Gravity causes constant
settling of the snow. Stellar crystals link arms. Layers bond or remain unbonded. The rate of change depends mostly on temperature.
As the winter progresses, each storm deposits a layer on the pack.
Water vapor moves within the pack, causing further change. In
stable conditions, with the earth, snowpack, and air at the same
temperature, water diffuses from the fine points of crystals to
the broader surfaces, gradually rounding them into grains. This reduces the airspace, settling the snow. The simple transfer of water
vapor in stable temperatures is called equitemperature (ET), or de-
structive metamorphism, because it destroys the complex form of
the crystals.

But the snow is not often the same temperature as the earth or
the air. Temperature can vary in the snowpack, layer to layer. This
changes the snowpack in complex ways lumped under the heading
of temperature-gradient (TG), or constructive metamorphism. Since
it takes place at any temperature difference greater than one-tenth
of a degree, it goes on almost all the time.

Imagine that it's night over Miller Park. The earth is warm compared to the winter air, so the bottom of the snowpack may be 30°F
while the surface, under winter stars, is − 10°F. The forty-degree
gradient drives water vapor from warmer, moister layers to colder,
drier ones. This is like laying a dry sponge over a wet one. To
anyone with the mildest dose of physics, the objection is that the
snow is nowhere warm enough to melt, making water vapor impossible.

Water, though, has its own rules. It sublimates, changing from
ice to vapor and back without becoming liquid. This allows the
transfer of water to the coldest, driest layers of the snowpack, where
it forms cup-shaped or flat crystals called hoar. The larger the temperature difference, the larger the crystals.

The largest temperature gradient may occur at the bottom of the snowpack, where the snow touches the comparatively warm earth. This gradient forms depth hoar, hollow crystals lacking strong bonds. Depth hoar may also form where an icy layer blocks the water vapor. Layers of hoar have a sugary feel, lacking cohesion. They are often the weak layer on which slab avalanches take off. In steep country, depth hoar, though unseen, is to be feared.

All this goes on under our skis, out of sight. But the changes can be felt. Experienced skiers can read the snow like a boatman can read the water, from the changes in texture, firmness, and resonance beneath their skis. I've followed blown-in ski tracks under a foot of new snow without being able to see them, by their feel. I wasn't even thinking hard about it. What seemed obvious to me proved mysterious to my partner, who kept plunging thigh deep off the old track when it was her turn to break trail.

Surface hoar, on the other hand, is both visible and exquisite. It forms on cold nights, in places open to the sky, where rapid cooling sublimates water vapor between the snow and the air. In the morning, thin plates like dragonfly wings catch the first light and give back prismatic color, then collapse as the sun heats them.

Across Miller Park, the wind has given the snow a thin, cake-frosting crust. My skis submarine and the crust ripples, lifting in a poof as the tip emerges at the end of a stride. The layer beneath is firm and trustworthy. In the woods above the park, the picketed lodgepoles give way to Engelmann spruce, subalpine fir, and white-bark pine as the sun begins to loosen the surface.

At this time of year the snowpack has a stratigraphy, like the earth's crust, which remains distinct until the spring thaws. Like time, the snow builds in layers, visible only at the surface. Ski mountaineers hunch over their beers and ponder the snowpack like fishermen mulling the mood of the sea. They take soundings by digging snowpits, brushing and shear-testing the strata to check for avalanche danger. The history of the snowpack can be reconstructed. A deep layer of fragile hoar represents ten clear, cold nights in succession. An ice layer marks a rare February thaw. Our history is a succession of surfaces. I like to think of historians as digging pits into the layers of memory, brushing and testing the strata, the stack of what we've said about ourselves.

We reach the campsite, on a gentle pass from which the country drops steeply away to north and south. We circle to the left and lay our red packs down. Laughing at our sudden lightness, we begin to circle again, packing a spot for the tent. Under our weight the layers compress. I recall an old print—Catlin?—of Indians dancing on snowshoes, circling to the left. Around we go, stomping our little history into the layers of snow, from the outside to the center. The snow yields and sinks until we have a level space. In a few storms, it will disappear, blown in, but under the surface the compressed layers will recall our stay.

We sit on our packs to eat, bagels and cheddar with an apple each. Tomorrow we will have bagels and Swiss. I'm not fond of bagels. When this set of samples is done, I'll shudder at the sight of one. But there are advantages to monotony. We don't have to decide what to have. We seldom overeat. And we tend not to linger over lunch, a bad idea when it's cold.

Clouds have floated in from the west, scattered like boats in a bay. There is a faint, intermittent breeze. The peaks of the Divide are close enough that individual features stand out, towers and headwalls, bare and gray where they are steep enough to shed the snow, otherwise white. Whitebark pines block our view to the west, over the broad valley.

What is the history of this place? you might ask. I've camped here twelve nights, perhaps more, I'd answer. Others have camped here before, I'd think, since it's a good spot, but there are no names carved in the bark of the pines. Frémont may have passed near here on his trip into the range, but carried his words and maps away with him and left no marks. But even that thin wash of history was laid on in summer. In winter, there has been nothing to draw attention: no gold, no prospect of gain, not even open water. There has been no reason to come this way except pure will: a few winter mountaineers trying for Gannett Peak. But will only stretches so far. "Hideous snow," they say, coming out. "We're going to the Tetons." A few groups from outdoor programs used to come, waddling in on snowshoes under frame packs, taking five days to reach this point. For most, one trip was enough.

One of my favorite professors came up here in winter with his son. "When it's clear enough to climb, it's too cold," he told me. "Then it warms up and snows so hard you can't see."

History requires human events and memory. Written history is a recent thing, standing on the shoulders of song, saga, epic, and legend. But in winter, high in this range, there has been so little human presence that nothing we could call history has ever developed. Natural history, the lives of trees, migrations of birds, the strata of glacial ice, the lift of rock from the earth's crust, all these, but little that takes place in words. The early explorers climbed their summits in summer or fall. Before Anglo settlement, the whole basin was deserted in winter, not just the mountains.

In 1867, when the transcontinental railroad was underway, itinerant loggers moved into the skirts of the range for the winter. They cut pine, spruce, and fir, then hacked it—squaring it on opposite sides with a broadax—and then sawed it to tie length. They lived in temporary cabins, banked with snow for warmth. Through the foothills on both sides of the upper Green there are old stumps three or four feet high, marking the snow depth when they were cut. The ties were decked—stacked in rows—on the snow and then skidded or sledded in bundles down to the banks of the Green. At the peak of snowmelt, they were tipped into the current and floated over a hundred miles to be caught by the boom at Green River City, a railhead. But the tie hacks, as they were called, never got much above the lowest skirts of the range.

Snook Moore used to snowshoe from his ranch on Tosi Creek to feed elk at the feedground below Green River Lakes. It was eight miles each way, done each day on snowshoes. Clem Skinner used to snowshoe up and core the federal snow courses to predict streamflow, but got pneumonia at Dutch Joe and had to build a sweat lodge and cook the congestion out. He left his set of coring tubes behind. I found them last spring in back of some horseshoeing tools, wrapped in cardboard and dust. Now, the Soil Conservation Service sends out a crew in a big, orange Tucker SnowCat. Most of the courses are next to roads, none very deep in the mountains. Recently, they put in instrumented snow pillows that beam signals up to a satellite, so they don't even have to leave the office in winter. Clem Skinner's sons, Monte, Courtney, and Bob, guide. Some years they've led a group of dude climbers in a New Year's attempt on Gannett Peak. Last year, they followed our December trail, and

Marty and I saw their campsites when we returned in February. They didn't make the summit.

Now, snowmobilers penetrate some of the easy high country, grinding around basins at timberline like one-legged tanks and leaving a spaghetti of tracks. There's little to keep them from crossing the wilderness boundary but a toothless law and a sense of honor, which is in shorter supply than gas or money.

There are NOLS trips, National Outdoor Leadership School, which take overburdened youth on a weaving, halting progress into the range. We call them Nolzoids. We see them in herds of twenty, struggling with their sleds, digging craters with their heads, camped in the cold spots, spending half a day to build a snow shelter. It looks like hard work. They pay for it. Occasionally, a helicopter roars overhead to pluck an unfortunate from winter's grip.

Marty, with his two complete winter traverses and forty-odd sampling trips, has probably spent more winter hours than anyone, alive or dead, in the heart of the range. If there was a list, John and I would be close behind him, but none of this is history. The mountains are named and mapped. We have no plans to establish a trading post or dig a mine. We aren't on our way to the Seven Golden Cities of Cíbola. There are no longer any native populations to be enslaved. We argue, but haven't started a war yet. That is, we don't *want* to make history up here. Let this be a history-free zone. We need a few.

Human events claim most of our attention, to the point where talking about the weather is regarded as a conversational failing. The storms of history float like black balloons in our skulls. But up here I feel a partial release: I'm free to notice details—finches, pines, clouds, the texture of the snow, the colors of the sky—things that have been subjugated to our self-interest. Character forms in a series of layers, some liquid, some frozen, some at the melting point. If history is a series of surfaces, like the snowpack, then it is also a series of justifications. We define ourselves as a frontier nation, a people who have overcome both howling wilderness and a horde of enemies in order to become great.

From here, from this cold, high place, it looks different. From here, I look into the world like someone gazing into a fire. I try to see our history as if I were a Wind River Shoshoni, dispossessed. Or, at the limit of thought, as a pine or a cloud. From here it seems our history has been inflicted, like smallpox, on an unwilling continent. It all seems, suddenly, like an immense weight, a flow of lava, churning with charred forests and melting engines, sending a sulfurous plume up to heaven. Suddenly, I want to protect this place from history. This is not my wish alone; the burden of our history is such that we try to keep places exempt by declaring them wilderness.

I try to raise the subject with John. He listens impatiently. I have the bad habit of pondering something for hours, then tossing out the final few particles of thought. He rolls his eyes up to the sky and then cuts me off. "Free What? Free history? History free? I don't get it. Didn't we have some more nuts in another bag?"

I decide to save this for my notebook. John has his own needs, closer to hand. Even after the bagel and cheese he looks hungry, which on his face takes the form of noble yearning, so we dig out the stuff-sack of trail food and eat the mixed nuts, sitting on our packs, watching a lone cloud form over Frémont Peak. We plan to catch the Hobbs Lake sample today and carry it to the A-frame cabin, a round-trip of about sixteen miles. Tomorrow, we'll return on our packed trail with the sled. By then the tent platform will be set up.

The advantage of this camp, which took a few years to discover, is that it sits above a hidden shortcut. The summer trail continues east. In winter, the trail is an opening through the thick woods. Other than that, it doesn't mean much to a skier. Missing our camp, it winds an extra mile east through rocky glades before dropping to a pair of lakes and much-used campsites.

Like rumors, shortcuts are sweetest when shared by only a few. This one looks improbable, diving off the high contour into a steep defile that drops to Suicide Lake. Most skiers—of the few that make it this far—see our branching track as evidence of either masochism or madness. They follow the dotted line on the map and are happy. Unlike Lander or Hastings, we don't proselytize for our cut-off. Let the main trail be swarmed. We're happiest off it.

Leaving the campsite, we loop down two narrow bowls that feed the gorge, telemarking past ragged outcrops and weathered white-bark pines. As the gorge steepens to a boulder-choked V, we exit to the right and traverse a short, steep slope into boulders fallen from a cliff. We link narrow tongues of snow into a route that sneaks through house-size chunks of granite. There is barely enough snow to bridge the gaps, so we go slowly, testing dubious spots with a cautiously extended pole. Beyond the talus, we slide off a low cornice where currents of wind shoot around a three-story boulder, sculpting the snow like hot-rod fenders. We avoid the air scoops, then climb a rubble moraine that dams a frozen lake. We stop for breath before going out on the ice.

North of the lake's outlet, the summer trail follows the right side of a slope down into switchbacks and a wet meadow. It crosses the grain of the land, the direction in which glaciers cut steep grooves, flowing west down the flanks of the range, so it drops wildly before climbing back up to the rocky cup that holds Hobbs Lake. Marty named this hole Depression Depression. "Yonder lies Depression Depression. Where marriages break up and self-concepts falter," I tell John.

"Yeah. That's what Marty calls it."

"Abandon all hope, ye who enter here," I intone.

"Wasn't there a bag of nuts somewhere in your pack?" he says.

In previous years, Marty and I camped farther in, on a pass at the south end of Seneca Lake. From there we returned with our camp and two large snow samples: full packs and about a hundred and fifty pounds on the sled, ripping down into this hole and then struggling back up toward Photographer's Point. Even Marty, a glutton for this sort of self-abuse, didn't like it much. As he pulled the sled up the steepest part, his eyes bulged. That's the only time I saw him really straining; it hurt his pride, so it was easy to talk him into using the new camp.

The shortcut allows us to whip down the two bowls, traverse, and take a steeper drop down another gorge that the trail avoids as it zigzags into Depression Depression. The second gorge holds a stream that froths down stairs of shattered rock, a scramble in the summer. With enough well-set snow, it offers a winter way of reaching the bottom quickly, with style. If the snow's good, as it often is in the sheltered, north-facing gorge, we carve luxurious turns above the frozen creek, then swoop across it with something less than caution. Below is a west-facing shield of talus and long, traversing turns to the bottom. Without the sled, we can cover this part fast.

On the return, we aren't dragging a full load of camp gear along with both samples. This change in tactics means more distance on skis—forty-four miles for both samples rather than twenty-eight—but lets us go lighter and quicker, in sum, less pain.

Today, the snow in the gorges is heavy and we schuss, dropping straight in. In faster conditions, this would be suicidal, but today we never get quite enough speed for fun, let alone fear. We cross the talus slope and thread a narrow V-gorge, traversing the steep south flank. Popping out into the bottom of Depression Depression, we shuck a layer of clothes before starting the climb out, looking around at the cliffs and slopes of talus, crowned with patches of pines, that rise on all sides.

Courtney Skinner, an outfitter from Pinedale and longtime Wind Rivers guide, claims he made one of the coldest camps of his life here, returning from a winter attempt on Gannett Peak. Since Courtney has tented out from Antarctica to Everest, it must have been cold indeed. The air from a lot of chilly country drains into this hole. Researchers in the Bear River Mountains, two hundred miles south and west, found that nighttime temperatures in limestone sinks, with no outlet for either water or air, could be as much as sixty degrees lower than on the surrounding slopes. This drainage opens in a steep funnel to the west, but the outlet is narrow enough to trap the cold. From our camp above to the bottom of Depression Depression the temperature drop is probably about twenty degrees on a clear, winter night. When that's subtracted from an ambient temperature of twenty below zero, not unusual up here, there is potential for fabulous discomfort. The tracks of hares and pine marten, common in the woods above, are much less so down here. The animals know what's what. Today, there is still surface hoar on the snow in midafternoon.

Starting again, we cut traverses up the short, steep pitch to the basin of Hobbs Lake, coasting down through the knuckled glades, crossing the ice and curving off east, skiing briskly to reach the far shore. There is no weakness or slush now, as there was in December. When the ice and snow cooperate, crossing lakes is easy. By definition, the surface is level, though I don't care much for the thought of water underneath my skis, no matter how much ice there is between.

We climb up short rises into a complex of small basins, each fringed with whitebark pines that give way to Engelmann spruce in protected spots. I stashed the collector in an unlikely spot, well off the ski-way that continues higher into the range. We follow my short but devious route to reach the collector at two o'clock in fierce sun. The tube is full, with a bit of snow mushroomed over the rim.

We drop our packs and peer up at it, deciding what to do. I slip my mitten inside a plastic bag and push the edges into the center, compacting the snow inside the rim. Then we unscrew the giant hoseclamp that cinches the bags, strip off two layers of duct tape, and have a brief struggle pulling the sample in its bag up and half out of the tube. I jump down with John still perched on the flange, grunting and heaving as I stretch a clean bag beneath to catch the top half of the sample. Floomp. Got it.

This is a recent innovation. Before, Marty and I took the entire sample in its bag and hauled it in the sled or crammed it into a pack, so one of us suffered with a monstrous load coming out, falling through the packed trail, sweating up each climb, swearing while the other loafed and tried not to snicker. Splitting the burden makes good democratic sense: we average the suffering.

Telemarking down steep slopes with ninety-pound loads is certain, sooner or later, to cause major grief. One screw-up and your knee is blown for life. Some tests convinced me that we could split the bulky sample for transport and then combine it to melt in the lab without contamination, so we do that, distributing the five-foot-long column of snow between two packs and four legs.

Coring, we find the snow about five feet on the level, a bit less than average. This winter we've missed the heroic storms that can dump two or three feet at once, but we still have a substantial snowpack, about three-quarters of the average at least, better than the 25 or 30 percent in the drought-stricken southern Rockies.

In the winter, our big storms come from the northwest. The snow they carry is cold, small flakes that build layers of light powder. Other storms come from the collision of frigid, polar air with moist Pacific fronts from the west or southwest. The snow from these boundary storms can be wet, windblown blasts that stick to pines and parkas, usually slowing as the cold front crosses, the flakes diminishing, becoming fine and dry.

The snow from the northwest is clean. In Oregon and Washington and western Canada, there are few large sources of pollution, other than the commuter traffic of cities, Portland, Seattle, and Vancouver, which is rich in the oxides of nitrogen. At this remove, our snowpack tends to be relatively clean. The warm season brings a southwest flow, and our winds pass over Los Angeles, Las Vegas, Salt Lake City, and the various coal-fired power plants and industries that light their lights and keep their people employed. Nearer these mountains, in southwest Wyoming, are an open-pit coal mine, two large power plants, and major oil and gas fields, giving off oxides of sulfur and nitrogen. Combining with the water in the air, these become acids. Thus does our natural history become unnatural. These mountains, by our early reckoning, receive about ten times the amounts of sulfuric and nitric acids that they did in preindustrial times.

Most of the sulfuric and nitric acid that is deposited arrives as rain, with a strong summer peak in both concentration and amount per acre. If our snowpack came to us on the same airshed as our summer thunderstorms, then it is possible that some of our high lakes would be acidified, like those in the Adirondacks. Once the smoke and dust are airborne, we lose any possibility of control. The air has its own rules. We can't—by wish or law—exempt this place from what we do.

I like the winter up here better than the summer, which seems perverse. I wonder if this knowledge figures in. In late summer when I look southwest over the heat waves of the desert, I gaze into a wall of dirty air, yellowing and blurring the far ridges of the Wyoming Range, obscuring the Uintas. Then, I feel like something awful closes in, a gray army, riding the wind.

In winter the storms loom, clean and blue as wet steel; they devour the horizon and pass. In their wake are nights of cold, perfectly starred, with Orion leaping up above the ridges, looking like a hunter on skis. There are chill, flawless days when the horizon is the earth's distant curve.

Leaving the collector with a clean bag, we ski with heavy packs through the knotted whitebarks to a hollow stump, where we cache the sampling gear for the next day's trip, higher and four miles farther in. Even split, the sample gives us oppressive loads, and we trudge like refugees across the frozen lake and climb out to the southwest, heading for the drop-off.

How can I describe this: the icy pressure at the base of the spine, the strain in the thighs, the grip of pack-straps on each shoulder? Skiing with a heavy pack is like a bad dream. My center of gravity is not at my hips but up under my sternum, making any sidewise slip a disaster. Ripping down the funnel from Hobbs Lake, I decide the safest course is to squat as low as I can and bore straight in, but every change in the snow threatens my balance. I wobble and my skis spread too far. I force them back together. The pack rides me like an NFL linebacker, arms around my chest. I make it down, drafting into the cupped bottom, losing momentum as I thread between small pines. John follows, more confident in his stance.

As I grope with my poles, the straps gnaw into the tendons strung from neck to shoulder. I loosen the straps, but the waistbelt slips down over my hips, and my left leg begins to go numb. I shorten the straps and the gnawing starts again. I bend forward and hump the weight up on my back, trying to cinch the waistbelt. I stand up and it slips down. Every movement is labored, even each breath. The chest strap squeezes like a vise. Loosen it and the shoulder straps spread, putting a worse strain on the arms. After skiing with light packs, this is pure punishment.

Below the talus shield, we drop the packs. I can feel the discs in my spine drawing back into their normal shape, no longer bulging like doughnuts. We stretch on climbing skins for the long, uphill crunch, then hoist the packs, first from the snow to one knee, then, with a gasp and a swing, onto our backs. Heading up the track, we joke about being dogs. We bark a few times until we run out of breath. Soon, all we can do is climb, ratcheting each step into the slope, our thighs creaking like hawsers.

We dump the packs and strip the skins off above Photographer's Point, named for its space-gulping view. From here, it is mostly downhill. We cruise down ramps and follow meadows into the pines, our track as usual, not as fast as we hoped. On flat stretches, we shuffle along our trail, getting quieter and quieter as the sun sinks. I decide to straighten a kink in the track and—whoosh—my heart tries to kick its way out of my rib cage. Grouse flush from under my ski tips, one, two, three, four-five-six. They flap up to sit on low branches and look at me. I stand and catch my breath. Their tails are slate gray, with dove gray tips. Blue grouse. They use the snow like we use a down sleeping bag, to wait out the freezing nights. The sky is clear, with a corona of high ice-haze to the west. The sun is almost gone. In the meadows, the snow glows like a silk scarf stretched above live coals.

The forest at sunset grows a different shadow than it wears before sunrise, deeper and less transparent. The strong last light flattens the receding pines into a single plane that rises and falls at our side as we continue. I am thinking quietly again, no longer about walls or history. I am thinking about Nelson Mandela and of Winnie Mandela, his wife. I am wondering how her name felt in his mouth, how the latch clicked when he pulled the door shut with his own hand for the first time in a quarter century. I am thinking about how it would feel, after twenty-seven years staring at a wall, to lose my face between a woman's breasts.

We slip into the thick woods above Faler Creek, southing down the slow waves of the land before the turn that will take us west to the cabin. I wish I knew a better word for blue. In winter, after the sun sets, there is blue in every particle of matter, in every pool of air, a watery transparency to every solid thing.

As I grow tired, as it grows darker, my vision becomes less than my will to move. My shoulders burn, and my upper arms and my thighs. My hands begin to numb with cold and the constriction of the straps. There is ice inside my mittens. I should change them, but I don't trust myself to do it. Only a couple of miles to go.

I no longer try to think, letting my mind drift into vague rhythms, alternations of light and dark. I'm used to pushing on when I can hardly think. Following John's black shape along a north-facing hill, I see lumps of snow shifting under the spruces and firs. Disoriented, I stop, thinking it's a dizzy spell brought on by fatigue. John disappears, skis crunching in the icy track.

Eyes shut, I breathe deeply. The cold air burns my nostrils. I open my eyes. Patches of snow still flick through the dark. I shut my eyes and open them: the snow jumps. Then, one of the white lumps grows a shiny black eye. It blinks and hops behind a pine. Then I realize that it's a gathering of snowshoe hares, white in their winter coats, blipping through the dusk, conducting their winter rites, nipping the needles and bark from snow-muffled twigs.

5

*History, as yet, has left in the United States but so thin and
impalpable a deposit that we very soon touch the hard
substratum of nature; and nature herself, in the Western World,
has the peculiarity of seeming rather crude and immature.*

Henry James, *Hawthorne,* 1879

I wake, knowing who I am but not where. I hear someone breathing
and see the rosy coals of a fire outlined in black. John. The cabin.
My internal compass spins and finally settles. I feel the cold air
drafting from the window above the bed and lift the blind. The
window is plated with hard frost. I roll toward the table and fumble
for my watch. There is a tiny button for light. 4:02. Slipping into
down booties, I kindle the stove, shut its glass-paned door, then step
out to pee. The snow squeaks and crunches under my feet.

The clouds are gone, and the stars are distinct from horizon to
horizon, almost palpable, like handfuls of snow scattered on a black
marble floor. In the clear darkness, the country seems to open at
my feet: I can feel the gulf of air to the north, where Frémont Creek
follows a two-thousand-foot canyon that was cut by a glacier. When
it melted, the glacier left an emptiness in the heart of the range, a
void that echoes with the presence of the ice.

It's strange to be here. Improbable, on a February night, to be
up this high in a cold range of mountains, preparing to go higher.

Even though I've spent half my life scheming to be in this time and place, it's hard to live in it easily, the way one lives in a room. Yet, in a room, I never feel the weight of a glacier, the hollow in the air it leaves behind. What I've been told, I can imagine. I see the canyon filled from rim to rim with moving ice.

There were people here, tracking the herds in the long valley, though they probably didn't see the glaciers from above. The snout of an advancing glacier, with house-size boulders tumbling, serac towers falling, and low-frequency groans vibrating through the bed-rock, is not a hospitable campsite, but as the glaciers retreated they left lakes dammed behind their terminal moraines. On the shore-lines are buried campsites, often only rings of charcoal, bone frag-ments, and broken hunting points. A Yuma point thought to be from 7,000 to 9,000 years old was found near the Divide at the northern end of the range where there are also ancient enclosures for trapping bighorns.

Any people who walked the distances it would take to survive in this country wouldn't be frightened by these mountains. They had softer shoes—bark sandals and leather moccasins—but harder feet. Between the rivers of ice were tongues of bedrock and boreal forest giving onto high tundra. Why would they bother to climb? There may have been particular roots or herbs, prized for their remote-ness. Breezes, to drive the summer hordes of flies and mosquitos to ground. The need for initiation, for a vision of the land from above. Curiosity or a touch of madness. Maybe those people did look down at glaciers, not all but at least a wild minority.

The last glacial advance, from 10,000 to 25,000 years ago, is named after the nearby town of Pinedale, which lies just below its moraines. The rough Pinedale moraines are studded with granite boulders like a cookie with nuts. Before the Pinedale glaciation were the Bull Lake advances, 50,000 to 140,000 years ago, which left great, smooth sweeps of terrace, and the Buffalo advance, over two hundred thousand years back. I picture the Wind Rivers on a win-ter night then, before there was anyone here to see them, a glittering mass a hundred miles long, floating above the valley like an iceberg.

Each glaciation filled the low points with ice and carved the heads of drainages toward ridgelines, narrowing them into cirques. The V-canyons of streams were scooped into rounded gorges with steep walls, torn and polished by the burden of ice and rock. When the ice receded, the steep valley walls lacked support. The ice that carved them away also held them up. Gravity is slowly dismantling them, burying their feet in talus, reducing them to shallow Vs at the angle of repose.

In the dry air on the roof of the continent, stars look like drifting ice; the universe might be the end of a snowstorm, when the last flakes sharpen against clear, black sky. My neck gets stiff and chill runs up the insides of my thighs; realizing that except for down booties I'm naked out here in the dark, I shudder and go back. The lesser dark, flame-lit through the stove's glass, welcomes me in.

A slow awakening and a sumptuous breakfast—omelettes with salsa—ease us through dawn. We have *café solo*, dripped through a cotton filter carried back from Peru. *Caliente, fuerte, sabroso.* I can feel it filtering through my passages. Before long, John leaves to scamper over to the campground outhouse in his longjohns, down parka, and booties while I wash the dishes. He returns to say he startled a lone skier headed up to higher country in our tracks. An early riser. The guy managed a spectacular leap, considering his skis, when John waddled up behind him on the path and grunted "G'morning."

I bathe with a wet rag and suit up, then we pack the sled with camping gear and issue into a clamor of light rather than the usual darkness. The trail register is duly signed, this time as Sid Vicious and Johnny Rotten, and we hoist up familiar tracks toward the camp-site, about seven miles in. Despite hauling the sled, this is almost a rest day. The samples from Hobbs Lake repose in a well-shaded hole we dug by the cabin. The next site is farther in and will require a night in camp, but experience has taught us not to haul both samples out at once. A pulk sled loaded with a hundred and fifty pounds of ice is not the best companion for backcountry skiing.

A pulk sled, for those unharnessed, looks like the bottom of one of those old claw-footed bathtubs. Take the bathtub and cut it hor-izontally six inches from the bottom. With the appropriate tool, slice off the claw feet. The remaining portion closely resembles a pulk sled. Look at it—your ruined bathtub—carefully. The slanted foot of the tub is the front of the sled. The best ones—made in Norway—are fiberglass. Ours is blue plastic, heavily abused.

It has a tubular hinge bolted to the front, which extends into long aluminum tubes—the traces. On a normal pulk sled, these relate to the skier like the shafts of a buggy relate to the horse. On our supermodified sled, I sawed off the traces and plugged the ends into pieces of heater hose just above the hinge, which makes them flex at the sled. This makes it possible to cross them into an X between sled and skier, enabling the latter, with a deft twist of the hips, to steer the sled around curves. A double loop of shock cord goes loosely around the junction of the X.

Since the hose-joints flex downward each time the skier slows, they act as brakes, digging into the snow. While this is convenient for the timid, it is hell for John and me, who regard out-of-control downhill runs as a way of completing our official duties more quickly.

More shock cord, run through d-rings in the front and knotted and duct-taped to the traces, keeps the joints from flopping down. No brakes. Good. Another innovation is the harness, which attaches the traces to the skier. The original waistbelt had to be strapped on under the hipbelt of the pack, which was typically heavy as shit. The pack's weight ended up resting on the traces and forcing them against the pelvic bones like giant tweezers. The stock system worked fine for day-trippers hauling pre-ski children, but for us it was a thoroughly evil arrangement. Each fall meant a tortuous double process of un-belting before one could move, then an equally onerous rebelting.

A bit of beer-fueled engineering, with The Replacements blasting from a cheap tapedeck, and I had it. I added female Fastex buckles to the hipbelt of the pack and sewed up little nylon-web units punched with two quarter-inch grommets, threaded through two male Fastex buckles. Clevis pins held them over the ends of the trace-tubes. The pack's hipbelt was then the belt for the sled. With two flicks of the fingers, the sled could be cut loose, nice if you happen to be up-ended in a crevasse or hear an avalanche whip loose above.

I tried the sled going uphill and it worked—*perfecto*. Going down, I tried a quick, sliding stop. Zang! The trace-tubes shot forward and almost drilled my elbows. Hmmmm. Too much flex in the front units. With the help of another Replacements tape, I devised a supermodified, ultralight type II harness that joined the two nylon-web grommet thingies with a strap and an adjustable buckle to prevent forward lunge.

Back up to the hill. I clipped the buckles to the pack's hipbelt. Snick. I reached around back and hauled on the dangling strap. Tight. It felt good. Solid. I hauled it around. Over logs. Around trees. Upslope, downslope, sideslope, leap, turn, stop. It worked. Tech-heaven.

The day blooms, clear and bright. The sky is snapping blue above the snow, and each object seems to have its own halo of color, light prismed from frost crystals. They coat the needles of the pines and firs, starting to melt on each dark, sun-facing plane, and form a layer of hoar that shines on the surface of the snow. Without cloud or wind, the day is warming. As we follow our track from sun to shadow, the snow begins to change texture.

Our faces are hot and the sun-warmed surface is melting slightly. Just below, where our skis are, the snowpack is night-cold. Like down or milkweed fluff, airy snow is a superb insulator. It keeps the ground from freezing deeply and allows small animals to live near the soil, burrowing through fragile layers of hoar for seeds or frozen vegetation, protected from subzero air. The snowpack also has a sort of memory for cold: last night's chill pulse will travel slowly down the layers of the pack, not reaching the bottom for about two days, diminishing as it goes from a ten-degree drop at the surface to one of less than a degree near the soil.

This morning as the surface begins to melt, the night's low temperature lingers six inches down. Surface moisture clings to our ski bases as they break through, and the colder snow beneath freezes to them with each step. The same thing happens when we ski out of a sunny meadow into the shade. We stop and scrape and rewax, though it doesn't help much. We rummage through snow of several temperatures with each step: a ski-waxer's dilemma. The sticky progress starts to get tiresome. John takes a fantasy break while I go ahead with the pulk sled, which is like dragging a dead pig through mud. O Sisyphus.

What we need now, I think, is a new sled, one that doesn't have rips and gouges all over the bottom. The Blue Hog. Jeez. It feels as if John's sitting on it. I flip it and find intricate ice formations, like white coral, a perfect snow anchor. After admiring them for three or four seconds, I whack away with the grip of my ski pole. The sled resumes its normal, mildly irritating drag.

I meet the returning skier, one Harold from Pinedale, a chess champion and pleasant chap when not crept up on from behind. He failed to make his objective, Wall Lake, saying that beyond our packed track the trail-breaking got too strenuous for a day's solo travel. A quarter-mile higher, the sled gets mulish again, calling for a flip and a whack.

Chickadees are burring and beeping in the conifers, picking the seeds from fir cones. Crossing the backbone of Photographer's Point, the sled gets impossible again, and the ice mushrooms growing from the blue plastic of its belly strike me as some sort of visual pun, so I find myself whacking the sled and laughing at it when John tops the rise. He pulls up with a grave look, though as a seasoned traveler he tries to conceal his dismay. I explain. He nods and gives a tiny shrug, as if to agree that it's quite natural to laugh at the bottom of a sled. Ice is funny stuff. We eat handfuls of nuts and he takes over in the traces. In stages, we haul and whack our way under sunny skies toward the campsite on the pass.

Watching John struggle up a hill with the sled, I recall accounts of polar exploration. Scott, for instance, counted on the ability of his men, harnessed in fours, to haul wooden sledges loaded with over two hundred pounds of supplies. Amundsen, more realistic about conditions near the Pole, elected to use dogs, a notion derided by the English, who worshiped the unfortunate Scott. A crucial problem not apparent to anyone from a temperate climate is that, in extreme cold, snow is not slippery.

Down to about $-30°F$, the pressure of a moving ski or sled runner will melt the snow, allowing it to slip forward on a film of water. Below this temperature the crystals no longer melt easily, so the ski or sledge no longer glides. One might as well be towing a bale of hay through sand. At very low temperatures, when every scrap of energy is precious, a dog team, with multiple small feet, has a tremendous mechanical advantage over a man on skis or snowshoes in pulling a sled. The skier has to lift or shove the skis over the abrasive snow in addition to dragging the sledge. For Scott's party, towing a sledge under such conditions was a fatal regimen. Amundsen learned tactics from the people of the north polar regions and, as far as he could, adopted their ways. Scott, counting on martial courage and English pluck, did not. His diaries are a record of courage, but not of good sense.

We reach a high point and slip down the north slope to the camp. It's a spot I picked out two years ago, on a height well sheltered by pines. We ski out of a sloping meadow into a small, level glade. The day is still calm, warm enough to lounge on a friendly boulder, but we resist. We pull the tent from its sack, and it blooms like a sunflower in the afternoon sun as we flex black rods into sleeves, tensing them so the metal ends pop into their grommets. We place it in the center of the packed snow, careful not to punch holes into the surface, shake out the dove gray fly and stretch it over the yellow body, then slip aluminum stakes into loops and extend the vestibule that shields the entrance. Into the tent go our pads, sleeping bags, extra clothes, food, and books. Since it's a rest day of sorts, there being too little daylight to reach the highest site and return, we devour a late lunch and drain a can of Foster's each— ballast for the sled—before setting off in search of some unencumbered runs.

I recall a steep, wooded slope above a small lake to the southeast that might be right for the conditions, shaded and sheltered from the wind. John roars off in Harold's track, which wanders north and loops to the top of a knoll, so I catch up and point us south along the slope and up a convoluted ridge. The climb provides devious trail-breaking through snags and gargoyles, so I take over when John's bullish approach dead-ends us on a bench.

Looking down, I can see a frozen lake to the north, no tracks on its surface. I scan the west shore, but see no sign of the Nolzoid camp's igloolike snow shelters that usually pimple the slope above the lake. The groups of twenty would build four or five of the snowhuts, called *quinzhees*, spending hours with shovels. The *quinzhee* is built by the Athabascan tribes of the interior north by piling loose snow into a mound, then beating it with sticks to pack the surface and promote the sintering—freezing together—of the crystals. The Nolzoids use grain shovels and ski poles. After the mound sinters and settles—about two hours—it is carefully hollowed out. The ground plan is like that of an igloo, except it lacks the low entrance tunnel, which is hard to build without solid snowblocks. There is a recess inside the door to trap cold air, a raised sleeping shelf and a vent hole. Often, there is an L-shaped wall attached to the outside near the door, to baffle the wind. "No Nolzoids this year," I say to John. "They usually camp along the lake."

"They're invading Teton Pass," he tells me. "The Ski-Huns of Wilson are up in arms about it. They come in with herds of novice skiers and hack up the bowls. *Muy malvado.*"

I've slept in their abandoned *quinzhees* on solo trips and found them comfortable, but they're far too much work for two people who intend to spend only a night or two in the spot. "I miss them, sort of," I tell John. "They make me feel honed. Skiing with Marty I don't get to feel like an expert very often." He laughs.

As we rest, I tell him a story. Our original route went by this lake, so we skied close to the Nolzoid camp and sometimes met them. Two years ago, Marty and I stopped to look at the recently occupied *quinzhees*. There were weird ski tracks on the lake, arrayed in rectangles and squares. "Marching lessons?" I asked.

"Probably practicing rescue stuff, packing a landing for a helicopter. 'Air evac' is what they call it. Remember the helicopter that flew over us at Seneca Lake last year?"

"Yeah. We tried to flag them down to haul our sample out, too. Do you smell that?" I scented something delicious, but not quite identifiable. We circled through the little village, and I saw a splash of brown at the door of the last snowhut. The smell was richer: "Chocolate!"

My skis in cocoa-flavored snow, I stooped and peered inside the hut. The aroma of chocolate was strong. I could feel saliva beading up on my tongue. Marty leaned down to look over my shoulder. As our eyes adjusted, we both laughed at once.

There were tatters of red nylon spread on the floor of the hut, the remains of a stuff sack. But the funny part was the deep brown chocolate color of the hut's interior—floor, walls, sleeping shelf. "Marten!" I roared.

"Hahh?" he blurted, jumping back.

"Not you. Not Martin. Marten. Pine marten."

"Oh. Yeah. That must've been what ripped up the stuff sack they cached."

A pine marten looks like a slick compromise between a cat and a fox, but in reality it is a larger, forest-dwelling cousin to the weasel. They prey on voles and squirrels, and apparently on Nolzoid

food caches. The image of the marten or martens dancing and shaking the red stuff sack was too much, and I laughed again as Marty joined in. Do martens growl? I imagined them making muffled, high snarls like battling pups, sun-fishing and shimmying in a wild tug-of-war over the sack, enveloped in a chocolate whirlwind.

"The poor babies are gonna be waaaay bummed when they get back and find this," Marty observed. "It'd be torture to sleep in this thing."

"Yeah, no hot drinks and your sleeping bag soaked with drool."

John laughs aloud, which he doesn't do often. I lead out, climbing through humps and cornices, snaking up the ridgetop, feeling clever. When we top out, it's evident that my scheme for a direct route brought us up the dumbest possible way. I mention this and he nods forgiveness. We break tracks from the open spine along a contour south onto a forested bench above the ski run.

From above, the slope looks madly steep, curving out of sight as our gaze drops to the frozen lake. We put on parkas and hedge a bit. "No sweat," I say as I think about ramming trees or dropping off unseen cliffs.

"Piece of cake," John agrees.

We choose lines and I tip off first. The snow is slightly heavy, giving just enough resistance that I choose the fall line, whipping into turns and swoops, wowing between big spruces. I can feel my parka slapping and my hair blustering against my ears as I try to catch a thin edge of control, dodging trees and snow-backed rocks, tearing a blue hole in the air. I break from the trees and hit faster snow, wind woofing in my ears as I slalom the open runout, hearing John howl "Tram Shred!" above, tears forming at the outer corners of my eyes with the rush of cold. Then I run out of steep. Raising my poles like two scalps, I glide the runout, crossing onto the ice of the lake.

John rips down on a different vector, whooping, slashing turns down a ridge that wishbones into a little bowl, then cutting right to catch my track on the runout. He whizzes past me, forty feet farther onto the ice. There are wind-tears on his cheeks.

"Jah Rockin' Shred," he proclaims. "Almost as good as the Pass." Two sine waves lace the mountain's flank, converging where we stand.

This kind of skiing is like sailing a light boat in a high wind. More often, laboring under a pack and towing the sled, I feel like a lugger wallowing inshore with a hold full of cod. Skiing with a pack is usually nicer than hiking bare ground, but skiing unburdened is exponentially better, like flying low.

From the lake, we get a face-on look at the slope, picking the best lines, finding markers for the start, scoping the rock faces and deadfalls. John leads up the obvious gully from the lake, traversing onto the sideslope. Ten kickturns later, we reach a bench below the ridge and look out, gathering breath. This ridge parallels the Divide, the razorbacks of Jackson, Frémont, Sacajawea, and Helen catching roseate sun three thousand feet above our heads, a heaven for the eye. There, under the burning sky are buttresses, walls, towers, blocks, a wild chiaroscuro from which couloirs of ice snake like lava into the violet depths of Titcomb Basin. The sky tilts, like a rolling iceberg; the light slides off it to the west. We stand and let words fail, as they seem to do up here.

After the quiet, I clear ice from my ski bases and take another shot farther north, steeper, with a catchy drop midway like stepping off the high board into a cloud, hitting a patch of speed, and banking into desperation turns, link, lift, overbalance, recover, cut, cut, and ooze out onto the frozen lake without a single breath in my body. This is a magic that lights the body from inside.

As the wave of alpenglow fades out on the Divide, we hasten up one more time, set on untracked lines, and drop. With the advantage of a preview, I veer toward a convex bulge that looks dangerous from above, but which falls nicely into a clean ridge that plummets through spruces to a stylish runout. Coasting to a stop, I cavort and howl and see John's alarmed face poke from the tree-gloom above. "The bump," I shriek and stab a pole, "Do It!"

He rolls a rakish turn off the edge, cutting telemarks across mine down the ridge to make figure eights all the way to the ice. It's a poem no one else will see.

I get breathless watching. For a moment I relax my arms and let my ski poles hang, let the air back in, feel my chest lift, looking up, full to the brim, tired. My knees ache. Enough. It's cold, getting dark. Nothing to do but go home.

Strange, how the word *home* comes up rather than *camp*. Being a professional nomad, I've grown used to how an unknown bit of earth can, by adding a tent or a fire, be called home. Do I own my home? Hardly. It owns me. Something Wallace Stevens said comes back to me: *Life is an affair of people not of places. But for me life is an affair of places and that is the trouble.*

In lieu of a fire, we pump the stove up and begin melting blocks of snow, alternately slouching and stomping our feet until the flame sends steam out from under the pot lid. We make cocoa to drive the teeth from our bellies. We melt more snow and spread the commissary, sipping Wild Turkey from a plastic bottle. Dinner is spare, a packet of freeze-dried rice and beans alleged to be Cajun-style.

Evening in camp. What do we talk about? In my notebooks I seldom record dialogue. I note other details: colors, sensations, insights. The truth is we don't talk about much except particulars. What shall we eat, the rice stuff or the stew? What did the clouds look like to you? Will it storm tonight? Shall I set my watch for an early start or shall we take it easy?

This evening we don't talk, but we grin every few seconds. We needed the ski runs; now we feel relaxed. Mug in hand, I look out from the tent at my red baseball cap hung on the tip of a ski, the triumphal arch of the crown seam, the right-to-left slope of the twill, three white eyelet vents, and the dolphin smile of the brim.

Tonight the cold is not punishing. We can take off our mittens to handle pots and put them back on quickly enough that our fingers don't start to freeze. Marty and I camped higher, often on the pass at the south end of Seneca Lake, in a windspill that had the single advantage of a stunning view.

In 1986, Marty and I skied to that camp in a day, direct from the trailhead in a cold snowstorm. It was a long and punishing climb. We were tired from trail-breaking with heavy packs and from dragging the sled through deep snow. The clouds blew away and as the sun set the sky cleared. The temperature fell precipitously, ten below, fifteen, twenty. In the wake of the storm, there were gusty north winds, which combined with the cold to make it hard to keep the stove going. We couldn't cook in the tent, since the steam would build a thick layer of frost inside to fall onto our sleeping bags and melt. Cooking in a tent is also a good way to die of carbon monoxide poisoning.

We built a little partial igloo of snowblocks for the stove, outside the door of the tent. It took two hours to melt water for a mug of chocolate each and to heat food. Marty would unzip the tent, tend the stove, and then spend five minutes rewarming his hands. Then it was time to tend the stove again. The wind pounded us, gusts whacking the stormfly against the tent like an oak board against the side of a barn.

We were dehydrated and exhausted, unable to find warmth even in our down bags with layers of underwear and pile. When the wind stopped about midnight, it felt like thirty-five below. The next morning, we felt like we had been running all night.

In severe cold, the wilderness starts just outside your skin. If you have good clothing, then that is your house, and it goes with you wherever you go. The Shoshoni knew how to twine rabbit fur and feathers into winter robes, how to line oversized moccasins with fur or shredded bark. We have synthetic underwear, vapor-barrier liners, pile jackets, down coats, parkas, overboots, and down sleeping bags of sleek nylon. They seem to work, though not without understanding and care. In five years of these trips, we have lost no fingers or toes.

In deep cold you must guard your heat, guard your water, since to gain water you must give up heat. If you are thirsty and want to eat snow, you must keep moving. Otherwise, you must make fire or find a patch of open water. The water straight out of a winter stream is cold enough to crack your teeth. It freezes instantly on the rim of your water bottle. When you drink it, it goes down the center of your body like an iron rod. Then you must warm it inside until it becomes part of you. The Shoshoni liked to camp near hot springs in winter, like the springs on the Bear River to the southwest, where a whole village was murdered by the California Volunteer Militia who had been brought into Utah to watch the rebellious Mormons. The massacre took place in deep cold. The returning troops lost hands and feet to frostbite. More than three hundred Shoshoni lost their lives.

In winter, not encumbered by notions of real property, not living within self-built fences, the Shoshoni moved to more clement spots, lower valleys and south-facing slopes out of the wind where the sun's heat could warm them, dry out the robes, make it possible to sit outside and watch the country. In deep cold, people slept together for warmth, children at the center.

Out here, at night, your sleeping bag is like a burrow under the roots, warm and dark like the earth. You take your book or your Walkman inside your bag. It may be zero in the tent, and your breath freezes to white fur on the fabric. The tent keeps the wind off, it keeps the snow off, it keeps the white peaks and the stars at bay so that you can sleep without hearing their voices in your head; but in deep cold it is not your house. Your body is your house and the cold wants to come in.

Tonight, the cold is not an enemy. It is easy to be grateful for the world's mercy, even when it bears no trace of recognition. Tonight we may eat and rest without struggle. This is an honest benediction. We eat, steam flowing up the sides of our faces as we bend toward the food.

After, we brew up mint tea and shuck layers. The air in the tent is around 10°F, and we get into our bags to hold the heat of the meal. John turns on his headlamp, and I use the spill of light to get out of my gaiters and boots. Then he snaps his light off, so I turn mine on to get out of my bibs. Then I cut my light off. There are sparks as I draw the layers of fabric apart: tiny lightning bolts between the nylon and the polyester. I get lost in snaps and zippers, so I turn my light back on. He uses the scatter to rummage the food sack for the whiskey. In mid-rummage I click my light off.

We are playing aggravation chess, but the first rule is that neither of us acknowledges it. The winner keeps a higher charge on his headlamp battery. John fumbles at his lamp—a feint—and then goes on rummaging in the dark. I wait, declining the gambit. He grumbles and lights up. I poach his illumination to fold my pile coat into a pillow. We both wear sneaky grins. This can go on for hours.

He gets up and exits the tent to pee, so I grab the whiskey flask and stow it in my sleeping bag, snapping my light off as he stoops back into the tent, his breath clouding the entrance. Headlamp on, he takes his booties off, shrugs into his bag, finds his Walkman, warms a cassette tape in his armpit, engages it, dons the headset and snuggles down, groping for the whiskey. I choke back a snicker. He glances at me with suspicion while I feign a deep interest in the stuck zipper of my sleeping bag. He gropes on, then subsides into glaring at me and tapping the fabric of the tent. Some frost drifts down. Off goes his light. I hear further groping and then the clack of a switch and the weasel voices of Camper van Beethoven.

Turning away, I ease the flask out and slowly rotate the lid. As I touch it to my lips, the tent lights up. I take an indolent, innocent sip before passing the bottle to John, who is pursing his lips and waggling gloved fingers in my direction. I see Aha! in his eyes.

I switch my lamp on and try to read a decrepit copy of Gide, through the ice-fog of my own breath. *I am going to speak at length of my body. I will speak of it so much that you will think at first I have forgotten my soul.* My fingers get cold and I lose hold of the book, rear up, and ask John for the whiskey. He takes a gulp before passing it, his shoulders rising and falling slightly to the music. The tape ends.

"What's the book about?" he says.

"The Immoralist," I say.

He smiles. "Sounds way Jah good," he says.

With the fruity mellifluousness of a BBC announcer, I read from the back cover. *As sheer story, Michel's rebellion has all the narrative excitement usually called forth only by tales of physical adventure.* John crosses his eyes. *How deep and secure is the protective veneer of civilization? What is the meaning of death to a man who has never realized life?*

"Sounds French," says John, and goes back to his Walkman, and The Cure or The Call or The Cult or maybe The Curse. I can't quite make out the label before he snaps off his light, and I hear only a thin, metallic yammer. This goes on until about eight-thirty, when I stow the book. I take a last small drop of the blessed milk, brush my teeth, and spit out the door, avoiding the snowblocks stacked for next morning's brew-up. John hunches up and deploys for sleep, getting tangled in his headphone cord and windmilling his elbows.

I'd like for you to know John as I do, to like him, but I hate to put words in his mouth. On these trips, we know each other not as much through words as through our bodies: grunts and moans, inhalations, the glint of our eyes under thickets of wool and hair, the dance of sleep. Words mean less than everything else. Posture, gesture, breath, the angle of wrist or elbow, the grudging relinquishment of a block of chocolate: these would fill volumes. But we don't say much. The Thoreau doll in my head shakes his finger. "The circumstances demand," he says, "something with marrow."

But I promised a degree of truth, so I'll tell you this: what matters up here is what we can't say. I can't ask John if he would die trying to get me out if I fell through the ice, nor would he ask me. Neither of us knows, but we still have to trust. We can't cram the pleasure of the sunset ski runs into mere words. The density of language often depends on a sparsity of experience. If you read almost any account of traveling with Eskimos or hunter-gatherers on any continent, there is a frustrating lack of articulation, but only for the explorer. *The natives communicate with rude grunts and a sly flutter of the hands, as if they had something to conceal. Their eyes slant toward a common object, a spot on the horizon, indistinguishable to me, and they utter a simultaneous breath, as if some great truth has been revealed.*

The more one shares a physical world, a realm of nerve and skin and bone, with another, the fewer words it takes to declare a meaning, to form a bond. How do bears communicate? What do lovers say? Does it bear the definition of print? Why do polar explorers recount so little in the way of dialogue? If living out here plunges us into a bodily closeness, it also makes us aware of the profound barriers between any two human selves. I'm suddenly tired. I slip down into my bag, grope for the zipper, and set my headlamp aside.

As I nest, John spills his entire bottle of water between our sleeping bags. "Shit!" he says, appalled. With resounding groans we hoist our bags like the skirts of maiden aunts, seize snowblocks from the pile at the entrance, and mop at the freezing puddle, an Inuit trick. The dry, hard chunks of snow soak up water. John's honor is saved for the moment, spills being serious breaches of camp decorum. He tells me that his ex-girlfriend, Susan, the one-woman safari who is now my ex-partner Marty's great love, once spilled her badly capped water bottle under their bags at twenty thousand feet in the Himalayas. It went unnoticed until the water soaked into both bags and began to freeze.

"Could be worse," he concludes as we chuck the last soggy snowblocks out and burrow into our bags to rewarm our hands.

"Worse indeed," I say, and we laugh. He's forgiven.

Aside from the mishap we feel good, and the bags are still warm and fairly dry. Such things—skin temperature, blood sugar, hormone balance—have more to do with our feelings than we like to acknowledge. On the verge of hypothermia I slip into a universal hate: I loathe my partner and all natural phenomena below freezing. When I warm up, I rediscover compassion. It's almost as if I need these alternations.

If you treat your body with too much solicitude, you will never learn to live with it. We depend so fully on our bodies that we are never able to forget them, to pretend that we are mostly mind or mostly words. Out here we are voluntary peasants: our speech is like black bread and ale. Yet the lack of speech engenders a richness of thought and perception. For sheer interest, what we say seldom compares to what we see. I look at the snow and see it, in a hundred ways, as my life. I grasp how a gathering of Inuit can sing a few words—*The White One, The White One, Aieeeeee*—repeatedly and with profound emotion. In a world that outweighs speech, one speaks more humbly.

Now, we think with our kidneys, hoping that the cups of chocolate and wee drams will not quite hydrate us enough to make any three o'clock dashes necessary, that being one of the rankest indignities of winter camping. Marty—who tends to be the hero in such tales—had urgent and unpredictable bowels, having all too frequently to exit the tent with a snarl, into snow-swirling dark. If you ever need to feel mortal, that's a particularly good way. He never accomplished his journeys in silence, but would snort and flail as if he had waked to hear a bear whoofing outside the tent and had to bust out there and jab a spear into it. Wide-Ax, I called him. The Barbarian.

If I dwell on this, it is because the body and its ways assume a larger role out here. Amundsen's first dash for the South Pole was turned back not by weather or starvation, but by hemorrhoids. A low-bulk diet brought the explorers to a painful halt.

I'm lucky, being able to call my shots. I usually know to the ounce how much water to drink in order to wake at sunrise, or just how to stretch the first cup of coffee in order to get my bibs and boots and gaiters on before the morning rush. *Schatzo perfecto.*

Easy stuff—getting a drink from the tap—comes hard out here. There's no morning shower or Mr. Coffee. We have to melt every drop of water. When John spilled his liter of water, he was spilling about a half cup of fuel and the work of dragging it in on the balky sled, the effort of pumping and priming the stove and the wait for a block of snow to melt. Wasted effort, lost heat. The difficulties seem most poignant in the morning, trying to come awake, dress, melt snow, drink, eat, load packs, and get up on skis before the sun. When you breathe in, your front teeth ache. When you breathe out, your glasses fog. Getting dressed in ice-needled dark, with stiff limbs, indecipherable zippers, straps, buckles, frozen bootlaces, armless parkas, and other puzzles, can wear you out before you even manage to get upright.

If the stove won't heat (ice in the pump? soot in the nozzle?) or a bootlace snaps or a mitten is lost in the jumble of gear or the toilet paper isn't where it goddamn well was last night, your fury grows by logarithmic bounds. Some of my finest oaths—*By the Bloody, Black, Frostbitten Fingers of the Cross-Eyed Siberian Christ*—have been issued about that time of day, early, when the pines are like inky demerits on the deep blue snow.

Something always goes wrong out here. Sometimes multiples of things do. Discomfort is a given. Real suffering is a possibility. The stove could give out. My binding could rip out of the ski. A blizzard could bury the tent and smother us. They could declare this place a national park.

It's either very late or early. Since it's cold and I don't need anything, I hate to lift my head out of the hood and switch on the headlamp and find my watch. John is inert, breathing heavily. I was dreaming and in the dream I began thinking and the thought woke me up. The dream was folkloric, with a foul cloud spreading over the land from evil furnaces and smoldering pits. I was filling a bag with creekstones and pieces of amber, getting ready to fight some goblins when I realized that I was dreaming about a fact, air pollution, which woke me up.

Underneath the love I have for being up here in winter and my love for the snow and the intoxication of skiing and big rock peaks and alpenglow is a kind of dread. I don't yet know how bad the air is way up here. The numbers have yet to be crunched. Our work doesn't translate directly into knowledge. Until the columns of figures on deposition and chemical concentrations get analyzed, I can't interpret them, other than to know that there are particulates and aerosols on the wind that ought not to be here.

The notion that L.A. and Vegas and Salt Lake City and Geneva Steel and the Naughton Power Plant, all that commuting and fabricating and burning, can taint the air three hundred or five hundred or a thousand miles downwind scares me. From the perspective of these mountains, our elaborate houses, glossy cars, hulking furniture, hot tubs, the blue burn of TV cathodes, and the heaps of status junk that we accumulate are monstrous. The stench rising from the cities is like the plume from the stack of a crematorium.

Sometimes a dream or a story is the only way out. Frodo overcomes the Dark Lord. Hayduke blows up the dam. The No-Good Shits retreat in disorder, and we all gather for drinks on the veranda. I like stories like that, but I'm always waking up in the middle, during the fight.

There have long been refugees, ones who crawled and swam and lied their way out of the fires. But in a poisoned world what happens to the possibility of escape? What sanctuary exists when the air itself has been despoiled?

On all continents, saints have struggled to free their souls from a world tainted figuratively by evil, a real world of plagues and boils and starvation that made the promise of another world, beyond death, sweet.

Yet their world was clean by comparison. Smoke was smoke, rain was not a witch's brew, and the earth grew hemlock and nightshade and cobra, poisons which were old and could be learned.

This is a different world, soft, deadly, altered beyond recall, and we must live in it and try not to kill each other. We must bear unprecedented threat, the anger that rises from fear, and the loss that yawns beneath our streets.

The wilderness is good, but it is only a respite. Only the self-deluding could find Eden up here, knowing what we know. But this is my heart's country. Five generations of my family sleep at the foot of the western cordillera, eight more above the bedrock of this continent.

Dissenters, Puritans, Democrats, Mormons, Greens, each generation with an urgent vision. We still aren't sure whether we found Zion here or simply dreamed it. After all the years moving west, we still lack a testimony to the land, a covenant to match its wild, spacious life. This is a part of what I'm trying to learn out here, to construct a plausible self beyond the border of language and law, before I join those pilgrims and pillagers and their victims in the earth.

Regardless of this, faraway cities burn their night lights, coil like dragons around their heaps of gold, the sources of bad air and grievous harm. The land has never failed us, but we've made the hasty choice a million too many times. We live apart now, in our hearts and minds and ways. Eden's a dead word; Zion's a convulsion.

Sometimes I dream and the dream wakes me and I have to probe this wound, scrub it till it bleeds, stitch it up with the coarse thread of regret. All this I do in order to regain my sleep. And I do, somehow, again.

6

In the winter mountains,
Praying to the wind and snow:
Get on with it.

after Bashō

Climbing out of Depression Depression's cold shadow toward the sun, I feel the blood beat its way into aching fingers and toes. It was cold in camp, rising in the dark, packing gear before sunrise. I took my leather ski boots into my sleeping bag for a half hour before lacing them on, but they still felt like frozen rocks on my feet. Breakfast was a sequence of small mishaps. The stove went out. I spilled boiling water into my hat. John's sunglasses were elusive. We mended our affairs with strong coffee and granola bars. Out of the tent, we both groaned, soft protests against shouldering the packs, clipping into our skis.

The snow was a frigid blue as we skied down the two bowls and traversed the talus slope, and the ice on Barbara Lake had a layer of gleaming hoar, mayfly wings collapsing under our ski tips as the sun opened the horizon above thick pines. Everything was perfectly still except where we touched it. To be skiing at first light made me feel like I was violating some winter law, breaking some vital silence.

We dropped down the stream-gully, faces burning with the air's bite. It was still colder at the bottom of Depression Depression, where sunlight wouldn't reach for another hour. Cold air flows

downhill. It drains off the ridges and then pools in the glacially scooped basins so plentiful in the Wind Rivers. In the low spots the air is noticeably colder than on nearby heights. In winter, it's foolish to camp in the bottom of a rocky pocket where morning sun arrives two hours late.

The cold presses against me like the body of silence. I can hear cloth scuffing against cloth, the creak of my boots in the bindings, the soft hiss of snow under my skis. Nothing moves but us and the sun's rising glow. No wind, no animals. In winter, most of what life there is hides, mice huddled in communal burrows, shrews threading the tunnels of snow-covered streams. Skiing down, we crossed the tracks of hares, but so far there is no movement in the landscape except John and me as we climb along the contour toward the sun line. The light comes down toward us, descending the slope, snow glinting like trapped stars. We break into light. It almost hurts. I can feel my pupils stopping down. Then I feel the sudden heat, soaking into my dark blue ski pants, and the right arm of my parka, reaching through the layers of my skin. *Gloria*, I sing, stretching it up the scale, then down, a one-word chant. John says, "What?"

"Gloria," I sing again. "G-L-O-R-I-A."

"Pretty nice in the sun," says John. When we stop moving, the quiet is absolute: no brush of wind, no far-off jet, no rumbling traffic, no skate wheels on a sidewalk, no muffled voices. It's hard to say whether this silence feels good or lonely. John is taking out his Walkman and putting on the headset. He grins and wobbles his head in time to the music, which sounds from here like a mouse chorus. Since the flood of television and films, our lives seem to need music for support. I can sweep the floor to music. I can make love to music. I can listen in the dark in my sleeping bag, but not out here in the light. Not while I'm on the move. I tried skiing with a Walkman, but hated it, like having one eye covered. Earplugs are earplugs.

It gives me a lot of room for thought, this wealth of light, this lack of sound. I recall "The Snow Man," by Wallace Stevens. It begins,

> *One must have a mind of winter*
> *To regard the frost and the boughs*
> *Of the pine-trees crusted with snow*

And have been cold a long time
To behold the junipers shagged with ice,
The spruces rough in the distant glitter

Of the January sun; and not to think
Of any misery in the sound of the wind . . .

I first heard the poem in 1967. I have a book at home that falls open to it. It's a lonely poem, desolate as this high place. When I follow its lines, something looms over me like the cold and silence, like this sky, this dark thin air.

Is the world a terrible place? Does it rest on suffering? I look around as we climb. "John," I say to his back, but he's lost in his music and doesn't answer. Nothing answers: pines, rock, snow. All beautiful, all mute.

But it's not bad. There's no anger. Just quiet. It doesn't obey. It doesn't resist. It's just here, like I'm here. In the light, I climb and look around, which seems like enough. I search my memory for the rest of the poem. The last line reads *Nothing that is not there and the nothing that is.*

John stops. I edge by and take the lead. We leave the sideslope and gain a raggedly forested saddle above, meandering through bent whitebarks. I hear the brrrrp of a chickadee, which clips down to a pine branch, setting loose gathered snow. The fine, dry crystals dust down between me and the rising sun in a fall of tiny rainbows. The sight stops me, stops the breath in my throat, gives me back a world which is briefly whole and unhurried, going nowhere, each part clean and perfectly placed.

To imagine is our special grace.

Through the pines and firs are more chickadees, picking and flitting. We descend, cross the lake ice, and climb through pocket meadows where only the tips of tall willows appear above the snow. The woods are warmer here. There are hare tracks, squirrel tracks, and those of a pine marten, but each footmark is filled with frost: old tracks, days old.

We cross the ice of Hobbs Lake, climb the rocky folds east. We recover the tools and bags and bottle from the gray stump, and I notice again the light lime green of lichens that beard the dead wood. It is possible, up here where wood decays so slowly, that this tree died before I was born. There is a different sense of time where the trees grow only a few months each year and sleep in dormancy for the nine months of winter, guarding their water and strength.

The stump is old. The tree died before any of us was born. Dead of lightning or winter's desiccation, its bark and the thin, resinous varnish stripped from the needles by the abrasion of drifting snow that cuts like grains of sand, a dead pine may stand rooted for ten or twenty or fifty years, bark falling like torn garments around its feet, insects gnawing the marrow, woodpeckers boring after them, squirrels nesting in those friendly cavities, hawks breaking away the finer branches for nests, people reaching up to snap limbs for fires, bare wood weathering to austere grays and golds, polished and re-fined by snow, heavy branches borne down by gravity and late-summer gusts, the whorled grain checking and opening up into pillows of mulch, fostering currants and creeping juniper, growing fat grubs for bears to dig, loosening, letting in air and light until there is only a silver shell, the bare idea of uprightness, a hollow in which to hide things.

John veers off the track, drops his pack and digs out a roll of paper, then skis into the pines. As I load my pack, a bird swoops boldly down to perch on the grip of my ski pole, large, with subtle whites and grays and deep black fenders. It has a black slash behind the eye, and the beak is a fine, black hook. The beak cues me: it's a northern shrike, a predator. I'm surprised to see one up here. They're uncommon and, I thought, furtive. It seems equally curious about me, tipping its head to focus its gaze. Another lights on a limb close by. Two shrikes. Linda—my bird-crazy wife—won't be-lieve this.

There are two species that resemble this one, both large, with the same palette of grays and whites. One, the Clark's nutcracker, feeds on the nuts of whitebark pines, which it caches in spots, like crev-ices in granite cliffs, where squirrels won't find them. It has black wings with white tips, but it lacks the muscular shoulders and head, and especially the hooked beak. The nutcracker has a tapered, finely pointed beak for extracting pine nuts from ripe cones, not this lethal hook. It's not shy, but swoops down on humans, usually with an abrasive *kra-a-a-a*. These birds arrived quietly and watch me in silence, feathers fluffed. The near one begins to quiver so slightly that I can barely see the motion. I remember reading that wintering birds carry so little body fat that they must shiver constantly to generate heat when they aren't flying.

The other species is the gray jay, common, seen up here year-round. This jay and its cousin, the blue-and-black Steller's jay, often pester us in camp, trying to steal scraps, perching on the tent and berating us. But the gray jay has a stubbier scavenger's beak and none of this silky black on wings or tail.

John skis back into view, shaking his head and muttering, and the shrikes fly off to the east. Loaded with gear, we ascend the drainage east toward a rock wall that looks impossible on skis. Where it nearly intersects with a rocky dome, we turn north, up a narrow chute, a short, steep climb topping out on a hidden pass which looks out on the expanse of Seneca Lake. This is the key to the winter route into the heart of the range. The official trail drops off to the west, into a steep gorge, all rock and roaring water. It climbs out, then wanders through glacial pockets before dropping again, farther, into another drainage. From the bottom it crawls back up to Seneca Lake. On skis, it is not a good way to go.

We count on the lake ice for almost two miles of level skiing. The lake is shaped like a bow tied hurriedly in string, the lesser loop, at our feet, about a half mile long and the greater stretching a mile north beyond the knot, a narrow, rockbound strait which shows open water all winter. Much of the shoreline is granite cliff.

One April, after Marty had broken his ankle by skiing into a tree, I made this trip with Eric, a soil scientist who had been on the ski team at Montana State. At Miller Park, we struck a fox track and followed it all the way in, over passes, across frozen lakes, here to this high point. The track went the length of Seneca Lake. This is strange, because foxes won't usually cross a big opening. They'll skirt it in the woods or hug rock outcrops. Foxes also travel in loops and curves, seldom going straight for long. Coyotes don't mind open expanses and often cross them in straight lines. But this track looks like a fox's—smaller than a coyote's and less distinct because of hair partly covering the pads— the track feels foxy.

The track doesn't show what I think of as normal fox behavior, but you could say the same about John, or about me. We leave some strange tracks, too. The fox—a male I think, by the size of the track, and alone—traveled with few turnings, continuing over the pass toward Island Lake, where we traversed off to the collector. A fox can live in this place, with nothing but his body: no parka, no sleeping bag, no skis.

In winter, a red fox grows a dense undercoat. It can sleep in a furry ball under the stars, on the snow. The red fox also reduces the ambient heat level—called the lower critical temperature—at which its metabolic rate must increase for survival. When a creature's surroundings reach this temperature, its body kicks into high gear, burning fat reserves. For a red fox in summer, this is about 46°F; in winter it drops to 8°F. In winter, when there is less prey and it takes more energy to catch it, this metabolic shift is costly, so the fox changes its critical temperature to survive. And the track of this fox shows not just survival, but exploration. In winter, the fox has a freedom that we can only approximate with all our clumsy gear. This fox found our old track and used it to gain the high country. The same set of tracks returned the way they had come, still lacking the innumerable loops and spirals that mark the path of a hunt. The fox had gone directly in, accomplished some unknown thing, and returned.

I picture the reddish gold ruff gleaming in the strong light, the black nose sampling the thin air, the eyes like intelligent onyx, shifting their gaze, the slightly sidling trot, the black legs outlined by snow. Suddenly, I want to be that fox, to give up what I am, what I know. To live a wordless life, without meaning.

Around the lake are faulted domes, burnished by glacial passage with long grooves and scratches tracing the flow of the ice. To our right is a spur of Lester Peak, gullys curving blue between cracked shields of granite. Farther north, a confusion of low summits fronts Island Lake and the treeless defile of Titcomb Basin. Beyond, the rampart of the Divide juts up impossibly, a prospect as forbidding and fine as any on the continent.

We stand a bit, catching our breaths. John observes innocently that on such a perfect day we should be climbing something instead of humping big clots of snow around on our backs. I only sigh. The temptation is to invoke our leave time, bag a winter ascent, and then get the sample the following day. Good weather makes us itchy.

To be up here would make it, if not easy, then at least easier. My Puritan forebears shake long fingers at me. Work, they say, is a Sacred Trust. Thou shalt not bag peaks on government time. I don't rise to John's bait.

We stand around, all scratch and squint. I'm reluctant to strike out across the ice, hoping he'll lead. He blinks and shifts and makes his owl-eyes at me, hoping the same. He is more patient, so I glide down the north side of the pass, making broad telemarks, and set out, skipping a breath as I cross the shoreline. On the lake, the snow is deeper and more breakable than I'd hoped, each drop of a ski reminding me that there's black water not far underneath. My imagination bothers me. I've skied the ice on this lake many times and never fallen through; the ice is probably about six feet thick under two feet of snow, but . . . I climbed the rocky dome east of the lake one summer day and looked down. The water was clear as any water on earth, light jade at the very margin where the rocky bottom dropped off and then quickly going emerald to tourmaline and off into jet, bottomless as a wolf's pupil.

From hydrographic maps I know it's deep. You could drown Yankee Stadium in it. All that black water under my feet unnerves me. It's a mild phobia, quite understandable, but I always have to screw myself a little tighter to step out onto the ice of this lake. Eyes ahead and thighs tensed, I move briskly across, not stopping until I reach the narrows and ski back onto snow-covered rock.

From this spot, two winters back, I saw Marty dancing on the ice a quarter-mile ahead. I looked harder, tried to focus. He's jumping. Why is he jumping on the ice? Is something biting him? Has he come unclipped? I skied quickly and heard a stream of curses, unbroken, staccato. I saw that he was dancing with both skis clanking on a ski pole, which lay scratched and somewhat dented on the ice. He stopped, looked sheepish. "What's the deal?" I said.

"Fucking dogshit Yo-Von pole," he explained.

The offending pole was a high-priced model designed by an august mountaineer. But the pole had an infuriating way of freezing up inside, whereon the adjusting part would stick. Marty had tried to adjust the pole and it had frozen, so he couldn't retighten it at the new length. When he applied weight, the pole would telescope to dwarf length. He couldn't grip the pole with gloves, and his bare fingers were getting frost nipped.

It seemed to me that yowling and jumping on the pole, on skis, on a frozen lake, even though richly satisfying, shouldn't be taken too far. Madness feeds on itself. In the arctic winter, depressed Eskimos tear off their parkas, charge outside, and eat frozen dog-shit. Sometimes they run away into storms and are never found. They call this *perlerorneq*, which means "feeling the burden of existence," what we might call existential distress. It is often brought on by the smallest causes. We call it cabin fever. The seven-year itch. Mid-life crisis.

I watched until he stopped for breath. Pirate-eyed, he proposed several interesting applications of the pole to the anatomies of all makers, agents, and dealers of said device, past and present.

"Amen. Can we fix it?" I asked.

He retrieved the pole and started to explain why we couldn't, then ground his teeth and threw it as far as he could. It made a nice whoosh.

"Maybe we can duct-tape it," I said. "If you need to adjust it, we'll duct-tape it again." To mountaineers, duct tape is sacred. In emergencies, you can invoke its healing powers. I dropped my pack and took out the roll we use to secure the bags to the collectors. He stared at it. The dull silver tape glinted in the light. It seemed to calm him.

He shuffled over to the pole, stared at it, picked it up, muttered, and shuffled back. The metal had to be dried before the tape would stick, but it worked.

Marty was host to an elemental fury that would emerge when some object thwarted him. As one of those souls who find grace in movement and risk, he hated to interrupt his headlong progress. When a snowmobile bogged or a ski binding failed to latch, he would pass from invective to action, kicking, slapping, and spitting. Once he threw his ski at a lodgepole pine. Another time he spat all over the windscreen of his stalled snowmobile, which tempted me so sorely that I walked over and gobbed on it, too. For the rest of the trip, the clear plastic was laced with frozen spit.

When he was immobile by choice, he could be choice company:

intelligent, funny, ironic, the source of surprising phrases and weird tales, full of stories about climbing and skiing. We talked, in snatches, in tents or snowbound cabins, but came to know each other more in the oblique way of mountaineering partners, by act and observation.

On the move, Marty concentrated on the object of the trip with a frightening single-mindedness. The most successful mountaineers share this pinpoint focus. The summit becomes all. It allows them to ignore danger or suffering that might otherwise hold them back. As a personal trait, it leads one to go faster, higher, harder, to attempt great things, to kick death in the face.

It can also destroy. It causes mountaineering expeditions to degenerate into running skirmishes. It hardens the heart. You might ditch your girlfriend in a blizzard because she isn't moving fast enough: her fault. It prompts the sacrifice of friends to ambition, and the acrimony that surfaces when there is a rupture of basic trust. Whole books have been written on the impetus that will cause one human being to abandon another in order to gain a peak or plant a flag. At heart, the struggle is that between self and community.

In Marty, the tension was close to the surface. We joked that he was the engine and I was the brake. His impatience was huge. At times, he would stride past me, glowering, to take a steeper traverse or simply leave me behind to drag the sled, disappearing for hours until I reached camp and saw him grinning with a touch of contempt. I hated him at such times, blindly and purely.

He could only sustain his compulsion on the move. Back at the camp or cabin, it gave way to embarrassment over the breach, an eagerness to make amends. He would feed me broken chocolate, vaguely apologetic.

I turn back to the south. John reaches the narrows, scraping a ski edge over a boulder as he steps up by the low cliff and shuts off the Walkman. There is a small patch of open water between the rocks. To our right is an overhanging cliff. The granite has reddish crystals, a live glow as the sun hits it. Lichens of an intense, acid green are frescoed along the tight joints in the face. Uncountable tons of ice slid over this spot, carving it down to the hardest rock and polishing that. Friendships erode. This rock will last. I think again of the fox track, turning to the open water for a drink, then going on. One brief snowstorm would hide it.

We relax, drink from a water bottle, and unwrap hard candy, recouping energy for the longer part of the lake ice ahead. It stretches, glittering, faintly rippled by the wind, like a plain of salt. At times, Marty and I saw open spots or encountered slush pools under the buttress at the north end, where the water is deepest. As John sets out I mention skiing into some slush last year.

"Bummer," he says, "was it bad?"

"It was deep and a couple hundred feet wide. No way around it. Coming out with the samples, we were too heavy and sank in. The slush froze on contact. It was like skiing on fenceposts. Hideous. There was nothing to do but shove through. I had ice up to my ankles. I had to chip my boots out of the bindings before I could start chipping the ice off my skis."

"Sounds pretty awful," he says, picturing our curses and flailings. He grins, eyes hidden behind dark glasses, then sets out. Near the buttress, he takes a long curve to miss the spot, though today it looks no worse than anyplace else on the ice. The snow above the ice is softer than usual. Sometimes the snowpack on the lake is thin and the surface like velvet or cat fur. Marty used to skate across the entire lake on his touring skis and arrive at the inlet ten or fifteen minutes ahead of me. Once, in December of 1988, the lake ice was blown almost clear of snow by high winds, and we both had to skate in gusts that sent me skidding sideways under my big pack, veering around black spots, thin ice above the deep, careening like a stagecoach in a cheap western.

One of the most enjoyable—I say this without irony—aspects of these trips is the unexpected range of conditions, the variousness of weather and snowfall. It calls for constant improvisation with waxes and tactics, constant attention to the rhythm of the country. We beat our way in with a chilly high, pull the sample in radiant sun, and haul ass out at night under a storm front, headlamps making weird shadows in the blowing snow. Since the sampling gear and the samples are heavy, we carry the minimum of extra clothing and fuel. Though we move steadily, we also have to stay alert and grab good weather for the high trips.

Once, in my first winter, we left town in such haste that we forgot the duct tape, which, besides being sacred, is needed to hold the bags at the rim of the collector. I skied down five miles to the ramshackle resort at White Pine and used the phone, sweet-talking someone into driving up with a roll of tape, while Marty headed toward Hobbs Lake, busting tracks in new snow. With the tape, I charged back five miles to the cabin, ate, and followed his tracks in the eight miles to Hobbs, reaching the collector at 3:00 P.M. Marty was perched on the flange of the collector, struggling silently to get the sample out. When he saw me, he let out a cougar scream. We loaded the sample—a big one—into a pack as the sun set. We were both tired, but I reached burnout and then passed it. My body took over. I remember a blurred procession of steep drops, climbs, and tree-studded slaloms in the dark. Then my headlamp gave out in the extreme cold.

Marty skied ahead and I strained after, staring at the black shadow his mittened hands made as they protruded into the beam of light. In my torture-trance, the shifting outline looked like a huge, black lobster crawling down the tracks ahead. I blinked and mumbled to myself and shook my head, gradually forgetting Marty and becoming grimly fascinated by that big, black lobster—uggh. It was ugly, and I didn't particularly want it for a skiing partner. I stopped abruptly, staring, and he pushed on, his light dimming out into pines until he stopped and turned and was Marty again, impatient.

"What's the problem now," he croaked. "Let's go. S'too late to mess with all this stuff." I nodded and kept slogging toward his light as it receded. We made it to the cabin at about eight-thirty, twenty-six miles of snow under my skis that day and the job done. But I was too thrashed to enjoy it. I blinked out in the middle of my first Dos Equis.

Today, we encounter neither thin ice nor phantom crustaceans. We pass the steep, black buttress and then rest just at the shoreline before fetching up the inlet gully. Above the lake, the trail-breaking is harder. Where the wind funnels down, there are patches of breakable crust. The tip of each ski rides up on the hard shell, but breaks through when weighted. It's like climbing steps that collapse in succession. Under the crust is sugary depth hoar. At times, the ski tip gets wedged under the crust, and it takes a grunt to knife it back to the surface. We trade leads, one fighting ahead, the other following contentedly in the broken track.

The route winds through talus boulders and flagged pines up to Little Seneca Lake, a white stage in a Greek theater of broken domes, where we cross the ice again and climb a step to a smaller lake. Two drainages come together here. The largest swings east and south below Lester Peak, a broad basin full of nameless lakes, a hundred ponds, a puzzle of scoured bedrock and jumbled moraines. We will climb up a tighter **V**, to the north, toward a rocky pass. Under the windblown snow, the trail switchbacks up through scree, following the shins of rock above a gully stacked with boulders big as junked cars. We look up at the slope, noting the shifting textures of wind-slabbed snow, the high glare under the noon sun. We halt and stretch the climbing skins onto the skis for the last push to the collector. John takes off his headset and stows it in his pack. Now we can talk again.

I tell John about the fox tracks last year and then about the fox. Two years before, I saw a big, red fox in February on this pass, running away on the crust, dodging between sharp boulders into a talus cave. I remember the way it balanced on the incline, looking back as it ran, the coat a carroty gold, ruffling in the wind, the only living thing we saw up there.

We're carrying light shovels and avalanche transceivers, plastic beepers that theoretically allow a partner to dig one's sorry ass out of a heap of avalanche debris, assuming the partner isn't also buried. It would be a bad wait in either case. In fact, there have been few live recoveries of buried victims, beepers or not. The slope leading to the collector hasn't slid but is just within the range of angle that it might, so we trigger the little devices and listen to the faint wheep-wheep-wheep as we start the first traverse, me leading as John watches, edging the skis into the windslab, then falling through soft patches between.

Traversing avalanche slopes is a delicate and serious art. One approach is to follow the ridges, taking a steep line in exchange for safety. This slope is too steep for a direct line and is punctuated by blocky outcrops of rock. It lacks the clean arête that would be a natural route, so we cut across the slope. A few moves into the traverse, I can tell we're safe. There is none of the weird, hollow snow I've learned to avoid. Avalanches are not always predictable, but I can tell this slope is safe. I take a longer stride, switchbacking, traversing, and sweating hard. Even though the air is chill, the sun at this altitude heats exposed surfaces, and we broil as we gain height. By a house-size boulder I stop, unzip my collar, and let John take over until we top out.

From the pass we can see the heart country of the range. Slanting east to west across the north are Frémont and the accompanying peaks, Jackson, Sacajawea, and Helen, above the chilly stronghold of Titcomb Basin. On the summits hang lenticular clouds—evidence of cold fronts and strong winds, predictors of storm. Up here we feel sheerly distant, a frozen ocean away from our cars and post-office boxes.

I think of an old photo, from the 1928 Byrd Expedition to the South Pole. There is a wooden sailing ship tied at the edge of the ice. In the foreground is a figure on skis, a Norwegian, Bernt Balchen. He was an accomplished pilot, a great mountaineer, and a legendary skier. You have read much of Richard Byrd, but little of him. They were a team, but it was Balchen's ability that carried the Byrd expeditions in the field. Byrd raised the money; Balchen designed and made the gear. Byrd navigated while Balchen flew the plane. Byrd drafted the plans; Balchen executed them in the most trying conditions. Byrd was a hustler, hungry for recognition; he became a public man, jealous of his renown. Balchen gritted his teeth and broke the trail. On one polar flight, Byrd was so frightened that he drank himself to oblivion. Balchen carried him from the plane and held his tongue about it afterward.

Their relationship was a long and uneasy one. Byrd stood up at testimonials and collected medals. He became a national hero. During the expeditions on the polar ice, Balchen got to do what he most loved. He was a supremely skillful man and an arrogant one. He craved the elemental test of the ice and storms, which confirmed him in his superiority. Despite the smoldering distrust between them, Byrd's organizing abilities made it all possible.

Have you ever heard of Bernt Balchen? I think more often of him than of Admiral Byrd; dressed in sweater and gaiters, skis bound to his leather boots, he traverses my imagination. In the photograph, he skis away from the ship. His gaiters are canvas, and his long skis are varnished wood, but the stance and silhouette are familiar. The figure on skis could be John, or Marty, headed into the theater of ice, poised against the harsh light.

On the pass, the wind slaps at us, then stops. Frémont Peak has been measured at 13,745 feet. There is a higher peak to the north, Gannett, at 13,804, but the difference is not apparent to the eye. From the fur-trappers' rendezvous grounds in the valley to the west, Frémont Peak is the most prominent feature in any direction, while Gannett Peak is hidden by lower summits. From the valley of the Green, Frémont has a naked, whale-backed majesty, while Gannet is a snowy hump. Both are climbed frequently in summer, but in bodily terms it is easier for astronauts to stand on the moon than it is for anyone on foot to reach the summit of either peak in winter. This is where we stop, where the fox went on.

We drop back, three turns down, and carve left onto the rocky bench where the collector stands, a galvanized stele as emblematic of our way of life as the carved stone pillars of the Maya were of theirs. We lower the red packs and I climb up on the flange.

The collector is nearly full, the bag having been in place since last October. On our December trip the lake ice was thin, and we postponed the high sample. Now we have almost five months of snow to retrieve. Once again, we strain to lift it out, split it, and bundle it for the descent. The packs will be rude but bearable. We unlimber the coring tubes, hateful things, and push them into the snowpack. There are sixty inches in one place and thirty-five in another, since strong wind swirls the snow up here and deposits it unevenly. By random pokes, we try to strike an average.

Taking core samples for snow chemistry would be easier than hauling the bulky samples from the collectors, but cores seem not to be reliable indicators of deposition. The snowpack is host to complex exchanges of chemicals and vapors, absorbing some things from the ground, losing others to it, responsive to changes in temperature. Since I started this work, there has never been the same sequence of snow conditions: every year is unique. The large tube collectors isolate the snow as it comes from the sky and hold its chemistry intact. I often wish that the designer, a scientist named John Turk, who depends on helicopters for his winter sampling, had settled on a lesser diameter than eighteen inches, but it's too late to change that now.

We tape new bags into the collector and sit in the sun for our perennial lunch of onion bagels, cheese, and apples preserved from freezing by body heat. We luxuriate in the sun, but cold creeps into our feet, so we finish our packing and start down.

Going back is seldom—even with hallucinations—as interesting as going up, except for the quicker pace of skiing. Today we lack the solace of a fast descent of linked telemarks. The fragile crust is unstable, and we turn judiciously under our loads, managing to avoid flips and fractures. We thread the rocky defile, then slog out across the lakes, climb the passes, swoop into Depression Depression, skin up the gorges—three hours in a single sentence—and arrive in camp at sunset.

The stove doesn't work—iced up somehow. We try every trick short of a complete rebuild, and it still doesn't work. It takes us an hour to melt the first cup of chocolate, two hours for a meal. We grouse and grumble and invent tortures for the designers of stoves, our bosses, high government officials, and anyone else who occurs to us while hunching over the meager hiss of the flame. I'm grateful for John's good nature. He bitches and snarls, but never gets angry. We get through a dinner of pepperoni, peanuts, and lukewarm soup without flaring at each other, a gift under the circumstances. Too tired to do the obvious—make a platform of branches and build a real fire—we roll up in our bags, waiting for sleep's release.

We got the high sample. We didn't get frostbitten or fall through the ice or get avalanched. My feet hurt, but they'll warm up even if I go to sleep first. The air is calm; no storm will blow in tonight. Tomorrow we can sleep until the sun hits the tent. One long pull and we can get out of the mountains for a while, order pizzas and draft beer, listen to cheap rock on the radio, sleep with our loves. We got it done again. On the backside of the world, Nelson Mandela's loose.

Part III: Shining Mountains

7

What does the son do?
He turns away,
loses courage,
goes outdoors to feed with wild
things, lives among dens
and huts, eats distance and silence . . .

Robert Bly, "Fifty Males Sitting Together"

*I*ce-fog surrounds us like the atmosphere of old tales. This morning I can see ahead only five or six steps. We hike across the featureless sink of Depression Depression on mid-April boilerplate snow, melted and then refrozen, with our skis strapped to our packs. At our backs is a talus slope and then heavy firs bordering the gorge we just skied down. In its sheltered confines the snow had a breakable crust. As long as my weight was evenly distributed on both skis, it held me; as soon as I shifted my balance to turn, the crust let go, dropping me knee deep in an instant. After a few brave tries, we made slow traverses and discreet turns, finessing our way down the steep, snow-covered stream and into thick fog.

On my face it feels like linen bedsheets in an unheated room. As we left the gorge and skittered onto hard crust, traversing a talus slope, the trees disappeared, big Engelmann spruce and Douglas fir gone into white. As we took off our skis and strapped them to the sides of our packs, the fog gathered until there were only the nearby dwarf willows and then blankness. My eyes strain, but I can't find a focus. Tiny ice crystals fill the air, scattering light so perfectly that it arrives from all directions: this is called the white-out.

In a white-out there are no shadows, no way to judge distance or depth. I look down. I can feel the hard snow, but to my eyes, my boots might be floating over a mile of white air. Bent over, I get a flash of dizziness and straighten up. We move on, toward the snow-covered creek. A willow twig looks like an etching on the void. John has a sly, proprietary smile; he likes this uncanny remoteness, almost as if he had created it.

To our left is a narrowing drop where Barbara Lake's outlet stream and the drainage from Depression Depression meet, then fall a thousand and a half feet, entering Frémont Creek below Suicide Lake. To our right, sentinel pines and broken slopes lead up to the confused ridges and tarns of the Seven Lakes country. Ahead is a level expanse, grassy in summer, then a frozen pond, then a climb up a narrowing talus gully between cliffs streaked with mineral black. The summer trail climbs to the left, chopped and balconied into a boulder-stacked slope, working up a shallow pass that leads to Hobbs Lake: this is memory. None of it can be seen.

We navigate the land's image in our minds. Having skied this route in winter and hiked it in summer, I'd feel foolish with a compass in my hand. I've never carried one. A compass helps reckon a full day's course; it doesn't help between one move and the next.

Each step yields a dependable crunch, but my frustrated senses say the next might plunge me into the abyss. Does the surface lift or descend? It is simpler to judge with eyes closed, but unbearable to close them. Above us, an outcrop floats out of obscurity like a ragged, dark cloud. John climbs toward it, depthless, the outline of a man bent under a burden, leaning lightly on a staff. Lashed to his pack, his skis cross, their tips curving like antelope horns strangely extended: the symbol for unknown floating over his head. X over John.

Kick, step, kick, step, we labor up the funnel of the pass, edging bootsoles into the hard snow, climbing a staircase of our own making. Time is arrayed not in seconds but in steps. I begin to sweat and slow my pace. I see John's breath rising in puffs to join the fog. As we ascend, the white-out opens into slow rolls of cloud that curl

around us, reefed on granite and pine. We can see a hundred yards, then a quarter mile. The clouds build and ebb, changing the size of our world from one moment to the next. Our traverses narrow at the head of the bowl, three strides, then two, and then we are out.

At the top, we regain the freedom of skis. The land rolls in swales between granitic domes: good ski-touring terrain. A current of cold air leans in from the west, and it begins to snow, little, separate bits of soft ice called graupel. We slip down a gentle slope and across the lake, poling hard, skating fast with twenty-foot glides across firm snow specked with tiny pellets of new snow. In December, I nearly fell through the ice here. Later than this in April, two years ago, I flew across on green ice with creamy swirls, like malachite. Now we ski in the clouds, on a thin layer of snow, over ice, above the lake, mostly water ourselves, surrounded by water in all forms.

We can see about a hundred steps in any direction, enough to orient ourselves while crossing the lake. As surface crystals shave the red wax off our ski bases, the skis lose their forward kick, and we lapse into a waddling herringbone step to climb out of the lake basin. On the knoll above, I take my skis off. John looks dubious. Rightly so: the snow under the old whitebarks isn't set, and I go knee deep in sugar. John, who kept his skis on, laughs and waits. I stand thigh deep in a pit with sides caving around my boots. I once worked in a sugar factory, and my break-in job was shoveling white sugar from broken and underweight bags into the remelt tank. It stuck to my black rubber boots, and by the end of each shift, it stuck everywhere—behind my ears, between my fingers, under the waist of my pants. The memory makes me shudder. I'm glad this is snow.

John watches the expressions—surprise, dismay, embarrassment, memories, odd smirks—play over my face. He rolls his eyes up to the clouds, patient. John isn't prey to these waking dreams—he lives in his skin, quietly, with a relaxed grace. He's a smooth goer, alert to every pleasure, seldom shaken by meanings. I'm like a pond: I reflect what passes, whatever cloud, whatever wind. I can go from black to silver in a breath.

I marshal myself to practicality. Climbing skins go on my skis, bindings latch onto my boots, and I'm in a state of grace again, mobile, suspended by the snow. Skiing. It's like having a set of clip-on wings.

The collector is hidden now. It was once on the main track, the route I learned from Marty. In the Wind Rivers, exposed to extremes of sun and wind, the snow tends to be difficult for ski-touring most of the time, either too deep and soft for easy trail-breaking or covered with an unpredictable crust over layers of sugary hoar.

So, after Marty and I set the first track to the backcountry in December, other skiers would follow, two or three parties a month, helping to keep the trail somewhat packed. Since our track led right to the collector, they would swing around it, packing the snow over the guy lines, which are thin, stranded steel cables that will cut up through unpacked snow as it settles. The packed snow would freeze hard and the cables would be bound. As it settled, the cables would bear the weight of the surrounding snowpack until they snapped. Snowmobile tracks will do the same thing to a wire fence.

After digging out broken cables in a blizzard to splice them—a four-foot slit trench and the kiss of frostbite—I decided to move the collector slightly, just enough to get it off the trade route. In summer I found a small opening that would accord with our protocols. The only tracks were those of deer and elk. The opening wasn't on the way to any named feature, lake, or peak. So, in turn I tipped each section of the collector onto my shoulder and bushwhacked to the new spot.

We turn and slip up through a complex of bedrock ridges topped by a sculpture garden of old pines, then through an inconspicuous notch into the glade. We see the lonely little tower of the collector. It emerges and fades in the cloud, an eighteen-inch tube of thin steel, nine feet high, painted white, half-buried in snow. We are here. In the old tales there'd be a crescendo: a storm, an attack, a visitation, but nothing materializes. There's no sound but the scrape and hiss of our skis, the faint peck of the snow on our sleeves. No virgin calls from a high window. No dragon roars.

The meadow is ringed with old whitebarks, some hardy with five-bunched needles, shaggy as a horse's winter coat; others are scarred by lightning, beheaded by wind, burnished by drifting snow, the wounded and the noble dead. We cross the pocket meadow to the collector and leave skis and poles stubbed upright as we unpack our gear. There are clean bags for the collector, smaller bags to protect the sample as we pack it out, a wrench and driver for the bolts, our ever-present roll of duct tape, and the snow-coring kit bulky in its green canvas sheath. I loosen a screw-clamp on the collector's rim and rip the outer layer of tape free. John climbs onto the flange and hoists the sample up in its thick poly bag. Straining to clear the rim, he lowers it to me, and I slip it into a protective bag, an icy chunk melted and refrozen to the shape of a small washtub.

Such is our grail, rock hard and specific, with mysteries to be unraveled in distant laboratories by grad students and technicians. After we pack it out, I'll let the ice melt, and test it for pH and conductance. Then I'll bottle it in one-liter samples and ship it to the Central Analytical Laboratory, the acid ranger's Oz.

In return we'll get bad news, a printout of concentrations in columns under chemical abbreviations, SO_4, PO_4, NH_4, cations and anions, microequivalents per liter and kilograms per hectare. Bad news? Maybe I'm prejudging the case. The air up here is better than it is almost anywhere else in America. Maybe this ice is plain ice, benign as industry scientists claim. Air quality permit applications—licenses to pollute—are usually supported by computer models that lack much data from field studies, floating free as hot-air balloons. Much of what we read about air quality is based on industry estimates rather than on field monitoring. A well-plotted fantasy illustrated by color graphics—the product of high-bucks consulting companies—is much more impressive in court than lumps of dirty ice. The samples we bush-wolves drag out of the mountains yield heavy columns of numbers that even specialists may have trouble interpreting. Is the collection method accurate? What is the natural variation? Is the sulfate anthropomorphic or volcanic? What would the trend be without the drought effect? The lawyers and consultants, swarming from their hillside houses and telephone-equipped Volvos, will gnaw white-shark bites out of our attempt to find out what goes on up here. If this data ever goes to court, it will be attacked, stormed, undermined, and set about with fires. We catch the snow and the rain, and send it off to the chemical gnomes of Oz. After that, it's out of our hands. It's up to the statisticians, the analysts, the white-collar cruisers. In other words, all this struggle may be of no use, no help.

But even if I were convinced that this effort is futile, that our evidence wouldn't help, I'd still be here. For me, the point has become this place. I want to be here, by whatever means. In this, John and I are alike. We make enough money to replace the mountain gear we destroy, if we haunt the sale racks. With my savings I buy old books and odd tools—bow saws, rifflers, drawknives, scorps. John saves for his ventures in third-world climbing.

We get to know the mountains firsthand. We spend our days up high, on foot, moved by weather and light. It doesn't have to fit into a story. It's all as we find it. It doesn't have to be remembered to exist.

Yá' át' ééh. Navajo. It means something like Amen, Aloha, and *Spiritus Sancti* all together. For two years, I taught Navajo students to write while they subverted my sense of what is.

Yá' át' ééh. Yaa-Ott-Ay.

I mumble it and John says "What?" He is used to cryptic phrases tumbling out of nowhere, sometimes bored, sometimes curious. I'll think for two hours and then roll out the conclusive sentence as if it were perfectly evident.

Yá' át' ééh. What next? John wonders.

"It is good," I say. "*Diné bizaad*—Navajo-talk."

"It's okay. I wish it would clear up," he says. "We need some rays."

"Could be a lot clearer," I answer.

Instead, the fog rises again and overwhelms us. Pellets of icy snow fall through it and peck on the crust. I take out the sections of the coring tube, which are wrist-thick, hollow aluminum, slotted along the length and marked in inches. They bell faintly as they touch. I thread them together as John readies the bottle and juggles the notebook. I raise the tube to the vertical and stab the toothed cutter into the snowpack. Depth of snow, 62 inches. Length of core, 49 inches. We balance the tubes in a sling under the scale, calibrated in inches of water, 34.5. Bottle ready? I whack the silver tube and the core drops out. Here we are.

In late afternoon we come back to camp under a cloud, under heavy packs, quiet, fatigued. The fog has given way to a snowstorm, fine grained and cold, which we watch from the sunflower yellow womb of the tent. This yolk yellow is an excellent color for a winter tent: it reminds us that not all is cold. Allen Ginsberg's voice drums in my head: . . . *Sunflower poised against the sunset, crackly bleak and dusty with the smut and smog and smoke of olden locomotives in its eye.* We wrench off our ski boots, put on down booties, and drape our sleeping bags over our knees. We read, resting, eating what can be held in one hand. I read a paperback comparing the art of China and Japan, which I found in a library surplus bin.

The door of the tent is half-open. Outside it snows, layers of quiet descending from the sky. In this location, this snow-breathing hush, it seems that I'll never forget anything. There is nothing extra. It all fits. It can be trusted, even when it is most dangerous. I think of a chemist I met at a conference, scoffing at the wilderness as a source of religion. "Yeah, it's easy. You can say whatever you want. No witnesses." True.

The wind rises. The nearest pines are a green close to black, sharp outlines crossed by single flakes wheeling down the air in their last seconds of flight. Among the pines, snow comes from several directions, circulating sidewise through openings, spilling straight down in the calm behind thick foliage, slowing and wavering in updrafts around the trunks, whirling in eddies that spin tighter with each gust, when the flakes rise again and blur like smoke.

Across the meadow, the pines are a furry blue, softened by the passage of each flake until, looking farther, there is always a snowflake between the eye and its object. At that vanishing point, which is not a point but a plane, the snow is all there is to be seen. There is more movement in the landscape now than at almost any other time, millions of flakes within range of the eye, but paradoxically it holds the most absolute repose. In snowfall there is endless, active repetition that prevails over meaning and form.

My father died when I was close to here, camped in the next meadow east. It was in March, two years ago. He had a heart attack, riding a bicycle to the store to buy whole wheat flour. In his retirement, a long purgatory, my brother and I had taught him to make bread. He mixed and kneaded with an engineer's precision, always a single loaf of wheat and one of white. I came out from a long trip to a note, dated a week past: Urgent! Call your mother. I called. "He died a week ago," she told me. "They said you were in the mountains. He was cremated yesterday."

When I came back to town, he was already part of the air. Was the wind southwest? Maybe the finest trace of ash and smoke fell with the snow over the ranges. "It's over. Wait a while before you come home," she said. I wept, stared into space, and went back into the mountains the next day.

I couldn't talk to Marty about it. We had another sample to collect, and I didn't want to falter. There were no words.

I didn't know how to let him go. I still don't. He pedals off on that red bicycle, out of sight, clutches his chest, and falls. It happens again and again, until the repeated image obscures itself, like snowfall. There is no last word, no ceremony, no knife to cut the knot. Alone, I burned sage and smoked a pipe to the sky.

The snow taps on the taut skin of the tent, hisses down the steep sides. I read that in Japan, laughter and ebullience are seen as base and vulgar. Grief, mourning, and inconsolable sorrow are considered proper literary subjects. *Sabi* is not just loneliness, but aloneness; *wabi* is a looming distress; *hie* is a shivering eeriness; *shibusa* is astringency, a severe dignity, what stops the bleeding: these are the bones of the Noh drama. In the Japanese mind, they sum up to truth. Looking at the pines and the sky, I think of white masks, black robes. The actors move in measured patterns; there are words and shrieks and the clap of hardwood blocks; violence and harshness, and at the end, something absolutely still.

My father was born to cattle and sheep, hay and grain and sugar beets. When he was seven, my grandfather ran 10,000 cattle and 25,000 sheep, with ranches and range in Utah, Idaho, and Wyoming. In 1921, when my father was eight, the price of beef plunged from twenty-one cents to fifteen, and they lost everything except the family homestead. His mother was intelligent and gimlet eyed, a teacher and a tyrant. He went to Los Angeles with a championship basketball team, quit, and stayed there. He got a job as a junior engineer at Lockheed Aircraft. He drank whiskey with John Wayne, with whom he shared a way of looking at life.

In California he learned to fly. During WWII he went to England and tested Lockheed planes that had crossed the ocean in crates, in convoys. Sometimes the planes hadn't been assembled quite right, so he made crash landings in the fields. The Army Air Corps didn't mount the guns until the planes were delivered. Unarmed, he also got shot down by prowling Luftwaffe fighters. In all, he survived thirteen crashes.

He brought home pictures of P-38s, twin-engined fighters angled in ranks on the aprons of English airfields. Of crashed planes, twisted, smoking. Of himself and his wartime friends, drunk in Dublin or Belfast, women in dark dresses with lace collars sprawled in their laps, glasses of whiskey raised in salute. Once, in Belfast, IRA men stalked into the cinema and shot up the screen with machine guns, inviting the Yanks to "get the fughing hell out of our country."

When the war ended, reasoning that his luck in the air had been exhausted, he refused to fly home. He crossed the North Atlantic on a freighter fitted with pipe bunks, four deep. The weather was infernal. In the ship's gut, it rained vomit. The top bunks were worth black-market fortunes. He came back to the States, but not to the ranch. In Salt Lake City, he married a pretty, gifted painter who, in tune with the times, got a degree in elementary education instead of an artist's trip to postwar Paris. They managed radio stations in Salt Lake City and Laramie and had their first child, a son, me.

In Albuquerque he worked for the Sandia Corporation, a company that had much to do with the burgeoning atomic bomb industry. My brother and sister were born. My father transferred to Tonopah, the husk of a mining boomtown, to work on the northern end of the Nevada Atomic Test Site. Later, he was put in charge of the roads and buildings at the nexus, a place called Mercury, north of Las Vegas. We moved to Las Vegas. He never made bombs, but he planned the towers and pits for them. He signed contracts for the grading of roads and for structural steel. I remember, so vaguely that it seems like a dream, flashes in the northern sky and rumbles in the earth.

Before I was twenty, I read a book by John Hersey, *Hiroshima*, and the world tilted under my feet. I no longer had a place to stand. The war in Vietnam blew out of control. I applied for conscientious objector status, was cursed and investigated, and found a cave in a maze of red sandstone with a nearby spring: a place to hide. I wouldn't fight but I wouldn't leave. I intended to become a refugee in my own land.

My father couldn't bear my perversity, my lack of loyalty to the nation he carried in his head. I was loyal to the country, which to me meant the land itself and the people I knew—friends, family, teachers. But I didn't see them under any threat, except in their minds. I saw, instead, a mounting hysteria: fear, armed and dangerous.

The chairman of the draft board was my old cub scout leader, a retired Marine colonel. My den chief, a neighbor named Lawson who went to 'Nam, had gotten his guts blown out a few weeks before. I told the board that I didn't have anything against self-defense. I'm not a pacifist. Swing on me and I'll knock your lights out, I said. Then I said that I wouldn't fight people I wasn't mad at, who wouldn't shoot at me if I stayed out of their country and minded my own damn business. Then I burst into tears. They turned down my application.

I dropped out of school, lived on the road, hitchhiked, slept on floors in small apartments, traveled with musicians and Quakers, slept in basements next to stacks of cardboard boxes. After the war ended, my father and I reached an uneasy truce. He felt misunderstood, betrayed. I felt cut off, from both innocence and belief.

I recall the last lines of a poem: *I believe our Father's bones / turned to chains / and were lost to the century.* The poem, called "America," was written by an Navajo fifth-grader named Jasperson Tom, who lives in Arizona. He, too, is trying to reckon the losses and come up with a life.

All I'd been given seemed false, the fruit of war and suffering. I couldn't repeat the words, couldn't march, couldn't weld my link into the bloody chain. Plunged into disarray, we make decisions without articulating them, shift the weights that balance our lives without knowing the precise contents of either end of the scale. I decided I would believe eyes before voices, pledge allegiance to what I could see, hear, touch, taste. That the world where my body lived would be my guide, my teacher, my lover. Maybe there is something larger that stands beyond the rock and the flesh, that justifies and forgives. I don't know. I looked up and I saw mountains. I saw the sky. I trusted only what could never lie.

Turning the page of the book, I look at my fingertips: the pattern circulates, like the isobars on weather charts, diagrams of Coriolis force, the map of what I am. My Navajo students told me that the spirals on the pads of our feet are the marks of the wind that holds us to the earth. The whorls at our fingertips are the marks of the wind that holds us to the sky. They are the prints the world leaves on us, the visible signs of the forces that bind us to the world, so that we remain upright and in balance. I look out of the tent. Outside, the snow still falls, giving a body to time. As storm cells pass, the flakes shift their direction, circling: northeast, east, southeast, south.

West.

Place your upper teeth against your lower lip and draw the lightest possible breath. That is the sound snow makes when it lights, except a storm can go on for days. I used to be frightened when a storm caught us in a high camp, but now I have learned to watch and sleep. *Shibusa.*

I haven't told you of the storms. This winter, John and I have been lucky. With Marty, I skied into storms from which I thought I'd never return, the wind shrieking, the snow horizontal, the landscape obscured by white violence. By myself, I'd have stayed in camp, huddled in my bag, shivering. But I trusted Marty, in a way. That is, I trusted his self-interest.

Any circumstance, whether love or storm, had to fit into his personal scheme or be an obstacle. When Marty prepared to leave camp and climb into a howling storm, I followed his impulse. In his greater experience, with his sense of self-preservation, the storm was not as severe as it seemed to me. I knew he wasn't giving in to bravado. It was precisely his selfishness that I could trust.

We suffered. It was an effort, moment to moment, to move in those storms, when the wind body-punched us all day and the snow hid everything farther than a few steps. The mountains were a white hell. One day, it snowed eighteen inches from the time we left camp until our return in the dark. We couldn't even follow our own tracks back to camp. I strained to stay with him. He never looked back. He was right, insofar as we survived, insofar as we came back to camp with our fingers and toes intact. I was scared. He was right. We made it.

The hiss and whisper of flakes on the tent gives way to the tap of graupel, each contact a distinct *thup,* repeated a million times. There is no way you can make this sound with your lips. The snow breathes outside the tent, like the white sound of blood rushing in my ears. There's something calming in it, something fearful.

• • •

Just as I'm about to sleep, John wakes. We look out the door, to the east. The snowclouds have parted. Low sun is washing the peaks with fierce pinks and golds. It's good to know they are there, these mountains, but better to see them again, larger and finer than monuments.

John blinks and eats a bit more. I'm restless, needing to stretch, to be as thoughtless as a coyote, to move. I boot up and crawl outside. The new snow is like loose velvet, four fingers deep over a solid crust. I lay my skis down and clip into the bindings. One kick, one glide. I'm twenty feet from the tent. The surface is silent and almost frictionless. I see John's eyes glow from the mouth of the tent. He struggles into his parka and boots and issues forth.

"I was thinking about dinner," he says, "but the snow looks tempting."

I nod and smile. Without further discussion, we set off in different directions. We have been together in the tent, day in, day out, close enough to chafe. Neither of us is worried about getting lost or in trouble: if John doesn't return, I can follow his track and likewise. It's a comfort to be out of sight and hearing.

I wander south, swinging my skis into long glides, easy as breathing. There is a long meadow draped over the saddle, curving off southeast into shadow, edged by pine and fir. I stop where the slope breaks and look around, up, around. I close my eyes and inhale. The alpenglow burns its brightest on the Divide peaks and the mountains of cloud. I drift into an easy glide, looking back as the distant ridgeline shrinks into the soft crest at my back. I could ski this snow in my sleep. I hum an old fiddle tune, "The Cowboy Waltz," as I lean into a slow turn, left, then right, my skis tracking the melody. It seems a long time before I reach the frozen lake below. When I stop, I begin to itch with inertia. So I climb up through the woods toward a run farther east. The snow holds the light and extends it, keeping the dark an arm's length away.

I make another dreamy, southerly run down to Sweeney Lake, then climb back toward camp, shearing west into S-curves, heading toward the rim, through complex ridges and tight gorges overhung with weathered pines. Traversing below a cliff, I find a six-inch hole in steep snow under an overhanging rock, melted and iced inside, but without tracks. Something passes through, it says, but not on four feet. Wind, I think. I touch the skin of ice inside its mouth. Warmth. The breathing hole of a hibernating bear? What else could it be?

The place is right; thick whitebark pines on the ridges, favored by bears for their late fall crop of rich nuts. The bears head for whitebark country to lay on a final layer of fat before digging in. I squat on my skis, trying to sniff the air without falling. I expect a whiff of bear, clove brown, but can't smell anything. Doubled over, I lose my stance and almost plunge—forty feet, too far. Sleep in peace, bear.

Climbing up through a break in the ridge, I ski back, traveling east as the last light drains from high granite faces. A distinct line of violet, earth's shadow, rises from the Divide to the zenith as the light goes and the air fills up with chill blues. I hurry, following backbones and skirting drop-offs, ducking the limbs of dead pines, knees beginning to ache, cold and lonely, so that the sight of the tent strikes me with dumb sentiment. John peers out, his smile flashing white in the dusk. He nods in welcome, tending the stove. The lid of the pot rattles, steam lifting the rim. I smell the food, feel the juices start along my tongue. In from the dark. Back in camp. Home at last.

8

Though my eye meets nothing anywhere but ice,
though my belly is aching,
Ayaaaaa! I am full of joy!

Inuit Song, Greenland

*H*earing an animal outside the tent, I wake abruptly to freezing
black.

Nothing. I exhale carefully, trying to listen around breath and
heartbeat. Nothing. I must have dreamed it. There's not even a
night wind. The only sound is my breath brushing the nylon taffeta
of the sleeping bag, until John stirs and sniffs. I was dreaming about
a bear. Maybe he was the bear in my dream. Bear John. John Bear.

The snow under my pad is cupped by body heat into a shallow
trough that doesn't fit my body. Where my heat concentrates, from
shoulders to hips, the hole is deeper. I shift and can't settle. After
two nights, we should relevel the floor or move the tent. The storm
has cleared; I can tell by the quiet, by the sharpness of the air at
my face. Outside, the stars are brilliant, steady in their white gaze.
I imagine them, but I'm too warm to go out and look. The sky is
clear. It feels like about ten below, going down. Should I roll over
and check my watch?

If it's an hour to dawn, I can drag my boots inside my bag to
begin the morning drill: warm clothing inside the bags, put on pile
jacket, swap ends and unzip the tent to light the stove, melt snow

119

blocks, make a hot drink, then retire to the bag to sip and rewarm hands and toes. It takes about an hour to get out of the bag, hydrated, and into full kit. In deep cold, it can take another hour to eat, wax, and load. When it's cold, it's best to rehearse moves before making them. Already I'm plotting the day. On the other hand, if there's plenty of darkness left, I should stop thinking and go back to sleep.

For a while, I stare open-eyed at the dark.

One of our uniquely human qualities is our need to place ourselves in stories. Most animals probably don't, except through what we call instinct. Our instinct is for stories. From the sensory chaos of life, we build a narrative. This is how we make sense out of raw experience. We hope that in the course of our tale, some desire will be fulfilled or some point proven beyond a doubt. Against these self-made epics, we set our days as we understand them, judging, weighing, agonizing.

In some sense, our self-told stories may be remedies for the more

complex ones we have to live. Our creations have a steady purpose, a certainty. I read the work of a neurologist whose theory is that dreams are the relentless efforts of our minds to impose order on the random sparks of neurons during sleep. Dreams are the pursuit of form at the cellular level. Our thoughts require structure, harmony, proportion, and symmetry to exist.

Crossing the border from sleep, I test the evidence of my senses: the moist heat of my body in the down bag, the cold air outside, the rustle of nylon as I move. I open my eyes to the dark, recognizing nothing in it, no reply. Then John sighs, the sound muffled in his sleeping bag, and smacks his lips.

Often, we seem to get more joy from recognizing a pattern in things than from the things themselves. Do I love these mountains and our cold climbs, or do I love The Mountain and The Quest? Who cares about such things anymore? But a phrase of William Everson's has stuck with me: *. . . irrelevant to the needs and uses of an established urban hegemony, and therefore out of harmony with humanity as it is.*

Most of us live in cities, conceded. But there are places, beautiful ones, too high and cold for the majority, and likewise states of mind. To be in step with a majority may not be the highest good. The majority may itself be profoundly out of step with something greater.

Why is this drive for order so insistent? Even when I try to escape it, I can't. But maybe this process translates into freedom for the body. The mind is an organ which, in the process of evolving to serve the orderly transmission of primate DNA, has leaped off in some strange directions. Suddenly, in evolutionary time, our bodies are held hostage. Having grown so far into thought, we must now maintain not only health, but that other intangible balance: sanity. It's a double burden for the poor, naked beast.

I remember a fox on the snow at 11,000 feet, running. I think of the fox's track, the unseen animal crossing high passes and frozen lakes with no myths to guide it. Usually, a fox will stay in the coverts: forest, thicket, brush. Why does a fox go on a quest? It has the freedom of a body and a story in its genes.

So our love for myth may be biological convenience: it reduces the effort needed to derive a set of physical tactics from a complex set of perceptions. Patterns that work are passed on not just in the genes, but in the language, as songs, dances, and stories. A child hearing that first tale is suddenly a half-million years old. With a burnt stick we draw a deer, then trace the arrows piercing its heart.

After a certain point, our lives are mostly recognitions. And a good story is preferable to the frightful clamor of the world.

Or easier, out here, than silence. In the mountains, in the snow, in my mind, I get closest to what I am. I want to seize a look in which nothing else fills my eyes but what's here. All the classes and seminars are blindfolds, knotted over dark glasses. It's hard to assign meanings, but easy to tell rocks from trees. From up here, you can gaze down into America, like looking into a vast fire.

I recall an anthropology text, something about personality not being separable from culture. Most of us live in cities, dominated by our images of the world, by the current crisis and the latest spin. We go to the mountains not to find who we are, but to forget what we have become. And that may have much to do with my being here, in this dark moment.

It's still dark. John's breathing is a comfort. I raise my head and frost falls from the tent onto my face. I fumble for the digital watch and push the stud for light. Three o'clock. I roll over and try to stop my thoughts. Have you ever tried that? I can't sleep. I can't think in straight lines. My mind travels like a hunting coyote, or a fox: loops, sine waves, spirals. A dog will charge boldly right up to things. A coyote will watch from the bush, zigzag, then come at an angle. Approaching the object of desire, a fox will circle downwind.

I try to recall what the captain of a Mormon handcart company said in 1856. The poorer Mormon families emigrated on foot with belongings in wooden carts, each cart roughly the size of two coffins bound together. Levi Savage—that was his name—voted against leaving the safety of the Platte in August and striking out for Salt Lake City, across the high plains and Rockies, where in some years the passes fill with snow in September. The rest of the company voted to leave, saying that the Lord would protect his chosen, temper the wind to his lambs.

Savage replied—I will look this up and get it right—*My brothers and sisters, what I have said I know to be true; but seeing you are to go forward, I will go with you, help you all I can, will work with you, will rest with you, will suffer with you, and if necessary I will die with you.*

Levi Savage lived, but more than four hundred others did not. Why the Donners are an emblem of horror and these people are forgotten, I don't know. Maybe it's because the Donners ate each other. On a single morning, still three hundred miles from Salt Lake City, they buried thirteen bodies in a snowbank. A young girl awoke in a frozen tent to find an elder gnawing her fingers.

Sometimes I feel as if we're heading for a fate worse than that.

I'm not setting myself apart, except physically. I love it out here among all these broken peaks, these ranges with glacial scars beneath their breasts. It's good to forget about New York and L.A., about Politics and Money, about the Shove and the Stink, if this dance with snow and darkness is forgetting. More often, I feel like I'm awake up here and fall into nightmares below ten thousand feet, where there are people who know the price of everything, who can quote you a dollar value for clean air.

Years ago, I had visions of staying out, away, apart. In 1972 I stayed in the high Salt River Range for two months, until the snow hit hard. But I got lonely. Love drew me back into town. My life is like the fox's track, striking out for the high country after some unknown thing, then returning.

In April it seems possible to live out here, as it didn't in December. But we can't stay out, or we don't. We don't have the right ways—the right songs and stories—to conduct our lives up here, scattered in ones and twos, human fragments. So we live as we can, in a succession of escapes and returns, of risk and homecoming. We load our packs. We ski up into the storms.

We come home to tell our tale.

Five o'clock. Still rather dark. I lurch out on the pavement-hard snow to pee, naked except for down booties. Still rather cold. The pocket thermometer outside the tent insists that it is $-8°F$, the calendar on my little watch that it is April 6, a day in 1909 on which Admiral Robert Peary may have reached the North Pole. About this circumstance there is considerable doubt. Until his death Peary said that he did indeed reach the Pole. Others claim he turned back, in fear or simple exhaustion, before the Pole. I lurch back to the bag, sorely missing the sleep I lost to thought.

This is cold for so late in the season. Three years ago in April,

Marty and I were bivouacked in the open air. We sat on a boulder pile, on a point that dropped off two thousand feet into the gorge of Frémont Creek, trapped by thawing snow. I could feel the drop, the void humming like the low string on a bass. A warm front had turned skiing into a series of waist-deep plunges. We sat on rocks that formed an islet in the bottomless snow and ate the last of our food. We listened, with a Walkman and two headsets, to the growl of Hüsker Dü as we slapped at mosquitos. Neither of us had repellant, since neither of us had ever needed it on a ski trip. But the sun had melted enough snow to form pools in the rocks, and the rocks held enough of the sun's heat to keep the water from freezing. Mosquitos.

From our perch, we could see big soft-slab avalanches peeling from the Divide peaks, hear muffled booms rolling down the throat of the canyon. We expected spring avalanches. The mosquitos were a strange bonus.

Better the cold than the thaw, if one has to be up here depending on the snow for support. There are no mosquitos this morning. The sky, stars nesting in the first feathers of dawn, is blameless: not a cloud on that great, blue conscience.

After warming in the bag, I pump the stove into life and wake John with coffee. As we finish eating and ready the gear, light breaks across the meadow. A short run from the camp, we turn left and drop into shadow, making diplomatic turns on the fragile crust of a north exposure, wanting to cut loose but knowing too much. We skied this yesterday. With the new snow we want to give in, ski fast, crank turns, but know we will break through: Bingo, fracture. Two bowls down, we contour east on snow slots through what looks like a heap of Airstream trailers but isn't: just good old glacier-pummeled granite.

Depression Depression's north-facing drop is also fragile crust, but the new snow gives it a slight lubrication, and we make it down without fractures or even embarrassments. Where Marty had a brute courage about tipping off and skiing fast, John is somewhere between that wild excess of nerve and my own circumspect style of descent. Marty would treat the problem of bad turning conditions by not making turns: he'd boom straight down at a speed approaching free-fall.

John and I are good skiers. Marty is a phenomenal skier. In memory I can see Marty skiing fast, head down, red cap like an idol's eye set in the stony blues of his wool shirt and wool pants flapping, blue gaiters and big blue pack, dropping, the blue sled trailing him down, his lips tight under the red brim, hitching weight as the speed piles on, plucking a narrow thread of balance from the air.

I don't like to fall, nor to muse on my errors upside down in snow, to unbuckle the pack in order to move, dig snow out of my hair and collar and nostrils, untangle my legs, point both skis in the same direction, try to stand, heave the pack up, buckle in, and then have to tip off again. Marty, even out of control, didn't usually fall. He had spark-plug reflexes that equaled his courage, but his few failures were spectacular: smoking pinwheels and full-gainers, skis buzzing the air like sabers as his body salvoed against the crust. There was a confusion of impacts, then a silence that sizzled.

Marty?

Arghh!!!!!

Okay?

SHIT!!!!

Need help?

GROOAAHHHRRRR!!!!

I'd wait for him to cool before skiing into range.

Amazingly, we never actually broke anything on these trips, but we regularly bruised, twisted, wrenched, battered, and strained most of our bodily components. This kind of all-out backcountry skiing is hard on the body, hard on the gear, but easy on the soul: it's worth every knock. If you want to duplicate this wilderness experience—the ski dive—in the privacy of your home, fill a pack with dictionaries, lash an ironing board to each foot, then, gripping a curtain rod in each hand, dive down a flight of stairs.

Makes you dizzy, pushing the envelope. Did you land on your head? Nice, huh? Pay's lousy, too. Barely enough to keep a part-time carpenter in Bud Light. Not near enough to settle down, get a little piece of property, a new car, invest in the future.

Nevertheless, John and I are foolishly happy, Skid-Boys on per diem. We wear the duct tape on our gaiters like a badge of honor. We climb up to our first view and stop. The peaks are living up to their early name, what the colonists on the eastern seaboard first heard about the Rockies: Shining Mountains. As the sun finds its way down long arêtes and into the tops of high bowls, the snow coruscates with brilliance. Light is a wave, like sound, and this high gleam can almost be heard, zinging way up there above the high E, the lonesome note at the top of a coyote aria before it falls back to silence and dark.

Inhumanly bright. Even this early, the shadows of timberline whitebarks are a refuge from the hard gleam. In 1778, Jonathan Carver wrote the first account of the Rockies, not knowing that they even existed. The actual mountains he wrote of, never having seen them, were the Turtle Mountains at the western headwaters of the Mississippi, compared to the Rockies a low range of hills. These Shining Mountains, he claimed, were "the highest lands in North America." His fantasy rose to its object. They were the crest of the continent, he said, and lay two days west of the Minnesota River. The Shining Mountains, he wrote, stretched three thousand miles, from Mexico far into the heart of Canada. They shone, literally, because of an ... *infinite number of chrystal stones of an amazing size with which they are covered and which, when the sun shines full on them, sparkle so as to be seen at a very great distance.*

Rather than poking fun at the past, I'll tell you a story. In 1974, when I was guiding horseback trips in the Gros Ventre Range, I heard an argument between two clients. It was August. The wife rashly claimed that the white spills on the Grand Teton, visible high above Jackson Hole to the west, were snow. "Ridiculous," her husband spat back. "That's the dumbest thing I ever heard. It's too warm for snow." He fluttered a hand in the air. "It's obviously, *obviously*," he repeated, looking to me for confirmation, "salt."

We pick up the gear we cached above Hobbs Lake and sprint for the next pass, skis tied to our red packs, bootkicking up the frozen crust, locked into a nice traveling rhythm, stretching and cruising, higher and higher.

On the pass, we're at timberline, or properly, tree limit—the elevation above which full-sized trees can't develop or set cones to reproduce. To our left is a ragged forest of whitebark pine and fir. There are conifers higher up, but they grow as *krummholz*, German for "crooked wood." Each tree is dwarfed by the combination of

cold, wind, abrasion by blowing snow crystals, and the loss of moisture which can't be replaced during winter dormancy. On clear
days, even when the air temperature is near zero, the sun heats the
needle surfaces far above freezing. Before I painted it white, the galvanized steel of the snow collectors grew hot enough to melt the
sample inside, even in January. Sometimes the sample still melts.
Dark green, the needles of conifers absorb generous solar heat. Once,
at two o'clock in full sun, I set a dial thermometer with a black face
on the branch of a whitebark pine. Soon, it read 92°F. Moved to
the shade, it dropped to 20°F, a gradient of seventy-two degrees
between the surface temperature of a dark object in direct sun and
the temperature of the air. This difference creates a tremendous
amount of vapor pressure in a conifer needle: the heated water
inside wants to escape to the cold dry air outside. The only things
holding it in are the closed pores—stomates—and the cuticle. If its
fine, resinous coating has been damaged by wind-whipped snow,
the needle loses water to the air. The tree, which stores water in its
roots and trunk, can't replace this lost water, and the foliage dies
back. Dry snow is highly abrasive, like windblown razor blades.
Before choosing a campsite, I look at the northwest sides of pines.
If the bark is gone and the trunks are blasted down to the wood
fibers, I know the place catches high wind and heavy ground drift:
not a place to stay for long.

Another fatal circumstance is the large temperature drop as the
sun goes down. The foliage, warmed to 92°F, is abruptly deprived
of heat. On that same day, twenty minutes after sunset, my thermometer dropped to 10°F; forty minutes later, it read −5°F.
Conifers have mechanisms to keep ice crystals from piercing cell
membranes, but these take time to work. With nearly one hundred
degrees of temperature drop in one hour, ice crystals form like tiny
scalpels inside each cell. During the recent drought, there was a big
die-back of pines on southwest slopes, high up. The strong winter
winds seem to favor the northwest quarter, so snow abrasion wasn't
the fatal factor. I think it was a lack of water reserves going into
winter, and exposure to the sun's heat.

At high elevations, in addition to low temperatures, the extreme
alternation of temperatures is a source of winter stress. At still higher
elevations, the dwarf trees persist only where they are sheltered by

snowdrifts or boulders; instead of growing up, they spread out in dense mats, pruned low by cold winds, hard sun, and the gritty snow that drifts like sand over these passes.

Today, though, the wind is elsewhere. No plumes of spindrift trail from the summits, not even a wandering cloud; the sky is a sea without islands, a heaven without angels. In the Shining Mountains, John and I perform our obligatory dance to decide who goes first onto the lake ice. He takes a roll of tissue from his pack, sneaky ploy, and hides in the pines, so I ski alone onto the frozen plane of Seneca Lake.

The night's cold has roused the lake ice to speech, a murmur of snicks and pops as I weight each ski. The ice is solid, I tell myself. I always tell myself this, but my phobia howls about thin ice and black water, shifting darkness, the instant of breakage, knowledge, failure.

The fear of skiing on the ice of alpine lakes would be a convenient terror for most persons, since they would never have to face it. I may also be unknowingly frightened of thousand-dollar bills, Roederer Kristal, or Komodo dragons. But I have to face the frozen lake. The ice ticks as I weight each ski. It's solid. The Chicago Bears could roll out here on a flatbed semi with the Marine Band and do the Pogo. Solid. There are weird, lightning-bolt cracks in the overlying snowcrust, but don't worry. The ice beneath is solid. You couldn't break it with a sledge. Solid.

John catches me at the narrows, where we avoid the open water on the rocks to the right. We stand for a while, wiping the frost from our glacier glasses. He puts on his headset, starts a tape, stows the Walkman in his front pocket, pops a lemon drop, and takes the lead. Being on the ice bothers me, even following John. You'd think it would be easier to get accustomed to this; the Inuit, after all, live on the sea ice in winter and are still around after a couple of millennia. John can't hear the click and whisper from the ice, since he's listening to a tape; whether owing to rhythm or distraction, his track is a serpentine boogie. On the previous trip I pointed out the deepest part of the lake, and he makes a long radius west, congastepping and sine-waving around it.

Up the nick of the inlet gully, we climb over windslab and sastrugi—frozen waves scoured and deposited by high winds, arched and immobile as breakers in a Hiroshige print. The snow is stiff yet hollow, resonating slightly with each step. We wax up again and climb the stepped bowls northeast, then ski across the lesser ice of Little Seneca Lake, climbing again toward the high pass, under wind-carved scoops and sickles of snow.

At the foot of the last slope we stop, gauging the condition with practiced squints. I look at John for a call while he looks at me. Skiing with Marty, there are seldom such hesitations. He looks up, sees the snow, and reacts. "Green wax," he'll sing out, or "Skin up." No pause, no doubt.

Today, we stop and consider. John's attention wavers back to his earphones and the Pixies. "Shall we take off our skis?" I ask. He reaches into his kangaroo pocket and shuts off his little machine.

"Huh? What?"

"Let's take off our skis," I repeat. He pokes the crust with a pole. Solid.

"Yeah," he says, reluctant to leave his music. "Let's do that."

Skis tied to the packs, we kick up the steep, open slope with our avalanche beacons peeping over our hearts. The snow on this southeast aspect has been worked over by sun as well as wind, so it's hard and hollow, the surface just beginning to loosen with the sun. We make a switchback and decide it's safe. The heat is changing the surface to soft granules called corn snow. Corn is transient—the same heat that forms it soon dissolves it into slush. John—burning with an abrupt desire—wants to dump the packs and ski it now. He looks about eight years old. I want to crank it too, at the first flush, but I resist. I'm in favor of a few runs, but only after we finish our work. We'll get the sample first. John's face falls, and he starts up the slope, kicking a little harder than necessary.

I feel like a crabbed patriarch, gripping the plow handles. We have a constant, friendly argument, which I tend to win in the name of duty and responsibility. Usually, but not always. The sample comes first—our unholy grail—but we are not always devoted to Total Quality. We have significant lapses. A skid is a skid. If we didn't love to ski, they couldn't drag us up here with a D-9 Cat. "We'll ski it in a minute." John groans. "It's not quite ready," I say, poking the surface. "In a half hour it'll be perfect." Muttering, John heads up, a brilliant figure in his shorts, scarlet long underwear and blue gaiters, under a flag-red pack with yellow straps, a walking Mondrian against the snow and profound sky.

At the collector, we perform our usual sequence: I climb up on the flange and hoist the sample as John grips the emerging bag. As the block of ice and snow comes clear, I shift the weight to his uplifted arms and jump down to slide another bag over the inner covering. It's not massive, so we don't split it up, and he opts to carry it while I take all the gear. The coring kit is unlimbered and used, a bottle filled, the numbers logged, all in an itch of anticipation.

We shuffle objects, load up the evidence, then debate whether to eat before we ski. For John, this is a tough issue. He wants badly to ski that corn. He lives for it. It's a fire in his heart. But eating, well, to eat is life itself. He chooses to eat and takes a mouthful of nuts, chewing as fast as possible, not saying a word. "No," he says, stowing the bag, "let's ski." We heft the packs and start down, skiing toward the drop-off, looking southeast over a broad, white basin that glitters under high sun. We've got the sample. I feel noble and righteous for a moment, as knightly as it's possible to feel on touring skis.

A jet emerges from the ridge of Lester Peak, turbines spinning it west on trails of vapor. It's a corrective to fantasy: as surely as we place ourselves in a wilderness tale, adorn our situation with grand adjectives, magnify our snow sample to a grail and our task to a quest, that damned jet will fly over, nailing us to our century.

I'll consult you: shall I leave the jet in the story? It reminds us that the wilderness isn't endless, timeless, a way out. It says that winter in this lost range is not inviolable. I consider Afghani *muja-heddin* watching the flight of a Russian bomber. Or the Havasupai, down in the Grand Canyon, watching contrails build, eight thousand gallons per hour of Jet A, on the route from Phoenix to Vegas. It's harsh, this late-twentieth-century metallic tang.

We gaze at the silver needle, the long bars of white vapor dividing up the air. *The wild duck, flying, leaves neither track nor trace.* An old Buddhist metaphor for original mind, the jet not so. Three trails of fire, turned instantly to ice at thirty-five thousand feet, the only marks in the blue. *Mene, mene, tekel* . . . Thou art weighed in the balance . . .

. . .

Our packs reside on a patio-size boulder at the base of the pass. We came down carefully with the heavy packs, dumped them, and climbed recklessly back up. Unencumbered, we race up the high white toward the high blue. Heads in the sky, we stop, panting but unable to wait. This is not part of our job, but part of our joy.

Off the top. The snow is perfect, moist, easy, and our turns are damasked, rough on smooth, into the steep snow as we fly down, light-headed with elevation and empty bellies, wrapped in a sudden chill breeze and the sun's insistence, lost in the Shining Mountains.

It's good to leave that chunk of ice at the foot of the pass and climb back up to the ridge, to ski hard, without burden. First the climb, then the long, sweet fall, the state of grace or madness. Between turns, no time for thought. Hop and drop, give and go. The surface burns and shivers with light, gravity gives her strong tug, the skis bite and spring. As long as we can forget, we will.

9

Earth's breath becomes my breath, this is how I shall live.

The Blessing Way (Navajo)

I want to leave the snowmobiles in town. Likewise, the damned four-wheelers. Noise. Stink. Let's leave it behind. John is skeptical. "Remember the last trip," I argue, "dragging the stupid machines out of thawed snow and bogholes, breaking through the ice? Remember how we did powerslides down that gully off Big Flat-Top? How I had to dismantle the log fence with a rock? Remember carrying the four-wheelers across Dutch Joe Meadows?" I stomp and gesture.

In early May, after a winter of thin snowpack. It's been warm and the snowline has receded. We can hike up to the continuous snow, then ski. John isn't convinced. The packs will be too heavy. We may have to walk in a long way through mud. I bully as much as persuade. It'll be quieter. Easier. More aesthetic. More fun. John's not a motorhead, but neither does he want to plod through the lower (i.e., boring) country on foot. He tucks his chin into his collarbone and sets his sunburnt jaw.

"*¡Madrecita de Dios!*" I squawk in frustration. "Okay. *I'll* carry the beer." At that, he shrugs and finally agrees. He just finished his regular work week with a fiesta in Jackson and looks raffish. We leave the four-wheelers on their trailer in the Forest Service yard and drive south, truck tires whining on the pavement, then climb the desert apron of the range on dirt roads, following last year's ruts, newly emerged from the snow.

John sleeps as the day dawns. Across the broad valley of the Green River, I can see the crest of the Wyoming Range fifty or so miles away. Up north, Gannett Peak, Wyoming's highest, catches the first glow on summit snowfields. From high in the Wind Rivers, on clear, cold winter days, it is easy to see the Grand Teton, Wyoming's second highest peak, almost a hundred miles northwest. From high points, looking southwest, I might also see the snow-covered mass of the Uinta Range, about a hundred and fifty miles off, stretching like a low, blue cloud along the horizon. This is about as far as I can see in perfect conditions, dry, clear air, no haze or dust. Beyond this, the atmosphere itself scatters the light, and the contrast by which we distinguish object from background is lost as the earth curves away.

We drive into sunrise, the big peaks to the east like blue cutouts under a clear sky, their long slopes cold in early shadow. Later it will be warm and the snow will melt. We want to make it in to the cabin—probably about nine miles on foot—before it does. Otherwise, we may have to posthole or even bivouac if our skis fail to support us with these monster packs.

South and west of the range, the land lies in long, depositional planes, tawny with short grass, spotted with sage or pocketed with aspen and juniper where bluffs give shelter from the wind. The land stretches the eye, the horizon at least a day's walk in any direction, or two, or maybe a week's walk to the west and south. This country opens to the southwest, toward the prevailing wind. Where the wind is strong, over ridges and in saddles, the vegetation hugs the earth. Everything from bedrock up—soils, plants, animals, weather— depends on how the wind blows. It's the air's country more than ours.

We think of air as being the same as space—open space. This is easy to do in the West, where the air is most often dry and clear; out here, the sunset is fifty miles west. In humid regions, the air has more presence, coloring with changes in the light; there, sunset happens all around you. You can almost swallow mouthfuls of it. In cities, the air has a kind of malevolence, the medium for oppressive smells and tastes, but even there we think of the air as a kind of void, a region where things as we know them don't exist except in transience: the silver knife of a jet, a baseball rising from the bat, a flock of pigeons, wheeling.

Yet the earth's air is a vital medium, vital in more than one sense of the word. It is intimately connected with organic life, in fact partly the result of it. To that life, our life, it is essential. It sets life's boundaries by changes in its temperature, movement, and composition. And it is an organ of the biosphere, as crucial to the continuance of life on earth as lungs or heart to a human body.

In comparison with the mass of the earth, the mass of the atmosphere is not large, nor is it of great extent. The zone habitable by humans extends from near sea level to about 15,000 feet (4,600 m), just under three miles. Above this, the pressure of the oxygen is not sufficient to permeate our blood. Humans can adapt to work or climb above this elevation, but permanent settlement is impossible. Higher still, say above 20,000 feet (6,000 m), the body will break down. Mountaineers call it the Death Zone. Among the great distances of planet and surrounding space, we have livable atmosphere only three miles deep. Compared to the earth's four-thousand-mile radius, this is like the single outer layer of an onion's skin. More closely, it compares to the thickness of the outermost layer of cells in your skin.

The biosphere—the zone supporting life—is somewhat larger, from the ocean deeps to the highest point in the atmosphere at which floating spores can survive. The zone affected by life is still deeper, from the strata of carbonate rocks, like limestone, deposited in the crust, to the stratosphere where earth's distinctive, biologically oxygenated gas mixture burns up meteors rather neatly.

It's doing a good job. We don't see a single meteorite as we bounce around Big Sandy Ranch. Years ago the ranch belonged to the Leckie family. When I got here, it was owned by a handsome ski hound who spent winters in Jackson and summers down here. Now, it's occupied territory, snapped up by a man from New York City, but unoccupied at this season. To the rich indoorsman, this place is habitable for about three weeks out of the year—the span between mosquitos and the first snow. Turning north, we labor the green truck, battered as most Forest Service trucks are, up switchbacks, climbing out of the valley. I roll down the window and the air comes in cold. I take a breath, then send it back.

Without life, our planet's atmosphere would be like those of Venus and Mars, more than 95 percent carbon dioxide, around 2 percent nitrogen, with no free oxygen at all. The mean surface temperature of earth would be more than twice the boiling point of water. Instead, we have about .03 percent carbon dioxide, 79 percent nitrogen, and 21 percent oxygen; our mean surface temperature is about 13°C, or 55°F.

There are purely physical models that attempt to explain the development of our atmosphere, but they all grind to a halt, with oxygen and nitrogen locked in compounds, hydrogen escaped, no free water, no available energy. The major physical difference between the earth and Venus or Mars is temperature: distance from the sun. Yet, by this measure, our planet should be much hotter than it is. The habitability of our world owes to our unique atmosphere, which is biogenic: created by living organisms.

What does this mean? Simply that our present atmosphere is the sum of millions, perhaps billions of years of life and death. The first life is thought to have been anaerobic, unable to live in the presence of free oxygen, like the bacteria that still live in the mud of swamps. Anaerobes also live inside us, in our guts, where they produce methane, the same natural gas we drill for and burn.

Obviously, I've been reading about the air. I try, between bounces, to tell John about it. He knows quite a bit, it turns out, but he's not in the mood for science.

"I had a lot of that shit in classes," he says. "I don't know why I remember it. They told me I could get a real job. Lies." He scowls and burrows into a pile of coats.

We pull out on top of a hill, the ruts getting more serious, the snowbanks deeper. We creep through a patch of thick lodgepoles, avoiding a wallow-pit where someone got stuck. We cross an open meadow and see the wallow-pit of all wallow-pits, a Rock Springs Special. Someone got stuck once, got unstuck, and then, in defiance of good sense, roared back, trying to blast through a deep drift. The truck went sideways and then spun out, hacking its way into the snow like four chainsaws. I can see the tiremarks, shovelmarks, kneemarks, and bootprints. Cowboy boots, needle toed, low heeled.

Truck-driver models. Two pairs, about sizes 10 and 12. Chunks of aspen and lodgepole, jammed and jackstrawed. Mud sprayed out from deep gouges onto the snow. Mats of sagebrush, mashed by spinning wheels. Cigarette butts. Seven empty cans, Coors Light. They must have been stuck for at least an hour. They were here last night. The tiny sagebrush leaves are still soft, their broken edges still moist. I can smell them, a sharp green scent.

Photosynthesis, the trick that leaves do, didn't happen overnight. Before there were plants as we know them, simpler species—called cyanobacteria for the blue-green pigment cyanin—started using sunlight to fix carbon directly from the CO_2-rich atmosphere. The carbon-based compounds photosynthesis yields are called organic matter. These photosynthesizers, a sort of chemical mirror image of the anaerobes, began giving off oxygen and other gases.

In photomicrographs, cyanobacteria look like the beaded name bracelets that hospitals placed around the wrists of babies in mid-century. The oxygen they gave off reacted almost immediately with the rocks or atmosphere. But colonies of photosynthesizers were the first habitat for complementary organisms that evolved to produce energy from oxidation. These creatures—I don't mind claiming them as family—were the forebears of all animals, a word whose root means "breathing one."

We park the truck, stuff our packs until we can barely lift them, and set out. Our breath forms clouds, each curse visible. Dutch Joe Meadows is a muskeg, all sponge and snowmelt. We hop and dance and sidle, stumbling under the weight, trying to keep our boots dry. We reach higher ground, a sagey hill, and strike for the guard station, a two-story cabin, built by the Civilian Conservation Corps. Even the high ground is spongy. The brush grabs at our ankles. John glares at me. We hike up the hill and see that the door has been forced by snowmobile vandals. We drop our packs and go in, boots booming on the hollow floor. Maybe *vandals* is too strong a word. There's no other damage. They just wanted to see what was inside, to build a fire in the fireplace. Maybe the cabin should be left unlocked. We shoulder our packs and head on, looking over the pines at the sky. There are a few stringers of cloud, but not the kind that herald storms. We go through the back gate, a groaning old timber one, and cut through the woods, wading drifts to a low crest.

On the downslope, we strike the road, untracked since last fall, and hike up it, avoiding the deepest snow. The road is cross-fenced by drifts. The alternation of mud and snow would make tough going for a vehicle, even a loathsome little ATV. It would be like driving over a dead cow every ten feet. Most of the mud is still frozen. Occasionally, though, a patch that looks hard as rock will prove not to be, oozing up as my boot sinks. We follow the road, then veer off it into the woods, following the open ground covered in pine needles and more solid than bare dirt. Crossing the snow-banked bridge on Dutch Joe Creek, I look down into the slow current. There is broken ice along the edge. Under my reflection, the silty bottom is blackish green with periphyton, the oozy stuff that grows on underwater surfaces. There are willow stems, chewed by beaver and weighted with rocks. I see a fine mist rising from the riffles up-stream, catching light, then disappearing a few feet above the water. Most of the stream flows downhill, in its meandering channel or through the ground, but a small part of it rises into the air, flowing back into the sky.

Not just water, but water vapor was essential to the development of life on earth. It is probable that this early atmosphere included a layer of smog, the product of photochemical reaction between methane and fog. This layer would moderate temperature changes—the first greenhouse effect—and filter ultraviolet radiation, allowing other photoreactive gases like ammonia and hydrogen sulfide to accumulate below. This would have improved the conditions for life in the oceans, and the resulting bloom of cyanobacteria may have produced oxygen in such quantities that all of it did not immedi-ately react: free oxygen, free at last.

Do I mind owing my existence to blue-green scum? Looking at my reflection filled in with streambottom colors, it seems natural. I can see the periphyton like a fuzzy coating on the stream's tongue, outlined by my shape, with my expression, my pair of eyes. All those little mothers working away down there in the primordial ooze. The thought makes me grin and the scum grins back.

While many complex species are extinct, the pioneer forms of life, such as viruses, anaerobic bacteria, cyanobacteria, algae, dia-toms, and zooplankton, are still common. Not only are they com-mon, but they are also the living foundation which supports all complex plants and animals. Little mothers indeed, they are still maintaining earth's atmosphere.

Around two billion years ago, the amount of carbon dioxide declined precipitously, perhaps because of all the frantic carbon-fixing going on under the atmospheric blanket, which deposited millions of tons of carbonates on the ocean floor in microskeletal remains. Every atom of carbon thus buried freed two atoms of oxygen. This increase in oxygen would have the further effect of binding hydrogen atoms in water molecules: we all know the for-mula H_2O. Hydrogen atoms have so little mass that earth's gravity can't hold them: they float off into space unless contained or com-bined. Even water vapor is broken up into its component atoms by the low pressure and solar energy high in the atmosphere, whereupon the hydrogen dissipates into space.

With a massive sigh, John flops his skis down on the snow. I slather my bases with red klister—a wax that looks like ruby-colored honey—and clip in. Showing his first grin of the trip, John forges ahead. The snow is sleek and firm, like a cat's back. We're so happy to be on skis that we forget to watch the sky. It's still clear ahead, north and east, so the sudden rise of clouds from the west catches us by surprise.

We ski west of the beaver ponds, where there are beaver trails and fresh-cut bolts of aspen. The terrain is glacial, full of gouges and moraines, the outwash pockets filled with beaver ponds. The clouds bear down on us and pass, each one spitting out what it holds, little pellets of graupel, then big pinwheel flakes. As the surface changes our wax balks, clumping with fresh snow, and then works again.

We schuss the road down the last hill and flat-track into Big Sandy Opening, noticing open ground on the south slopes and open water in the creek. John stops and groans. He has a headache. I can tell he's miserable, but he doesn't lash out or get broody. When Marty had an ache, the world was responsible. Between spates of temper, he would describe it in fine detail and ask, twenty times a day, if it could be serious. "Don't worry," I'd say for the first nineteen, "it'll go away by tomorrow." The twentieth time, I'd get impatient. "It's Terminal," I'd say. "You're buzzard shit, José."

We straggle through the succession of gentle, treeless swales that flank Big Sandy Creek. The Opening, as it is called, is glacial outwash, possibly a lake at some time, about two miles long. For a place that appears flat to the eye, it has a surprising number of ups and downs. John is suffering, but brave. The skiing is good until the last mile, when the snow reaches the melting point and the Opening changes to a huge bowl of cream soup. We thrash across a blank space, herringbone the hill, and fetch up at the *Casita Perdida*, the Little Lost House.

I unlock the door and we tumble in. John mumbles something about lunch and piles into the only chair. I build a fire in the stove and pull the foodsack out, spreading the table with everything we've got. We sit and stuff, not a word passing between us. It's quiet. I like it. Without the big snowmobile sled, we couldn't bring a boombox, to me a blessing. But John looks forlorn.

He finishes eating and clambers into the upper bunk, going to sleep in seconds. I lift the top plate and stoke the stove, then watch the flames eat the splits of pine, soaking in the heat. Oxidation. Where would we be without it?

We think of oxygen as a life-giving gas, but it is both poisonous and dangerous in high concentration. In ozone molecules, O_3, or in unstable combination with hydrogen, oxygen reacts wildly. If these were present at higher concentrations, steel would rust immediately, and the paper of this page would blossom into flame. There is a layer of concentrated ozone high in the atmosphere, where it forms in the strong sunlight. Ozone filters out ultraviolet rays, while allowing visible light to pass. Near the surface, though, high concentrations of ozone are poisonous. Oxygen is like the unpredictable guest at a dinner: three glasses of wine and he's delightful; four glasses turns him into a wild boar.

The proportion of oxygen is critical; with a 4 to 5 percent increase in oxygen concentration the entire vegetation of earth along with any exposed wood, coal, or organic soil would erupt in a burning that would make the fires in Yellowstone seem like a single lucifer match.

The incidence of fire is a powerful consequence of oxygen levels. On the other hand, with a 4 to 5 percent drop in oxygen, nothing would burn. Thus, the world we think of as ours is dependent on oxygen levels that vary within one or two percent.

In animal cells, oxidation is the major source of energy and also the largest part of the biological process we call aging. We oxidize nutrients to live and are in turn oxidized: the biological equivalent of rust. Clearly, the proportion of oxygen in our atmosphere has been maintained for a long time in order for the form of life that we know—that we are—to exist. So we not only evolved in earth's atmosphere, but in intimate connection with it. We depend on the air. The air depends on us. I smile up into the blue. It's like finding a long-lost brother.

It's too late to head for the collector. The thaw has taken over. We didn't have space in the packs for a tent—what with science junk and amenities—so we're committed to a lightweight ascent. In and out in a day. I push a few more splits into the stove and leave John to his dreams.

Outside, there are open spots under the pines on the southwest slope. Between snowbanks, the moist needles are rusty red, the earth is chocolate brown, and the rocks are splashed with lichens, orange, yellow, and lime green. The storm has blown past and the sun is bright and sweet. I find a dry patch and lounge on the matted needles, smelling the rise of the sap in the lodgepoles. With a boulder as a backrest, I lay my head on smooth granite and nap in the sun. When I wake up, buttercups have unfurled around me.

We speak of time as a river. By a river, though, we can choose to walk downstream or upstream. We can swim it. If it's shallow, we can wade across. Time has no banks, unless it washes the shores of the universe. Time is the sun's heat against my skin. Time is buttercups.

The sun is seductive. I strip off a layer at a time until I'm naked, lolling on my heap of clothes. I think of women. Ideas are too pure, either snow or flame. A living body has its own, dependable heat. I recall favorite sins, matchless transgressions. I think of Bella Linda, heavy hair resting at her collarbone, reading her mad Spanish novels, studying the forbidding ranks of irregular Spanish verbs. In the cabin, in the top bunk, John may be dreaming of his present girlfriend: Shana, Queen of the Greater Yellowstone Ecosystem. The thought of her—long and shy and crowned with auburn locks—claws at my heart.

Thinking of John, I reconsider: in his dreams, he's probably exhausted love and is hungry again. A Rabelaisian dinner, carpets of prime rib and sofas of mashed potatoes, where he reels to and fro, biting with a will. John may not be the hungriest person I've ever camped with, but he's a remarkable eater.

Marty had both appetite and capacity; I'd pack enough food for three and he would eat for two of us. If they both came, a party of three, I'd pack for five. While Marty stows food under his mustache with a wolfish dispatch, John has an almost saintly glow as he contemplates a pot of freeze-dried stroganoff. Quite simply, with a pure heart and a tight belly, he worships the miracle of food and drink, the literal body and blood.

This course of thought makes me hungry. Sleepy, horny, hungry. What a billygoat. I should try to meditate or do something noble. Sorry, Thoreau. I roll over and feel the sun nipping my winter-pale behind. The snow is impassable slush, but I'm on standby. This is unpredictable country: it might suddenly freeze. If it does, I'm ready. Still two hours until quitting time. Eat your heart out, midlevel computer bureaucrat.

John wakes up and smells the burritos. He slides from the upper bunk and gazes into the cast-iron pan with delight. He looks around for the boombox and then remembers that we left it in town, excess weight. His face falls. "You'll just have to imagine the music," I say.

John laughs. "I put in for another job."

"Where?"

"Puerto Rico," he says. "Tropical forestry. Cheap rum. Swimming in the ocean. The bad point would be the lack of snow. I'd have to come back to ski."

"You could water-ski."

He ignores me. "There's a biologist job in Washington, too, old-growth stuff. Spotted owl habitat."

"Into the combat zone. Do you get a bulletproof green vest?"

"The place is nice. It'd be good, but I'm more psyched for the tropics."

"It might be too warm and easy. Winter is a great rein on decadence."

We eat the burritos with great gouts of salsa. Lacking the hammer of loud music, we start a conversation. When John is desperate, he's a good talker. We talk about whatever enters our minds and go through a certain amount of rum. He describes the weird vegetation on the slopes of Mount Kenya and the black wilderness rangers with carabiners stuck through their ears. I describe the harvest dances at Jemez Pueblo and the molten splendor of their red chili. "To those people, chili isn't a spice; it's a vegetable."

We share a fascination with detail. We take turns describing the texture of places, the plants, the names of rivers, the night sounds, the feel of the air. John tells me about his brother, a guy with a good job who's bored out of his skull. "He sends me tapes of weird, cranked bands. He likes really twisted stuff. It's his release. He must spend thousands on tapes and CDs every year." We talk about the horrors of suburban life, the morass of possessions and debts. "I don't think it's worth the confinement," he says.

I don't miss the background music. It's good to talk. John's interested in sociobiology: how human and animal populations interact, so he discourses on that. We cram the stove and mix rum drinks. It gets dark. The cabin gets too hot. Our talk falters. We run smack into entropy.

This is Punk Physics, a violent simplification. The universal change from order to disorder is known as entropy. Some of this has to do with radioactive decay and the increasing heat generated by ongoing reactions, like solar fusion. There seems to be no corresponding reversal of such reactions. They run their course, the universe heats up, and order deteriorates. This quality is also present in our grasp of time, which feels to us both inexorable and irreversible.

The sweet trick of life is to forestall entropy. Living organisms develop boundaries—the cell wall is the most important—and run a sort of entropy exchange across them. In pencil sketch, the organism takes in nutrients that are low in entropy and, through chemical reaction, loads them with some of its internal entropic burden. Now high in entropy, they become toxic to the organism and must be jettisoned, along with excess heat. But back to the air.

There is evidence that the earth's surface temperature dropped abruptly as the greenhouse effect of a carbon dioxide–methane atmosphere was lost: the grandaddy ice age took place about 2.3 billion years ago. This ice age may have marked the shift from an oxygen-poor atmosphere to one rich in nitrogen and oxygen. Since then, there have been periodic swings in the earth's average temperature, but they cover a small range: a few degrees. The temperature swings are responsible for the pulses of glaciation which, we are told, are the earth's normal climate. We are living in a brief interval of warmth that is as rare as a clear, balmy day in the Aleutians. Some scientists hold that our biologic sins will trigger greater warming, a problem considering the ever-increasing output of the sun. Others say that despite a temporary warming, the natural shift to glaciation will ensue.

The cabin is murderously warm. John, lizardlike, sprawls on the top bunk and goes to sleep. I shuck down to a t-shirt and try to read. Our winter habits have become bad habits. Sweating, I shut the draft on the stove and open the windows.

For we living ones this heat regulation is critical. Our atmosphere stabilizes the solar heat, reflecting it from clouds and haze on earth's sunlit side while simultaneously trapping heat on the nightside, limiting the range of temperatures in one place. Without it, days would be too hot and nights too cold for life, as on the moon. Each of us has a boundary layer of air next to our skins that mimics this effect on a small scale. If you whirl your arm in a sauna, you can dissipate this boundary layer and get a serious burn. On cold days, the dissipation of this insulating boundary layer can lead to frostbite or hypothermia. Animals deepen this layer with fur, while we appropriate their skins or otherwise hold air stationary around our bodies, in wool, feathers, or synthetic fibers.

We also move around. John likes the top bunk, which is warmer. I always grab the bottom one. As the air in the cabin cools, John crawls, half-asleep, into his bag. I shut a window, stoke the stove discreetly, and retire.

We leave the cabin at a respectable hour: it's light but not bright. The snow is set up hard. We skate the flats and cross the bridge. I take this bridge, a rustic wooden structure, for granted. But without it, this would be a very different trip.

The creek rushes under our feet, over ice, between snowbanks. The water is two feet deep above the anchor ice, green and cold and fast. How would we cross it? We could wade across it, but walking barefoot across ice in a fast current would be dicey. We'd have to scout upstream until we found solid ice above the water— unlikely in May—or a fallen log. There's one I recall about a mile up. Then, we'd have to scramble across the icy trunk, skis lashed onto our packs. Nice for the film version, but not for now.

We cross the bridge in four seconds, then forget it. Our wax is working nicely, and the snow is pleasantly firm. Following the bend of the creek to the east, I can feel the cold air draining down from Meeks Lake and then the deeper current of chill from Big Sandy Lake and the Divide, not quite a breeze; more like a slow, deep breath.

Air moves with differences in temperature. It is a truism that hot air rises and cooler air rushes in to take its place. Warmer air is less dense, its molecules bumping each other for more space. So it's lighter. On a global scale, this circulation helps to even out temperature, just as a ceiling fan does indoors. The grander movement of the atmosphere is caused by big differences in temperature between high and low latitudes and by the rotation of the earth. Since the air isn't attached to the earth, it lags a bit. On our scale, these lags are major wind currents. All this moving air helps to smooth out the effect of the sun and the earth's spin and wobble, which by themselves would make the tropics and the summers too hot while the high latitudes and winters would be too cold: killing extremes.

As the air responds to temperature difference and spin, so do the oceans. It is the grand sum of these patterns that produces weather. Air circulates both vertically and horizontally, with the vertical pattern owing mainly to simple differences in heat, which cause local differences in pressure.

If you want to see this in miniature, slowly blow a mouthful of smoke over the lighted candles of a birthday cake. The candles create tiny highs, with lows in between. There are corresponding, slower patterns of circulation in the oceans that have much to do with both weather and with the conditions for life in the seas. Oceans have their deserts, their jungles, and their cold sea-floor tundras according to their depths and currents.

Surface winds result from the pressure difference between adjacent highs and lows. In the northern hemisphere, winds circulate clockwise around highs and counterclockwise around lows, a pattern seen in dustdevils and the gusts around thunderstorms. At a regional scale, this cyclonic movement blends with the earth's rotation to produce prevailing winds.

Now, in Wyoming, in May, our weather is changing. The flow from the northwest that brings the severe cold has weakened, and the prevailing southwest winds of summer are taking over, melting the snow. Soon, we'll have our first spring rain and the snowpack will melt as the streams fill to flood stage.

There are high clouds, thin stringers of vapor riding the high-level winds, southwest. As we climb the glaciated slopes, they disappear, leaving the sky open and bright. We move fast. The snow holds up, our klister wax works, and we cross the ice of Big Sandy Lake, seven miles in, at midmorning. The air over the lake is cold, since five steep drainages intersect, spilling cold air down to be trapped in the deep basin. Even with the colder air, we get hot crossing the ice, since the surrounding slopes are like a great, concave mirror, concentrating the sun's heat.

Air flow over the land encounters the surface friction of forests and the reefs of mountain ranges, around which it forms waves and eddies. This slows the air, just as a stream is slowest at its banks and bed, creating differences in water pressure that swirl the water. In the air, there are swirls—updrafts and downdrafts—along the surface while winds ride faster above. The earth has stratified wind patterns, slower and more complex at the surface, faster and simpler on high.

The wind leaves tracks. Choosing a campsite, I look at the plants and trees for clues: Are there a lot of ground-hugging and cushion-forming plants? Do the shrubs huddle behind boulders? Do the trees seem to lean in a common direction? Is the bark scoured off the pines on their northwest sides? That means strong winds and drifting snow.

We climb up the dull blade of a ridge, sweating, trying to beat the thaw. The downslope flow of cold air has ceased, and all is still. Before long, the heated air of the valleys, warmed where the ground is free of snow and dark, will begin to rise up the drainages. Combining with the heat of the sun, the upslope flow will help thaw the surface.

But we're fortunate. We make it to the collector on firm snow. Dropping our packs, we go through our drill, pull the sample, change the bags, split the bag of snow in two, pack the sample, take the snow cores, weigh them, slap them into a bottle, label it, and stow it away. It goes more quickly when our fingers aren't about to freeze. The sun is strong, high noon. We sit on our packs to eat, unable to resist basking in the warmth. John dozes. I listen to the creek booming under the ice, thinning it out from below, growing stronger with the day's melt. From the cliff to our north, icicles fall and shatter. From rocks and pines, water drips.

I feel the first breath of the upslope wind, warm and soft. I close my eyes and see the red mosaic of my inner eyelids, like bubbles in cherry jello, a rich design. Everything seems to circle around us as we rest: the swing of the planet, the roll of the seasons, the rising and falling air, the water cycle—snowflake to ice to snowmelt to rushing creek to lake to river to sea.

These powers and patterns are no less vital than the circulation of blood. From a high perspective, imagining the great whorls of air and water, some of our proudest edifices seem to make little permanent sense. Concrete and asphalt keep the soil from breathing out, keep the rain from soaking in. Glen Canyon Dam is a clot in a continental artery, filling its backwater with nutrients needed downstream. The City of Angels burns like a Lucky Strike between the chapped lips of the continent.

So it is said. The sun will become hotter, so the ability of the atmosphere to cool the earth's surface will be vital to the continuation of life. At present, much cooling comes from cycles that depend on the global movement of air, like the water cycle.

The presence of free water gives us the protection of clouds and moist haze, without which the tropics would broil. Some of this airborne moisture nucleates around salt or sulfur rising from the sea and its blooms of phytoplankton, while some of it is the result of the transpiration of plants: largely the tropical forests that girdle the earth's hot zones with green. Clouds increase the earth's albedo, or reflectivity, and bounce a lot of solar heat back into space each day. They also hold warmth instead of allowing back radiation at night.

If we deforest the tropics and also manage to dump enough toxic waste into the ocean to affect the growth of phytoplankton, we could succeed in temporarily harming the earth's cooling plant. The effect would not be permanent—in Olympian terms—but the wild climatic swings might last long enough to eliminate not only us but large vertebrates in general. So it is said.

I blink at the other large vertebrate and say his name. "John. *Juanito*. We'd better go."

He sits up. "I wasn't really asleep," he says.

"I wasn't either," I say.

"Nice day," we say at the same time, then laugh. The snow is beginning to loosen, but is still skiable. We make a fast slither down to Big Sandy Lake, mush across the ice, then climb out to the west and start down our track. I can feel the sample, a cold block, low in my pack. I hope it doesn't melt and start to leak. That would mean not only a loss for science, but wet pants for me. We have to guard the samples, keep them uncontaminated and get them out, to keep the chemists happy back there in Oz. I try to recall my reading on the air's chemistry, wanting to tax John with some of it, but he takes one look at my pensive expression and disappears over the hill.

So I keep the chemistry to myself and think. A lot happens in the air: it's a chemical boogie. Incoming solar energy kindles all possible chemical reactions, and the diffusion of gases ensures that they take place all over, so the air has the same general composition throughout each layer.

One factor that supports the rapid chemical interchange and diffusion of the atmosphere is its smallness: the air has only a tiny mass compared to the mass of the planet. Another crucial characteristic of the atmosphere is that it supports the action of chemicals essential to life, such as enzymes. Much of our present atmosphere—nitrogen, oxygen, carbon—has been part of living cells before. Through many means—transpiration, respiration, decomposition—it is reemitted in a gaseous state. But it will be part of living cells again and again.

So all the mystical Hindu-Buddhist-Hopi stuff about breath and circles and cycles, all that softheaded, mushy, unscientific Redskin mumbo-jumbo . . . it's true. It's a bit short on specifics, but it's a good, sound summary. I take a couple of big breaths. I can smell the sap rising in the pines. I should be reverent, but I'm not. My appreciation for the world is active. I don't enjoy watching it from a state of transcendental calm. I want to get up and dance. Aer, aire, air, aria.

The snow goes to slush. We slop down our track, graceless, falling through into pits of white goop. I catch up with John, but spare him further enlightening comments on the atmosphere. We stand in the sun, eat some peppermints, and are content to breathe. How much do you need to know to do that? The top four inches of snow goes absolutely liquid, so we surf down the last part of the trail. Our skis make sucking noises with each change of lead, splashes with each awkward stride.

The bridge has melted out and the tread is all sand, so we take off our skis to walk across. When I bend down, both legs cramp, so I stagger and curse until the pain goes away—all this much to John's amusement. Then I shoulder my skis and walk across. The creek leaps and races. The ice has broken up, and I see the gold sand of the bottom, glittering and drifting under fast green water. On the other side, I stoop to latch my bindings, and the cramps return: more ugliness. John laughs out loud.

We take off our skis again to reach the cabin. We bury the samples—which haven't leaked—in the shaded snow, and lounge outside in the sun with bottles of dark ale. We share a bag of roasted peanuts, grinding them with our teeth, washing them down with luxurious gulps. John spills a few foamy drops and rubs them into his bare chest.

We'll ski and slog out tomorrow, starting early to get out on the frost. After the long cold season, these first warm days make us coyote-lazy. "Wish we had the boombox," John says every six minutes. "No life without music." Waving my ale bottle, I make up a little song:

> *There once were two rangers, Demons for dangers,*
> *Who risked all for Science and Sin.*
> *They brought home bananas, To Linda and Shana,*
> *Who welcomed them both home . . . and in.*

John salutes and drains his bottle of ale. We dig up two more, shining wet out of the snowbank, and uncap them with my Swiss Army knife. To be lying on this warm patch of ground, under this particularly bright sky, to be guarded by a thousand square miles of impassable, gleaming slush, is to know rare bliss. I can smell the lodgepoles waking up, their pitch pushing out to the green point of every needle. Like newly awakened bears, we loll, aromatic and hairy, in the sun. John hums scattered lines from a song in a drowsy voice. Every time I start to talk about the atmosphere, he replies with a global yawn.

Part IV: Headwaters

10

Water travels far below us,
Going on, going down.
Whatever walks, whatever passes
Goes forever on its round.

Peyote Song, Shoshoni

*E*arly June. The south flank of the mountain, under the aspens, is already dry. On the north-facing slope, melting snow holds out. The mountain, more a stretched foothill against the lift of the main range, has steep sides and a flat top that grades east into rolling forest. I stay on the south side, following muddy elk tracks up. The aspen buds are opening. There are dime-size leaves, tentatively green. Last season's grass is matted like wet hair, with white marsh marigold starred across the swales. Above a milky stream are snowbanks in the thick spruce and fir; over there I'd have to posthole, boots plunging through saturated snow to the sodden ground. Slushwhacking.

The thought of it makes me tired. I stop on the warm side, before the end of the ridge turns east and north. I'm scouting for our next trip, hiking on my day off. I unbutton my shirt and tie it to my daypack, feeling the sweat cool against my back. The sunlight is soaking into the ground; the boulders are warm enough to be backrests. I slouch under a patch of orange lichen and look south and west, into the sea of space.

Distant mountains ripple above the brown steppe, slanting south like a long train, out of sight. Above their woolly, coniferous blue is the snowcap. The crest cuts precisely into the sky, a flaring white that leaps out as the deep sky blue recedes above, falling away, untouchable.

I'm so absorbed in going that I forget about getting back. Each spring I'm caught out on ridges by nightfall. But the weather is not always this fine. Once, on the summer solstice, I sat out a three-day storm with a crew in the valley below. The clouds broke after four inches of snow. The next morning was summer, full and hot, creeks flooding, fresh snow melting into anarchies of green.

It's a fortnight before the solstice: old words, good ones. I can feel the land waking, like a cat stretching under my hand. Scent rises: earth, must, rot, moss, melt, bud, pitch, sap, leaf, all whirling up to crowd each breath. The air is full-bellied, pungent, pregnant. I forget my name and duties. The hard fatality of winter is past. On sunny slopes, the last elk are giving birth.

Last year, I was surprised by a face that lifted from a low thicket. Coffee-dark eyes took me in, widening with gentle shock. An elk calf: it stood up for the first time, saw me, and went still in every delicate bone. I was the second living thing in its world, and it knew I was to be feared. Behind, the mother strained to rise, blood and mucus still blackening her side.

I circled quietly, out of her wind. There were coyote tracks in a drift, ravens and eagles on the updrafts. I didn't want to drive her away from the calf. When I came back a week later, I searched for blood or innocent bones, widening my circle until it took in half the hill. There was no blood trace, no fly-grazed mat of baby hair.

In the valley, by the cabin, our garden is begun. We burned off last year's grass, pushed barrows of manure, and left barefoot prints in the frost-fluffed soil. We aren't the first to live here, though we like to think of ourselves that way. Our ways may not be the best ways for this place. But the ground is warm and wet, ready for seed, so we work according to what we know, like the homesteaders who started the garden patch, like the Shoshoni before them, watching the deer and antelope move along the sage-covered hills to the north and east.

Signs of human residence in the upper Green River Valley date back at least 12,000 years, though this may be a shallow estimate. The sites dug so far tell of big-game hunting in the basin and a foraging way of life in the benches and foothills, the country that opens at my feet.

Near Mill Creek, north of here, an outfitter found a pot carved from pepper-colored diorite, with a conical profile, a flat base, and thin walls. Probably a cooking vessel, it may date back 12,000 years, to the end of the last glaciation. If so, it would be one of the oldest artifacts found. It rests on display in a glass box in the bank in Pinedale, en route to the Smithsonian.

Clovis and Folsom points from early hunters are found on the surface, but such finds are hard to date. Archaeologists try to locate them in a buried context, with soil strata or datable charcoal. Clovis points, large and sturdy, are found with mammoth and bison bones in eastern Wyoming. Folsom points, long and center-fluted, were a favorite tool of bison hunters in the West.

Last week I saw a piece of flaked obsidian, volcanic glass, as long as my palm is wide. It was picked up a generation ago, due west of here. Held up to the light, it had an angled grain, black streaks in translucent gray like weeds in a slow current. The maker lifted parallel flakes along the grain from the convex face, narrowing the ends. The concave face was rougher, irregularly flaked. His intention was perhaps a dovetail point: a rounded tip, gently swelling margins and deep notches angled up from the base for binding to a shaft. The point was never finished. Viewed from the edge, it's unsymmetrical, too deeply curved to strike well into flesh.

Blades struck from a core often show deep concavity. Perhaps the curve was too strong, and after a hopeful try he saw that and left it on the ground. Maybe he was interrupted: a lightning strike, a bellyache, a passing herd. In my palm, it was an open question.

Obsidian forms when lava cools quickly. Chemically, it resembles the granite that forms the Wind Rivers, but their heart rock cooled slowly, deep in the crust. Slow cooling allows crystals to form, giving granitic rocks a speckled look. Obsidian cools so fast that it is amorphous, lacking crystal structure. Thus, it fractures along molecular boundaries and has the sharpest edges of any stone. This also makes it easy to flake.

I've never seen obsidian in the Wind Rivers, nor is there any in the Wyoming Range, where the point was found. One likely source would be young lava flows that stretch north of the Tetons, on the southern lobe of the Yellowstone Plateau. Another parent bed might be Eocene volcanics, forty to fifty million years old, that form the Absaroka Range, an empty grandeur north of the Wind Rivers, howling all the way to the Montana border.

The obsidian was carried at least a hundred miles on foot. Like the diorite pot, it may be a relic of a people moving south. Even unfinished, it may have been too pretty or too useful to leave behind. The edges were slightly dulled; it may have been used to scrape a wooden shaft. It fit my fingertips, my thumb resting firm in the concave side.

A dry period, the Altithermal, succeeded the cool, wet glacial age. In sight of our cabin are deposits of windblown sand from this time, 4,000 to 10,500 years ago. For the long dry spell, human evidence in the Upper Green is sparse. The hot, dry summers and frigid winters were a severe test. Throughout the West, some species, mammoths and giant sloths, became extinct. Others, like bison, were dwarfed in size. The horn spread of the largest living bison equals that of the smallest skulls from postglacial deposits. The big-game hunters migrated or became foragers, clinging to the mountain slopes with their perennial streams, hunting the few herds only sporadically. When the grand drought passed, both large herds and human bands returned to the upper basin.

In the most recent climate, with dry summers, vicious winters, and a sixty-day frost-free growing season, the lives of these people were bound to the movement of herds and to the use of favorable microclimates. Spring allowed them to spread out after game and the first shoots, while summer was given to foraging and individual hunting of small animals, deer, and antelope. In fall they stored plant foods, such as pine nuts and dried berries, and made a trek to a migration path for communal big-game hunts that drew the scattered families together. Successful hunts meant blood, marriage, and merriment.

The fall hunt was a chance to stock dried meat and fat for winter, when hunting or foraging were tough. Winter campsites were made in caves and rockshelters, or built: pithouses or skin tents reinforced with piled brush. The camps sat on the south-facing slopes to shed cold air and to catch winter sun.

From here the antelope move a hundred miles or more, south into the open steppe, where strong winds expose the sage and curly grass. Deer migrate in small bands up and down the rivers, browsing the thickets, or on dry slopes where bitterbrush grows. A winter of deep snow kills nine out of ten deer. The elk herds seek out grass along the rivers, bedding together on sun-facing bluffs. Moose gather by twos and threes in willow bogs, nipping the twigs.

Except for a small herd that roams near South Pass, the buffalo are gone. Yet the country, once tracked by their seasonal floods, echoes with their passing. Bones and skulls heave up out of bogs under Union Pass, and there are wallows, circular pits dug by rolling, pawing, fly-plagued bison, that range cattle have taken over.

The extreme cold and insistent winds made winter a bitter time. Frostbite was a hazard. The people had ingenious ways of twining rabbit fur or feathers into warm robes, but it was hard to make shoes that could withstand not only cold, but the sharp edges and abrasion of crusted snow. Most winter camps were set up near a known winter range for herds, to allow hunting during spells of good weather.

During storms or extreme cold, the families stayed in shelter, sharing fur robes and twined feather blankets. Many western tribes reserve certain stories and songs for winter's dark, when the circles of human warmth are small. Stories heard on the edge of sleep, in the closeness of a winter lodge, would afterward seem to have been recalled from the womb.

There are circles of stone everywhere people lived, small ones for fires, larger ones for tipis, and great ones, ceremonial calendars, for tracking the sun and moon. Fires were possible in rockshelters, pithouses, or tipis with roof vents. The firewood available in the basins, sagebrush, cottonwood, and juniper, tends to have acrid, stinging smoke. My brother Chris once wintered in a Utah canyon in a tipi heated by juniper fires. The smoke layer hung about three feet above the earth. Stand up and your eyes filled with tears.

Low earth-and-wood lodges may have been heated without smoke by rocks warmed in a fire outside. Archaeological digs have uncovered rounded structures with pits full of heat-cracked stone, but no ash. This would be a way to heat the lodge in daylight, for cooking and crafts. The nights would have been spent cocooned in robes. The traditional sweatlodge is built and heated in this way, and can be made excruciatingly hot. Sweatlodge rites, a complex of songs, stories, and initiations, are older than any of today's major religions. It might be that the sweatlodge memorializes the still more ancient practice of heating with fire-warmed stone.

Early spring brought relief from grinding cold, but not from hunger. The animals were in poor condition, with little body fat. Without fat, lean meat is indigestible and can cause fatal dysentery, called "rabbit starvation." The daytime air was warmer, but, until May or even June, soil temperatures were too low for robust growth. The people were weak after long abstinence and sharing. There are nineteenth-century accounts of Shoshoni families literally crawling from winter lodges to grub for bulbs and to chew the first spears of grass. It is an unkind paradox that the first flush of spring could mean a concentration of deaths.

From its high point, the sun wanders down the sky. This spring stayed cold until the first week of May and then warmed up fast. Too eager, Linda and I had seedlings ready when the ground was still frozen and then had to work at a frenzied pace after the thaw. The old-timers said it was an early spring. "When I was young," said one, "in May the cows would still be dragging their teats in the snow. You could see the little grooves between the hoofprints."

The weather of the high interior is shockingly variable, both on the scale of glaciations and from one year to the next. To survive on the land's yield, people need to be acutely sensitive to the land's mood. Before written history, the elders had to know the effect of changing conditions on the game, plants, and availability of water and shelter. They needed not only accurate observation and prediction, but a memory spanning the generations.

Because bare fact does not always lodge in human memory, the distilled experience of past seasons was set in rhyme and melody, given heart by the drum. Poetry, song, and story kept the hard lessons of the past within reach. They also comforted the harsh present, filling the house to seal out the shriek of the night wind.

There were no hospitals, no nursing homes, no funeral directors.

They lived risky lives and could not escape the consequences of injury, or the sight and sound and smell of pain. People who live thus have a terrible fear of death, yet they also have a relish for life, for the taste of food, for the warmth of spring days, and for the creation and care of children. They share resources not always apparent to outsiders. My forebears, crossing South Pass in 1847, were the outsiders.

I stand up from the boulder and stretch. Time to move. I look down at my rubber-soled boots, my blue nylon gaiters, my thighs in navy longjohns below tan cotton shorts. I have friends who kill their own meat, tan their own leather, make their own moccasins. I have other friends who only dream about the old ways, invoking Coyote or Grizzly along with Freud and Jung, to sweeten their lives as shopkeepers or ski-lift attendants.

Anyone rambling the hills in June can feel the generosity, the holy juice in the veins of the land. But it's a mistake to think of the world in terms of a few fair-weather rambles. What's missing is hunger. The green season and the fat summer days are short up here. The old ways weren't all drums and ecstasies. Scarcity is the diastole of the land's heartbeat, the drawing-in. There were seasons of suffering and privation to balance those of green leaves and the blood of abundance. As much as I want to know this place, I lack hunger's art. And it is an art.

During the recent drought in east Africa, traditional groups like the cattle-herding Samburu fared much better following ancient patterns of migration than semicivilized people of the same tribe who had converted to sedentary agriculture. While the traditional people had lower birthrates and higher infant mortality, their loose-jointed mobility meant that fewer of them starved. They knew the omens of climatic shift and had stories that told them where to go. They kept their wisdom intact. Lacking this depth of knowledge, under climatic stress like the thirties' Dustbowl, the boom-and-bust fringes of modern culture become quickly untenable.

Today in the basin of the upper Green, wet years followed by mild winters have swelled the herds. The Game Department hands out cheap additional hunting licenses, trying to cut the population. Long ago, such peaks were marked by communal hunts. This was done by trapping small herds in natural features like arroyos or crescent-shaped sand dunes. Dunefields south of the Wind River Range hold remains of bison kills from about nine thousand years ago, with long, meticulously flaked points that probably were used in darts with atlatls.

Dry years, with low populations of herd animals, were times of diaspora. Foraging efforts were organized at the family level, in which nothing, not mice nor bitter herbs nor crickets, was scorned. Hunger was the beat. The climate called the tune. What seems like two different cultures to an archaeologist may be wet- and dry-phase strategies of the same people. Beautiful spearpoints are not much use in hunting mice and scratching roots. Imagine comparing the relics of a dustbowl Okie with the personal kit of a 1980s bond trader.

Their lives would have required both alertness and mobility: think of it as low-impact backpacking, squared. It is an understatement to say that all clothing, shelter, and tools were made from natural materials. Some necessary things, such as grinding stones, were also cumbersome. Weighty items were often left in well-known spots, where they could be retrieved a season or a generation hence.

Around me are plants, rocks, bones, some with uses that I know and more that I don't. I make up for my lack of knowledge with money, a heavier pack, and tools from the stores in town. Dropped out here naked, I'd probably starve before I learned enough by trial and error to survive. Flake a good arrowpoint? Fabricate a snappy bow? Sorry. I couldn't do it, but those people did, and endured as families and souls.

Caches of elegant hunting points have also been found in the dunes south of the Wind River Range. They resemble a plains type, Scottsbluff, a slim triangular shape with a sharp point for piercing hide and finely flaked edges with a subtle outward curve. They narrow to a rectangular base, shaped and dulled to fit a foreshaft, bound with sinew and cemented with pitch. One large set of points, in the museum in Rock Springs, appears to have been made by a single person. The impression they give is neither crude nor primitive, but one of sophistication and exacting craft.

Riding range, I saw grinding platforms and handstones in the grassy flats. From the lichen growth on their abrasive surfaces, they had been unused a century or more. Hidden by sage, they hadn't been noticed by artifact collectors, who regularly truck them home to adorn the front stoop. I got off my horse and looked them over carefully, touched them once, and then left them. They were used to grind ripe grass seed gathered nearby. We might be needing them again someday. Too heavy to carry, they were laboriously pecked into shape and left where needed. Then, the warm-season population of the upper basin was probably fewer than two hundred souls, a few related family bands. They knew each other by face and name.

Friends of mine have found stone points in the Wind Rivers around lakes at 10,000 feet, relics of summer campsites. In the center of the range there are ancient quarries for steatite, an easily carved greenish soapstone that was valued for pipes, cooking vessels, and ornaments.

Much of the mystery in these old ways is imposed by the centrally heated sensory narrowness of our own. Classroom-educated scientists lack the bodily wisdom to be had by observing animals. The deer near our winter cabin bed down on south-facing slopes to soak up sun. They use the warmth for rest and good digestion. Feeding in the chill of dawn and dusk keeps them moving. Follow the deer in winter. There is mystery in what they are but not in what they do.

I traverse to the shady side, looping around snowbanks, scrabbling for rocky toeholds, tough after the open ground. I look for elk trails and find a subtle bench where muddy hoofmarks lead through drifts. I follow around deadfalls and under dark banks of pine to the top. Even in shadow I begin to sweat. When I break into sun, I'm hot, neck itching and sweat welling at the roots of my hair.

Summer hits the basin like a whip. After snowmelt the short grasses dry out, and the basin shimmers with heat. When dust rises and flies hum, there is good reason to be up high. The nights are cool, and there are daily breezes to clear the bugs away. There are fat mule deer and bighorn sheep. The mountain water is cold and clear. There are fresh greens and wild onions. There is plenty of firewood. And it is beautiful. It is beautiful. It is beautiful.

I head west, threading the broken pines along the rim. I can see across the basin to the river bluffs hiding the Wardell Site. It is the earliest-known communal bison-kill in the Rockies and Northwestern Plains where the bow was definitely used. It was found on ranch land close to the Green River, a low scarp at the joining of two arroyos. Bison were herded along the bench, driven over the edge to injure and disorient them, and trapped in a corral of juniper posts and cottonwood poles. The corral was used from about 1,600 until about 1,000 years ago, showing cycles of repair and rebuilding by its many postholes. It contains the jackstrawed bones of more than a thousand bison, mostly cows and calves. This was the choice of the hunters. A large herd or one with mature bulls would be likely to break down the trap. Study of the bison teeth shows that it was used in fall when the animals were fat. They were butchered and their meat cooked for immediate feasts or dried nearby.

In this and similar spots discovered in the region, there are drive-lines thriftily marked with wood or stone, not so much fences as templates, precise as to vector and timing. They show an exact knowledge of how bison respond to threat. There are also shallow pits, which may have concealed the people needed to give crucial nudges to the herd's direction. Lacking horses and long-range weapons, it's a brilliant strategy.

It was learned from observation. About a hundred miles south of here, last November, a herd of antelope plunged over a cliff. Game wardens examined their tracks and found no sign of humans or predators. Instead, there had been thick fog. In it, the herd spooked and charged off in a fatal direction, over a hundred-foot drop. Wardens counted 150 carcasses, most of them in a single heap. There are ancient piles of bone where stone butchering tools are found, but no signs of an intentional drive. Foragers must have come upon animals killed by accidental falls and moved in to salvage the meat. At some point, it occurred to the hunters that they could cause such mass plunges.

Some corral sites had small lodges nearby, probably used for blessing and prayer. The First Church of Meat. The people who used the Wardell Site probably followed the herds south to winter in the more clement valleys of the Wind or Bear rivers. At the Wardell Site there are points and ceramics much like those of the historic Navajo and Apache, Athabascan speakers. There seem to have been several migrations from Asia into North America. One of the latest was that of Athabascan groups, who settled in a long stripe from Alaska all the way to northern Mexico. Their collective name for themselves is *Dene* or *Diné*. They have a distinctive, handsome look, with slender, gracile builds and strongly Asiatic features.

Their languages, from interior Alaska to the Sierra Madre del Norte, are dialects of a common tongue. Like other pioneering peoples, they are powerful innovators, geniuses at learning and adopting new ways while keeping their cultural identity.

These ancestral Athabascan groups either occupied or continuously migrated through the Upper Green River basin. The Shoshonean people, with longer residence in the high West, probably gave way before them and then reoccupied the basin when they had passed.

Looping east again, I reach the snowline, more drifts than open ground. The elk stopped here too, milled, and then headed back. I work my way through forest toward a narrow park, hoping to see a band of yearlings. I sneak through a fringe of drifts and edge along the meadow. Too wet. The snow is gone, but the ground streams with snowmelt. I step onto a deadfall log and look north to the meadow's head, but see no elk. I count tracks in the mud, next to the little creek, then turn back. I know enough to plan our trip next week, to a snow collector two miles farther in. Through the heavy ranks of lodgepole on the mountaintop, the afternoon sky flashes blue.

At the time of the American invasion, the Seeds-ke-dee country was the home of the two eastern branches of Shoshoni. The more modern had adopted the horse and warbonnet, elements of Plains culture, and had ventured across the Divide onto the western edge of the buffalo plains. Speaking the same language, the traditional bands were cautious, sharp-eyed foragers of the foothills and mountains, called Shoshoko. They traveled on foot and the Anglo settlers called them sheepeaters, a vaguely insulting translation since the sheep they ate were mountain bighorns. The entire tribe had a reputation for physical beauty, fine leather, and bone beadwork. The Shoshoko were renowned for laminated bows of mountain mahogany, ash, serviceberry, or chokecherry, backed with boiled strips of sinew and horn from mountain sheep. At first, the division between the mounted and unmounted groups was small, probably like that between urban people and their country cousins. Later, it widened with time and the flood of history.

There is an 1871 photograph of a dark-faced family under a shelter of canvas and aspen. The husband is slim and sleek haired, eyes alert under bangs. Two women, faces slack with apprehension, hold babies. A pretty adolescent girl kneels in a striped blanket, eyes on the ground, three ropes of shell beads across her chest. To the right of the man sits his young image, a son who glares with haltered intent at the photographer, Mr. W. H. Jackson. Sheltering between them is a smaller boy, hair bushy and burred up from his head, stricken dumb by the booted gentleman and his terrible black box.

Do they look savage? No more so than any of us would appear in the same circumstance. With a closer look they are, in turn, cautious, scared, and angry, full of the strangeness. As a family, they share more than a common name; they know each other by touch and smell and appetite. They are strung together like the bones of a wolf, one body composed of separate ones, needing all of its parts to survive. They have a smoky dignity, more awake in their senses and in the world than may be possible for any of us, or even their descendants, now.

The Shoshoni, and their relatives the Lemhis, Bannocks, Utes, Goshutes, and Paiutes, have a long experience of the Great Basin and western Rockies. Their language belongs to the broadly dis-

persed Uto-Aztecan family, and they are specialists in dryland sub-sistence. Upon getting horses and modern weapons, they entered a brief cultural flowering like the more famous Plains tribes, a period of intense change and immense violence.

The trappers called them "the Snakes." There are few snakes in the basin of the upper Green, which is simply too cold for them. The basin was also claimed by the Absaroka, Sparrowhawk People in their own tongue. An old buffalo migration route runs north of here, between the Wind River and Gros Ventre ranges, over a high, rolling plateau. Buffalo skulls are still found there. Twelve years ago, I came on one bedded in the willows.

This plateau has a subtle but crucial set of drainage divides. The Continental Divide descends from the crest of the Wind Rivers and runs northwest over the plateau, hard to trace through the slow undulation of forest and grassy upland. The northeast rim falls off to the Wind River, with water that changes its name many times before it enters the Gulf of Mexico via the Mississippi. At the south edge of the plateau is Pinyon Ridge, named for the whitebark pines on its broad back, the boundary between the glacial trough of the upper Green and the Snake. The upper Green joins the Colorado and tries, despite dams and diversions, to reach the Sea of Cortez. The Snake churns through basalt canyons into the Columbia, drain-ing to the North Pacific. From the meeting of the three divides it is only two days on foot into the headwater valleys of three major rivers.

Drawn south by the buffalo over the broad pass, the Absaroka ventured into the valley of the upper Green. Called the *O-e-tun-i-o*, the Crow People, by their Cheyenne enemies, they were a Siouan-speaking tribe from the east, relatives to the Teton band of Lakota, the Hidatsa, and the Assiniboin. Frequent conflict between the Sho-shoni and Absaroka tribes is memorialized by names like Crow-heart, where Washakie, a Shoshoni leader, is said to have either devoured or merely hacked out and brandished the heart of an Absaroka. The following battle drove the Absaroka from the Wind River Valley, cutting off their access to the upper Green.

There was constant, natural friction between the Shoshoni and bordering tribes. The high valleys had limited food resources, most either seasonal like the camas lily or migratory like the bison. The quest for subsistence led different peoples to the same ground. Battles were fought on foot to protect vital hunting and gathering areas, but often in a formalized way that prevented heavy loss of life. Spears and bows were the weapons, with painted shields of buffalo hide. Like knightly armor, the shields fell into quick obsolescence with the arrival of guns.

The area was also visited by the Blackfeet, a formidable tribe from the northern Rockies. (When I counseled at a Bureau of Indian Affairs school, a smart and rather beautiful young woman named Tatsey explained that it is always Black*feet*. "A human being has *two*," she said.) By turns, they traded and fought with the Shoshoni and Absaroka.

With the horse came mobility and also a tremendous increase in friction between tribal bands. The fur trade brought not only smallpox and other plagues, but also moral epidemics of greed and opportunism among the tribes. This disturbed the edgy accommodation over hunting and gathering grounds while igniting a high-stakes weapons trade, as each tribe struggled to get the mechanics of defense. Soon, the newly acquired guns were used for aggression. We like to think of the tribes as mystically unified, but there was intense discord even within bands: there were peace parties and hawks. There was also latitude for individual action.

What followed was an era of slaughter, as tribes first allied with the whites against traditional enemies, then joined with traditional allies to stem the tide of invasion. There were waves of murder and cyclical revenge, with whole bands and lineages wiped out.

Jim Beckwourth, a black trapper who later joined the Absaroka tribe, tells of a casual massacre of Bannocks by Jim Bridger. The trappers were hoping to avenge the killing of a Shoshoni and the wounding of two whites by Bannocks, a corruption of the Shoshoni words for either "Hair-Thrown-Back" or "People Who Don't Give a Shit." A useful pun. The Bannocks, including many women and children, waded and hid on an island in the Green River. From the banks, the trappers shot and reloaded until there was "Not one Pun-nak left of either sex or age. . . . We carried back 488 scalps, and, as we then supposed, annihilated the Pun-nak band."

South Pass, a wind-blasted saddle at the southern end of the Wind Rivers, was the only route open to wagons for hundreds of miles north and south. For the immigrant parties, it was a bottleneck on which all routes converged from the east and diverged to the west. The impact of this migration on the land was great. After the charge of the Forty-Niners, Father Pierre-Jean De Smet brought a group of Indians from the upper Missouri to Fort Laramie in 1851, where he wrote:

> Our Indian companions, who had never seen but the narrow hunting paths by which they transport themselves and their lodges, were filled with admiration on seeing this noble highway, which is smooth as a bare floor swept by the winds, and not a blade of grass can shoot up on it on account of the continual passing.

The wholesale immigration of the 1840s ended the possibility of a native hunting-and-gathering way of life anywhere nearby. In 1857, the Lander survey party found the Shoshoni in difficult straits, with many close to starvation. C. H. Miller, an engineer, wrote:

> The new road in many instances follows the summer and fall trail of the Shoshonee tribe. The animals of the emigrants will destroy the grass in the valleys where the Indians have kept the pine timber and willows burnt out for years as halting places in going and coming from their great annual buffalo hunts, and I believe, even beyond the mere question of policy, that it would be a very unjust and cruel course of action for the government to pursue should we take the use of the land without reimbursement to the tribe.

Few of the immigrants were afflicted by such compassion. Most alternated between fear and disgust at the thought of Indians. While an elite minority lavished pity—from a comfortable distance—on the natives, the prevailing notion was that they were beastly impediments. With their aim of living dispersed across vast areas, they held back a more deserving people.

There were attacks, seen as a last resort by the harried tribes and as capricious brutality by the invaders. But despite movies and pulp fiction, Indian attacks weren't a significant cause of death on the westward march. It is not only probable but provable that more of these pioneers were killed by misadventures with whiskey and firearms than by hostile raids. Every heavily armed community had these incidents: drunken shootings, curious children with head wounds, and a roster of deaths and disfigurements from accidental discharge.

Nineteenth-century firearms were crude and dangerous, stoked with unstable black powder. Liquor and narcotics—laudanum, patent remedies, and others—also contributed to violence and accident. Many pioneers were red-eyed monsters, drunk, wasted, moody, sick, hemorrhoidic, and armed to the teeth. Even so, most loss of life was from diseases such as cholera, or from starvation.

For the tribes, it was the drop from a roller-coaster height, beginning a time of discord and starvation, of both bravery and the loss of hope. The Shoshoni, athwart the main line of advance, were attacked not only by immigrants but by Sioux from the east and by the Cheyenne and Arapaho from the southeast. They were held together by Washakie, whose sagacious dealings with the government saved them a prized hunting ground, a reservation, east of the Divide in the Wind River Valley.

Isolated groups of Shoshoko—the traditional people—responded to the Anglo influx by retreating to the mountains during the summers, when migrating whites were active in the basins below. There are drivelines and traps for bighorn sheep near timberline in the southern Absaroka and northern Wind River ranges, most of them either built or maintained in the 1800s. But the subsistence base at such high elevations is extremely fragile. As a population, bighorns are vulnerable to intense hunting and also to diseases such as pinkeye that are spread by domestic sheep. In the late 1800s, bighorn populations probably crashed, driving the family groups of Shoshoko into servile coexistence with early ranchers or to the reservation. A few holdouts, families or solitary men, have places named for them, like Togwotee Pass between Jackson Hole and the Wind River or Tosi Creek on the upper Green.

There are no landholding tribes on the upper Green today, unless one counts Republicans a tribe. Pressed by technology and force, the Shoshoni selected a reservation on their favorite winter ground, the valley of the Wind River on the east side of the range. They were joined, unwillingly, by Arapaho who fled from wholesale extermination in Colorado and spent several years raiding and starving in the drainages of the Platte, Bear, and upper Green.

These Arapaho survivors were captured and temporarily plunked onto the Wind River reservation much to the displeasure of the Shoshoni, who had offered their old enemies sanctuary rather than a permanent home. The two tribes remain in peaceful but uneasy accommodation, sharing a reservation but seldom intermarrying, as do the Shoshoni and Bannock on the Fort Hall Reservation in Idaho. Sadly, the major common ground between Shoshoni and Arapaho has been the incessant pressure of the surrounding Anglos.

I walk south on the rim of the mountain, following a strip of dry earth. There are fresh tracks and scat so recent that the surface of each egg-shaped pellet is moist, yet there isn't an elk in sight. They're close, though. Just off the feedground, they are probably glad to be away from humans and nervously aware of my smell. I can smell elk here. They can smell me.

My forebears were Mormon refugees, fleeing the United States after attacks in Illinois and Missouri. They rolled up the Sweetwater and over South Pass, descending the Big Sandy River and then striking for the narrow oasis of the upper Green. Winter found them settled, barely, in the valley of the Great Salt Lake, where Harvey McGalyard Rawlins and Margaret Frost began a farm, horse ranch, and sawmill at the mouth of Big Cottonwood Canyon. Their families had been on the continent for perhaps four or five generations. In a family history, I read this:

> All the battles that frontiersmen ever knew greeted these young people. No monument can portray their integrity, no picture can describe their heartaches, and yet no tongue can express their joy, their pride in conquering.

Sometimes I think of that: the intoxication of taking a country that felt new, of the feverish work and aspiration, of the urge to survive and acquire that translate to later generations as a kind of nobility. Even now, I like to stand at the end of a newly dug garden row, seeing how it looks in the world. Other times, in the hills, watching elk give birth, I feel as though something deep and patient, a human quality that rose from this place, was destroyed.

The sun is still four hands above the horizon. I stop and feel it on my face, its touch approving all. At my back, a squirrel yammers in the lodgepole. I hear the drip of snowmelt from limbs and rocks. I feel warm air lifting over the mountain rim, combed by the aspen, scented by pine. I shift my weight, and the clean, angular grit whispers under my soles.

The earth and I are of one mind. Chief Joseph, Thunder Traveling Over the Mountains, said this in 1879. It asks much in terms of belief.

We planted our garden seed and it grew out of virgin soil and everything was brand new. Frances Johnson, a settler on the upper Green, said that in 1988 in her old age. It asks much in terms of forgetting.

In school, I met a woman with long, black hair and a compact beauty. She was a Northwestern Shoshoni. Her family had lived for thousands of years in the mountain valleys later occupied by my great-great-grandparents. Her grandfather, Moroni Timbimboo, was the bishop of the Shoshoni farming village of Washakie. By the end of the Depression the Shoshoni farming effort collapsed, the people moving to Brigham City and Ogden.

Patty taught me the Shoshoni words for eyes, nose, and mouth, touching her lips with a fingertip. She had a child, over the mountain, in the care of her mother while she tried to finish college, a leap from her job as a beautician. As a project for a history class, we drove to the bend in the Bear River where Colonel P. E. Connor's militia had wiped out a winter camp of Shoshoni and Bannock.

There had been attacks on travelers. The militia, who were from California and eastern Nevada, were veteran butchers of Indians. Their orders were to go to Salt Lake City to watch the fractious Mormons. Since the Mormons remained quiet, they chafed for action. They were obliged by an outbreak of angry, roaming bands in southern Idaho, who attacked a wagon party, killing many of them at a place now called Massacre Rocks. Some of the attackers and their leaders were said to be camped with Bear Hunter's band of Shoshoni. In January 1863, as a cold wave spread over the Great Basin, the California Militia marched north.

Making sense of Connor's report of the battle—he claimed to have attacked uphill against a fortified Indian position—is difficult in the actual terrain, a slope cut by gravelly ravines. Militiamen claimed that the Indians "waved the scalps of white women" as a taunt. This seems an unlikely tactic even for the most reckless warriors, as they watched the militia surround them in a camp full of noncombatants: the elderly, women, and children. Earlier, in the fall of 1862, Bear Hunter had climbed a hill to wave a truce flag, which the troops under Major Edward McGarry didn't recognize as such until a civilian convinced them that the Indians wished to talk rather than fight. Likewise, Connor's troops may have seen scraps of cloth fluttering desperately in the predawn fog as scalps.

The troops poured heavy fire into the camp, then slaughtered women and children as they tried to escape up a gully, a fate echoed more than a century later in Vietnam in the village of My Lai. In the 1860s, there were no investigations unless the army lost. There was no disloyal press to raise a cry of indignation. Yet, in writing his report Connor seems to have concocted a lie. Did he feel guilt or was he simply bucking for military honors? Or did his guts turn, afterward, at what he had seen?

Walking over the place, it was hard to speak. To Patty's family, this was like Babi Yar, a place of horror. I felt indicted, though it wasn't a massacre of Indians by Mormons. The California Volunteers hated them both. My great-grandmother helped to nurse the frostbitten troops returning from the massacre. Other Mormons went to the scene to help survivors, finding two badly wounded women and three small children. In the gully, they saw the dead, frozen eight feet deep. I think of those women, great-great-aunts to Patty, with her heavy hair and smooth brown skin, women with her resolute brown eyes. Women with names, with songs, with children. When I am asked to recall my pioneer heritage, these images flicker behind the paintings of stalwart settlers, the sturdy oxen, the wagons with clean, white canvas tops.

In the late seventies, I lived in a Utah canyon, in a cluster of houses called White Horse Village. I was teaching and counseling, mostly with Indian students. When I got word that a group was walking from Alcatraz to Washington, D.C., to talk about broken treaties, I found my brother Chris and loaded half of the deer I'd gotten that fall into my rattly, orange Volkswagen. We met the procession, called the Longest Walk, after they crossed into Utah.

That night, we were gruffly welcomed, and the deer meat went into several big stewpots at a roadside pullout. A circle of young men talking in low voices, crowded around a fire, sneaked looks at us over their shoulders. They didn't appear pleased. A woman came over and said that someone thought they recognized us as Mormon missionaries from their reservation. We weren't even churchgoing Mormons, let alone missionaries, I said, upset.

The trouble was that ex–Mormon missionaries were frequently recruited by the FBI. Some of these men, Lakota sundancers and activists from other tribes, knew quite a bit about FBI ringers. My brother and I looked uneasily at each other, then fell into talk with some older women who were supervising the campstoves and big pans in which frybread bubbled in hot lard. From the increasing length of the glares from the men around the fire, I estimated we had about five minutes before being escorted to the junipers for some rough talk. I got ready to run.

"Mr. Chips! All right!" I whirled. A tall young woman in a denim jacket bounded toward us, glasses reflecting the firelight, long hair flying. "Hey! It's me—Mary Rose. The graduate." I drew a relieved breath.

She had been a student at a BIA boarding school where I set up a tutoring program for college-bound students. There were a few good teachers, but mostly it was a sad school, more custodial than educational. Graduating seniors had the equivalent of an eighth-grade education from a public school, so we met after classes to work up to college level in the basics.

The bright kids spent a lot of time smoking and talking behind the buildings, which is where I met Mary Rose, a Wind River Arapaho. We spent afternoons with a small circle of others on the dry grass, passing books and pamphlets, reading from them aloud. They told me they were discouraged by the classes inside the building and came out here to have their own.

'Skin History 101, they called it. We read the Code of Handsome Lake, a Seneca prophet who preached moral reformation in upstate New York, a quarter-century before Joseph Smith got his revelation there and founded Mormonism. We read the subtly stinging reply of Red Jacket to a missionary, and other words from Tecumseh and Smohalla and Chief Joseph. It was their standard works-in-translation, the Redskin Canon. It was an education for me.

Mary Rose. Her eyes crinkled at the corners as she smiled. She was glad to see me. She gave me a complicated handshake and then a scandalous hug. I introduced her to my brother. "He's pretty cute," she said. "What happened to you?"

We were known—it was enough. We ate, sitting on rocks, talking to Mary Rose and an older woman with waistlength braids. The word went around the camp, and some of the men from the fire came over to tell us that the deer stew was good, then asked us to join them in a song. We didn't know the words, but the fire was warm on our faces.

We walked across Utah, marching along I-70 as cars and diesels blasted by. When we crossed into Colorado, the leader—Bill Schweigmann, a Lakota—declared a rest, and my brother drove the orange bug ahead to help set up camp on the Colorado River, west of Grand Junction. My new Triple-A Springbar tent had been grinningly appropriated by Grandpa Bill as a Moon Lodge. This was traditionally the refuge of menstruating women, but some of the young, urban activists on the walk were chafing about such confinement. Those few who assented slept in my deluxe, mosquito-netted, canvas condo, while my brother and I, feeling virtuous, slept under a lean-to of poles and a tarp.

Schweigmann, whose Lakota name I can't recall, was called Grandpa Bill by everyone. It was said that he organized the Walk after a dream involving four colors that represented the holy directions and also the racial conflict of modern times. I didn't understand it very well. He drove an old pickup and towed a venerable, humpbacked trailer with burnished aluminum coming through the blue paint. He was tall, with long gray-white braids and a big, pocked nose. He would stride around camp and ask questions, like "Do you know what you're doing?" I was tying some feathers and beads to a peeled cottonwood branch when he asked me that.

"No," I said, embarrassed to be caught playing Indian.

He laughed. "Good. Let me know if you find out."

The last day we spent with the Walk there was a ceremony. Fresh recruits had arrived from Denver, and there was tension between the traditionalists and the urban folks with sunglasses and degrees. Even so, we looked forward to the gathering. Wands were planted and bundles of sweetgrass from the high plains were lit to clear the opening, their odor hovering in the morning air, mixing with the smell of crushed sage and the willows by the river. A pipe was passed and each of us, about sixty people, had a chance to talk. I don't recall what I said. Nothing eloquent, just thanks for the welcome from people who had every reason to treat us otherwise.

Grandpa Bill offered prayers in Lakota, then in English. I remember his voice above the liquid drum of the river, high with the red water of early spring. In the church I went to as a child, they admonished us not to drink coffee or smoke or drink Coca-Cola. We donated one-tenth of our money each year. The building was gray brick with white wood trim. The voices were a comforting murmur, like herd-sounds, all passions contained.

Religion was something we generally believed to be good, like a drop in taxes. Our prayers were self-assured, and we were smug with good incomes and new houses. Grandpa Bill was poor. He wore old jeans and faded shirts. His truck and trailer were relics. He didn't have that money-and-property gloss, assurance of a going thing, but he was easy to trust. An old man in old clothes, with big hands, open to us all.

He looked up at the sky, then spoke to the river and the hills. He talked to the sage and the cottonwoods, thanking the place that sheltered us. I had never heard anyone say prayers in this way, direct and yet uncertain, as if there were a listener. As if the prayer meant anything but comfort to the one who spoke.

Grandpa Bill talked to the winds and the directions. He prayed for the hate between races to cease, and for justice to be done in the form of respect, not charity. He talked to the river and to the water in the river and to the wet sand at its edge and to the dust at our feet. He talked as if his grandmother were sitting on the ground, looking up at him, old and sleepy, looking up at him with a patient squint. He talked as if the earth were listening.

When I thought about it later, I felt so lonely that I started to cry. I had never heard anyone do that in my life, nor had I thought of doing it myself. He talked as if the earth could hear.

11

The real is only the base, but it is the base.

Wallace Stevens

On the west side of the mountain, our colleagues are learning to run chainsaws, a training session which we escaped. We waved at them, a group of twenty, hunched and jerking at starter cords under a drift of oilsmoke. We could hear a chorus of two-cycle snarls and a shouted admonition—*Don't be askeered of it*—as we bounced by on the dirt road.

"Don't be askeered of it," I repeat, and Jim laughs.

"Askeered of what?" he asks.

"The elephant," I say, which sparks another attack of laughter. He has innocent eyes that make you want to either tease or protect him.

"Why is that funny?" he asks when his breath comes back. "There're no elephants in Wyoming."

"That's why." The road leads up, cutting contours and branching to reach abandoned drillpads where oil rigs sunk their mosquito beaks into the flank of the mountain twenty years ago. The road is all dugway, carved into the steep slope, slowly washing away. The drillpad is a sloping scar, the soil too compacted for the surrounding aspen to recolonize it. A rusty drillcasing pokes up ten feet into the

172

air, its top daubed with birdshit, where we swing the truck around and park.

Jim stows his lunch and assorted bundles into his daypack, along with poly bottles and bags for the snow sample. He knots a red bandanna around his head and puts on sunglasses. Eyes hidden, he looks pure jock, a tough guy. He sets his mouth in a grim line, looking up at the slope above.

I've always envied his type, the Naturals. Even after half a life spent in the Big and Scratchy, I still look like I just wandered out of the reading room of the Minneapolis Public Library, hunting for my tweed coat.

Ten days ago, when I scouted for this trip, the pine forest was pinto-spotted with snow. We climb through the aspens, their leaves now a distinct canopy, catching the sun and covering us in light, shifting green. We follow elk trails, and Jim mentions the fact every ten seconds.

"Elk tracks!"

"We're on an elk trail."

"Elk tracks—look at this one!"

"Nobody built this trail. It's an *elk* trail."

"Wow. Look at all these elk tracks!"

Climbing, we turn the end of the mountain, south to east to north, and follow a water draw to the top, hearing the lop and gush of snowmelt through rocks and deadfall. There is still snow in the woods, but the patches of open ground are enlarging, touching edges under the pines, and we're able to skirt the drifts, ducking under low limbs and walking the tops of logs. The open spots appear first around the bases of the pines and then grow larger. Grandpa Bill, the old Lakota with whom I shared a long walk, said the month when this happens is called Dry Around the Root. He was explaining when to harvest the inner bark of red osier dogwood for use in ceremonial pipes. Between the bare spots the snowbanks are hard frozen, but thawing quickly in the early sun.

In winter, each pine holds snow in its branches, keeping it from the ground around the trunk. The forest itself is warmer than the meadows, and the boles of trees absorb the spring sun's heat, melting the thinner snowpack around the pines first. Snow has the strange quality of being a perfect reflector of visible light, but a perfect absorber—termed a "black body"—for longer-wave radiation. The trunks and foliage of the pines absorb shorter light waves and radiate them as invisible long waves: heat. The exposed, needled ground absorbs further heat, and the pine, with warmed soil and free water trickling from the surrounding drifts, can begin its yearly surge of growth.

We come out of the pines into the open. Now the ground is like soaked burlap, sending up flowers along the morning side of a long meadow, which in this country is called a park. Spring beauty, five petaled, white to pink, about the size of a button, stars the dark soil, with marsh marigolds duck white and anemone silk yellow in the flooded spots. It is mid-June, three days before the solstice, but barely spring at 9,000 feet.

As the day heats up, there's water running everywhere, out from under snowbanks, around the pines, between tussocks in the meadow, through the soil. We stop to watch a freshet diving into a mole burrow and, looking through its collapsing roof, follow it a hundred feet down the gentle slope. Water speaks to me. Growing up in the arid heart, I have a reverence for it.

I chose to go to college in Logan, Utah, not only because it was close to the family homestead, but because in June the gutters sparkled with mountain water. The deep gutters along every street are part of the system of irrigation that is a Mormon legacy. I didn't care about that as much as I liked to wade, barefooted, up one block and down the next. Just as my devout aunts and uncles see the will of God moving in the conduct of their days, so I see the flow of water. The water cycle is my calendar, the names of lakes and streams my litany.

Most of the world's water is not fresh. Almost 97.6 percent of it is in the seas, and another 2 percent is in the polar ice caps. What does that leave? Accessible groundwater is 0.3 percent. The fresh water in all the lakes and streams is 0.0091 percent. Compared to the mass of your body this is less than a tear. Still less, 0.0009 percent, exists as vapor in the air.

But even that trace of water is important. The fall of rain and snow are vital. Hydrogen is so light that gravity can't hold it. It would diffuse into space and be lost: we'd end up as dry and as lifeless as Mars. When it is contained in a water molecule, the two oxygen atoms weigh it down.

Water vapor is happy to stay in the air. The hotter the air is, the more water it can hold. Deserts are dry because hot air is greedy for water. It takes 540 calories to turn a gram of liquid water to vapor. Given enough heat, the air holds on to the water it has and takes more from any moist surface, by evaporation.

Water leaves the air by condensing at a decrease in temperature. In doing so, it gives up all those calories. Water doesn't like to condense alone; it clings to objects. When fruit growers set out smudges, they are trying to get water vapor to condense by providing tiny particles, in the form of smoke.

Cloud seeding, blowing silver nitrate smoke, tries to provide more nuclei to condense droplets. Other sources are dust and particulate air pollution. The ski resorts east of Salt Lake City get heavy snow partly because of the "lake effect," moisture drawn off the Great Salt Lake, so salty that it stays ice free, and partly because the air pollution from the city seeds storm clouds with particles.

Water threads the dark ground, like silver chains laid across brown velvet. Our boots make spongy sounds—coosh, thrush—on the tussocks. Jim is an almost-graduate of Colorado State who had to drop the spring semester—his final one—after he wrecked his knee playing shortstop. The knee was surgically rebuilt, but got infected and swelled, says Jim, to the size of a football. After a month in the hospital with antibiotics and tube drains, he decided another summer in the mountains looked good. He worked with me last summer and we clicked. He's as good-natured as an otter, with dark brown hair about the same shade as an otter's coat and a sturdy, mesomorphic frame. Under a fresh crop of leg hair and a tan the scars are visible, but he chugs happily up the meadow as if he's never been off his feet at all.

I've promised him elk: this flat-topped mountain is tattooed with elk trails, and half the pines have elk hair stuck under the flakes of their bark. At times one can even smell elk, a rank, malty whiff through the pines, but we don't find them in the first little park where I thought they'd be, where I've seen spring bands of cows before, lolling with their new calves, grazing the earliest grass.

For two summers the rain collectors I set up here were knocked over and scattered when I returned to get the sample. At first, I suspected an outfitter who had hard feelings toward the Forest Service, but I noticed a profusion of elk tracks around the collector, with no suspicious bootprints among them, and decided to return at first light and watch from the woods.

I crept on my belly into a stack of deadfalls and tried not to breathe. The knees of my pants were soaked and my hands were muddy. Breath under control, I looked into the open park. There were about twenty elk, backlit by rising sun. Elk are big animals, rangy, slab sided, about the mass of an Arabian horse. A clutch of young bulls with velvety, sprouting antlers jostled around the collector—a simple plastic bottle which squatted under its white plastic funnel like a mushroom.

One of them sniffed it and began licking the rim of the funnel, rolling its eyes. Another joined in. They tongued it dreamily for a bit and then the first one stopped with a grimace, if you can picture a grimace on an elk. Its long face registered disappointment. Another elk started to lick, while the disillusioned one stretched his neck and bit the funnel's rim, his lip wrinkling. The second elk did likewise. Then they raised their heads with a look of having been cheated—*Mister, I put my quarter in and pulled the handle, but nothing came out, honest.*

The first elk ambled away disgustedly, and others came up to try licks and then hearty bites. After ten or so had tongued and chomped, the funnel came loose and was nosed in one direction while the bottle was subjected to repeated tasting, soccer kicks, and chagrined looks. What were they doing?

Then I recalled the salt blocks that a rancher set out just west for his cattle, white with a faint human scent. The elk, salt-lovers all, had concluded that white objects left by humans in the meadows were to be approached with eager tongues and dreamy eyes. Their disappointment seemed so natural that I forgot to be mad at them for breaking up my collector. I laughed and they leapt to attention, heads high, nostrils flared.

When I stood up, they scattered east with a pounding and cracking of twigs. I squished across the park into the circle of muddy hoofprints and picked up the funnel, in which I could see the

grooves of their incisors. The next week, I made a telescoping pole and mounted the collector on it, reasoning that elk didn't care much about objects above eye level. It worked. Aside from scratching themselves on the pole, they haven't bothered it since.

The big park is tough walking. The earth feels like a waterlogged mattress, all spring and squish. Water fills every low spot and wicks up into the tussocks, which compress to dip heel or toe into the surrounding soup. Many of the higher spots are tangled with dwarf willows, which twine around our ankles, so our feet must rise high in a slow, awkward parkhorse prance.

After months of being confined, Jim luxuriates in the movement. He stops often to stretch or wiggle his shoulders. He flexes his wrists, sucks air through his nose, stretches his neck, and looks like he's about to whinny. "This is great," he says, "to be out again."

I feel responsible for him, not simply as a boss. He lived with his mother, who was either widowed or divorced, I don't know which. He asks me about things that have nothing to do with work: how to handle a misunderstanding with a girlfriend, how to find out what he really wants to do in the world. I feel like an older brother or a maternal uncle. I don't know what I have to teach, unless it's a slant on the world. Or perhaps how to walk in the woods. That would be enough.

John, my winter partner, is up in the Teton Wilderness to the north, climbing pines to hoist meat poles—an odd summer occupation. The idea is to provide bearproof means of hanging elk and deer carcasses during hunting season. Not only are bears tempted to go after the fresh meat, but the hunters are tempted to shoot them for it. The object is to reduce grizzly bear mortality.

Marty, my ex–winter partner, has returned from Pakistan with Susan, John's ex–climbing partner/girlfriend, to start wilderness ranger jobs in the Cascades, where Susan is Marty's boss. I haven't seen them, but John said they had a good trip except for their attempt to do a ski-traverse of the Baltoro Glacier. After packing their skis for a month, they found skiable terrain on only two days of the traverse.

Jim and I cross the head of the park, looking back down the flattened V of the drainage, the meadow rising at the angle of an eagle's wings from a central streambed, hemmed by lodgepole pine for a mile to where it turns west and drops from sight. I've been told that these grassy parks are maintained by fire and also by local wind currents. The two might combine, since fire spreads along the wind, but being up here today I'd say that water plays the largest role. The edge of the lodgepole woods lies just above a necklace of springs and seeps. Below each seep are sedge, bulrush, and dwarf willow, plants that do best with their roots submerged for much of the growing season.

It's a mistake, though, to believe that any natural scape comes from a single cause. The spring wetness keeps pines from taking over the opening, favoring sedges and such in the wettest spots and grasses in others. The strong local winds—we've skied through howlers here in winter—break and uproot the lodgepoles at the forest edge and also, in late summer, dry out the grasses. Fine fuels such as grass will burn when the forest is still moist.

It could happen like this. The mountain rears abruptly from the valley of Willow Creek, across the prevailing late summer wind. This makes it a lightning rod of sorts, and there are many pines with dead tops and spiral lightning scars to testify that lightning, contrary to proverb, strikes repeatedly in the same place. A lightning strike from a rainless, late August thunderstorm could start a smolder in dry grass or in the fringe of deadwood along the park. The winds would fan it into the park, torching the fine grasses. In fine grass, fire moves quickly. With a backing wind, it would run up the park in minutes. Along the fire's edge, deadfalls would burn, but living lodgepole pines would not. Lodgepoles prune themselves by shedding low limbs; consequently, the branches of a mature tree begin slightly higher above the ground than flames from a grassfire tend to reach.

A grove of mature, healthy lodgepole resists fire. Ground fires course through, consuming deadfalls and diseased trees like a good housecleaning, but only drought and extreme wind conditions will ignite the crowns and kill the trees, as in the massive fires of the last season here and in Yellowstone.

Thunderstorm winds are strong but brief. As the storm cell moved northeast, the wind would cease, leaving the opening spotted with char, as scattered flames died out in the deadfall at the forest edge. The increasing humidity of evening or a dash of rain would put the fire to rest. In a normal year, with moisture in the ground, grassfires burn the dead stems but leave rootstocks unharmed. They also convert the grass into ash, which dissolves in water and returns nutrients to the soil.

Thus, topography, weather, microclimate, plants, and drainage are all vital to the state of this place. A change in any one will alter the relationship of all.

"We didn't see any elk there, either," Jim reminds me as we enter the woods at the head of the park.

"It's not like you schedule them," I snipe back.

What about the elk? They feed in these parks at dark and near dawn, then bed in the lodgepoles during the day. "Hiding cover" is what biologists call it. Do they nip the occasional tender pine seedling found among the grasses? Perhaps. Their grazing makes the grass vigorous, and they recycle nutrients in their manure. They need both forest and parkland: housing and food. In getting what they need, they help maintain the conditions that provide it. Right now they'll be in young pines or thick patches of deadfall, sleeping off the morning meal. Every twenty minutes or so I hear muffled cracks and hoofbeats off in the timber but say nothing to Jim. He'll think I'm fabricating elk signs to save my reputation.

The lodgepoles are regular, even-aged, about a foot in diameter, about ten feet apart. I can see old fire-scarred stumps, relics of a forest that burned hot over a hundred years ago and cleared the rocky soil for this cycle of growth. There are snowdrifts across the trail and we wade or zigzag. Another mile or so along, the trail breaks into a smaller park where the snow collector is still standing, guyed by three steel cables above the thawed soil. We drop our packs, unlimber tools, and unbolt the tube midway, lowering the sections containing the melted snow to the ground. The trapped water sloshes.

We raise the tripled plastic bags from the tube—no leaks—and agitate the water inside to mix it thoroughly. As Jim holds the bag, I snip a corner to let the snowmelt fill a one-liter sample bottle, then cap it. That's the chemical sample. Then I let the water spout into a two-liter bottle, to measure the remaining volume, one, two, three times full. Seven liters altogether. Since most of this moisture arrived as snow with a water content of 10 to 20 percent, it took between 35 and 70 liters of snow to yield this bagful.

We unbolt the snow collector and hide it in a maze of deadfall pines, where no one is likely to see it. It leaves a circular print in the moist earth. I mug and point. "Get the Instamatic, Lu-Dean!" I blurt. "The mark of a spacecraft! Extra-Tee-Restrills."

Jim dissolves. Making him laugh is like getting an otter to eat trout: no problem. Done with our work, we shuck and jive. "Wanna play Bears?" I ask. I point out a pert flower emerging in pink-and-white zillions from the moist ground and dig up a couple of bulbs, white fleshed and the size of peanuts. I eat one, give a satisfied growl, and hold the rest out. He cups them into his mouth.

"S'good," he says, jaws working, amazed. "Look how many there are." Spring beauties, like teeny potatoes but with a nicer taste. Jim is excited by all this unsuspected food right under our feet, so he digs more and chews them with his eyes closed. "I've seen those, but I didn't know you could eat them."

We amble down the park to a generous tree that has fallen into the meadow as if to offer a sunny seat for lunch. I lean back where a big buttress root forms a chaise, and Jim slips between two thick limbs. There are few bugs flying, a blessing for us if not for the swallows; two nights of hard frost have forestalled the annual swarm. Mosquitos, horseflies, and buffalo gnats: if they land on me, I swat 'em; no decent coyote would do less.

Here I sit on a shimmeringly green and untroubled day in June, clouds sheeping their way across the meadow of sky, and brood on my enmity for bugs. I gnash my crackers-and-cheese and shoot dark glances into the lodgepoles.

One of the liabilities of too much mind is to imagine scratching before commencing to itch. If Jim notices my mood, he's wise not to comment. What's up, he might say and I'd say bugs and he'd say no bugs here and I'd say I'm *thinking* about the little bastards and he'd say oh and look up at the sky. Glad we don't have to go through that.

Sitting in the sun is a pleasure. We doze, slouched against the silver hull of the windfall pine. I can smell the old wood and the wet ground. A memory rises: I'm bellied under a bush, dirt sticking to the cuffs of my Sunday shirt. The bush has a good smell, juniper. I watch the doors of the church across the road, gray brick with white wood trim. Then I look up.

The bush is a thousand greens, light, dark, shot with yellow. Its bark is rust red, silver, shaggy. My mother left me off in front of the church and drove away. I hid in the coat closet, musty with wool, and listened to the voices. When they went into the chapel, I escaped.

They are done with the singing. The low throb of the organ has stopped, and the hum of voices means that they are leaving the chapel, breaking up into Sunday school classes. A few kids come out the white doors and squint at the sun. A fat man in a blue bow tie comes out and herds them back.

Fallen needles prick my forearms and nip through my pants. When the people come out, I'll crawl out the back of the bushes and brush off, then wait for the gray Plymouth to roll up. Our car.

I feel good under the bush. At my back, there is a grassy slope down to a grove of cottonwoods. It's hot in the church, crowded with perfumes, hair oils, aftershave. I pick a few needles and break them under my nose. The good smell washes away the shame. From sprinklers, the smell of water rises. The dirt smells clean. Whatever I love in the world is here.

Lunch over, we start off to the west, but I notice a horse track crossing ours. We veer down the little park under the collector to walk out a different route and see what the horseman—horseperson, how about *rider*—was up to in the woods. The track comes up a muddy and badly eroding set of trails that braid through the grass. Once the snowmelt gouges a few little creekbeds, the trail gets too bad to use so all traffic—human, horse, elk, deer—detours, starting another track that braids along the first. When the original rut is freed from the impact of hoof and boot, fine sediment begins to collect behind rocks, roots, and twigs.

As the second track is getting pounded, grass grows back in the first, and the deposition of sediment begins to change the watercut Vs into shallow Us. Meanwhile, as the second track has been hammered, eroding into the rocky layer, becoming another cobble-filled gully, so a third track is etched by passing souls, forming a genuine braid.

By this time the first trail is filled up with soil and filled in with grass. Its turn has come again. As long as the amount of traffic doesn't increase significantly, as it might in a national park, or the flow become strong enough to shift the cobbles and twigs that form little check dams, the scarring and healing will go on side by side. The best land management is managed by the land.

We follow the horse track into the spongy woods and find an outfitter's hunting camp that I've heard about. There is a cook-tent frame with a moldering board floor, a big stove of welded sheet iron, and a rough table set upside down and ballasted with blocks of lodgepole. There are stump seats for the circle of bodies to gather around the stove for morning coffee and evening whiskey, both enjoyed in the dark during hunting season. Clustered about the cook tent are smaller frames of logs for the sleeping tents, in which city-living hunters no doubt miss a lot of sleep, starting at night noises, simmering with indigestion from the fried food, coffee, and whiskey. They roll in their sleeping bags, trying to ease thighs sore from riding cranky dude horses. Since an outfitted hunt costs about as much per day as a room in the Gramercy Park Hotel and three fair café meals, even the aches must be savored.

Between two pines is a seven-foot heap draped in black plastic, which we peer under only to find cheap tin heating stoves, a roll of plastic pipe to run water from a spring, toilet stools, and other artifacts.

We wander vaguely west from the camp, scouting in the heavy timber, dodging boggy spots, and walking fallen logs until we meet a little road in the pines that probably started from the camp a few yards north from where we did, along which most of the heavy items were hauled in a truck.

The old road is a thin slot through thick pines. We follow it southwest and break into the light of the big park, skirting back north and west to locate the trail we followed in so that I can fix the two on my mental map. Then we mush down the long, soaked meadow, each humming a different pop tune. My tune is a lot more exciting than Jim's, so he stops to listen. "Who recorded that?"

"Chrissie Hynde—Pretenders. 'Tattooed Love Boys.' It's ancient. Classical music."

We climb through spruce and fir up a north-facing slope. At the top, a trail leads through heavy lodgepole, descending gradually to a smaller, wet meadow. I warble happily. Jim stops. "Who recorded *that*?"

"The Pogues. An Irish folk-punk band. A major influence on modern music. I stayed in the same hotel after they visited New York City. The bartender had some vivid recollections."

"What's it called?"

"The Gramercy Park."

"No, the song."

" 'The Turkish Song of the Damned.' "

"That fits."

We cross a small park to bushwhack the heavy timber across the spine of Big Flat-Top Mountain. The sun throws long bars of shadow toward us. "No elk yet," Jim observes, lifting his brows.

"I'll stop singing."

"Thanks."

We hop deadfall, wind around bogs, walk fallen trunks, scurry under bushy limbs, and generally do all the things that children do given a really good playground. To be out and going, just that, feels good.

To parallel our hunger for knowing, we have a hunger for movement, not just in the limited sense of dance or exercise, but movement over the land. Our scavenging ancestors walked everywhere, prizing up bulbs, sniffing for carcasses, scuffling for small game. Since walking and watching were the means to life, they feel instinctively good.

These woodsy perambulations fill me with good spirits, while two successive days of office work can reduce me to numb despair, regardless of what's accomplished. My legs are the major part of me—forty inches from sole to hip, of seventy-six and one-quarter inches total, all that muscle and bone and bounce—and to use them is my chief delight.

Walking feels good. It helps me think. The practice of pilgrimage—walking trips to shrines to achieve recreation of the spirit—has been persistent enough to suggest that the act of walking, rather than the shrines, is vital. The physical process of moving over the land seems to swell the human heart with a conviction of finally, absolutely doing the right thing. The Grail, Mecca, Lourdes, the Frontier, Everest—all are simply good excuses for going.

For the pilgrims who arrive, a common feeling is disillusionment. Mountaineers report feeling sadness at the summit, where their absorption must cease and give way to descent. Perhaps the hoped-for miracle doesn't occur: the supplicants limp off, crutches still socked under armpits.

To go is the thing. Socrates strides across the dust in front of his students, pacing to mirror the gait of his thought. *Peripatetikos.* Aristotle, good peripatetic, circles the Lyceum, dispensing wisdom, confining his pilgrimage in space to open it up in mind. Our feet may have more to do with our thoughts than heaven.

"Our feet may have more to do with our thoughts than heaven."

Jim is unimpressed. "Elk. I want to see some elk."

"Okay. Let's go see the bastards. This way."

In gaining the mechanical means to travel long distances fast, we may have cheated ourselves of the human benefits of travel: a friend described his frequent jet flights as like being locked in refrigerators for a half day at a time, with little feeling of having done anything significant, though a continent had been crossed.

I like to walk in the woods. The woods teach patience but not subjugation, acceptance but not obedience. Maybe that explains the ruling tendency in the Forest Service to chain any promising person to a desk and a computer—a career. Get them out of the anarchic grip of the land into a nicely padded, rectangular slot. This replicates the original human sacrifice, giving up nomadism for the grain field, the hike for the hoe.

I stop and point at the ground, where there are fresh tracks. As we look down, a few pine needles topple into one. I tell Jim that elk can be smelled. He doesn't believe me.

"You can't smell an elk."

"Why not? You can smell a cow, can't you?"

"Yeah, but elk are wild animals."

"C'mon, James. They pee on their own feet and don't take baths. Just sniff."

He squeezes his eyes shut and inhales deeply. "Okay, I smell something."

"What does it smell like?"

"Funky. Like a locker-room after baseball practice. Or the bathroom in a bar."

I point to a pisshole in the duff, a foamy puddle around it. "That's what you smell. They were bedded here. When this one sensed us, it stood up and peed before moving out. Deer and bighorn sheep are pretty odorless in comparison. It's not elegant, but it's elk."

That there is an elk trail to follow through this tangle is itself a minor miracle, but I've seen an antlered bull dash full-bore through this snagpatch—like running through Macy's at Christmas holding two Shaker chairs above your head—while causing only an occasional clatter.

We stalk—ever slower than the elk—and emerge onto the open ridge and a long view to the southwest. I nod our direction and we hike out onto the ridgecrest and turn up a dry meadow, into the wind.

To the south and west is a sea of air above the seven-thousand-foot basin of the upper Green, the scalped buttes and coulees of the shortgrass steppe leading to the blue ranges farther west: nearby, the sedimentary tipis of the Gros Ventre and farther off the shattered ridgelines and talus bowls of the Wyoming Range, rock and forest showing blue against the snow. On a day like this before the industrial revolution, we might have seen nearly two hundred miles; now we see about eighty and count ourselves lucky. Of course without the industrial revolution, we wouldn't be up here at all, let alone in nice, lightweight boots and turquoise shorts and nylon gaiters, humming pop music, but allow me my objection. It doesn't take that much air pollution to make shorts, boots, and gaiters.

I get another whiff, on top of a hunch, so I wave Jim back into the edge of the timber where we creep like coyotes, trying to avoid dead twigs. I stop. Between us and the sky are two lanky young bulls, slick coated and ruddy, with velvet antlers mushrooming from their brows.

Jim gets that nervous, reverent look that urban college kids wear when they observe real critters. I'm wearing it too. The elk are as handsome as any animal has a right to be, long muscles rolling under reddish gold coats, heads lowered, grazing. We can hear the grinding of their teeth, the crunch of severed grass. Their jaws work and their throats pulse as they swallow. One stops and raises his head, edgily scenting the wind. The other follows suit. The first takes a few jerky strides. The second follows, then they turn as one. They know we are about, but don't have us located.

This is the old way to hunt elk in the mountains. Catch a trail, catch a whiff, sneak up on an island of timber, and then draw back the bowstring. When elk flush from their daybeds, they run willy-nilly, scattering in all directions. It's a good chance for a shot. But there aren't many elk bones in the ancient kill sites, though fragments of antler are often found in nearby camps. They probably were picked up for use in toolmaking. Elk bones don't show up in campsites before about 1200 A.D.

Journals of the fur trade mention herds of elk in the valleys, leading to the notion that elk avoided the mountains until ranching forced them out of the riverine pastures. Of course the fur-trappers—so-called mountain men—seldom spent much time in the mountains. They trapped the valleys, the rivers, and foothill streams, since that's where the beaver are, so that's where they would have observed the elk. Biologists tend to have more rigid ideas of elk habitat than elk do.

It's possible, too, that elk were overshadowed by the bison, both in competition for grassland habitat and as the choice of hunters. Bison have richer meat and tastier fat. Elk is tougher than bison. The current populations of elk may have been impossible before the buffalo were extinguished.

These elk are in no danger. They start to drop off the ridge, out of sight, so I step out and speak. "Howdy pardner—yonder lies Jackson Hole, last of the Old West." They plant their feet and stare. Two ear flicks and one exits—a survivor—while the other stops broadside in astonishment at the sounds coming from this pink-legged beast in the blue shorts. Some elk fall for it; most don't. Deer, easier marks, will stop and waggle their ears and even relax. Bucks are spookier than the does, who will listen to a whole song and then stand, waiting for more. Whether this is instinct or the result of Wyoming Game and Fish Department policy—buck-only hunts—I don't know.

Alas my love, you do me wrong, To treat me so discourteously . . . I sing a few measures of "Greensleeves." The credulous elk stands and goggles until I feel a little guilty. Then Jim steps out of the pines, and the elk vaults, thundering over the rim.

Jim is appropriately charmed by two animals as furry, brown, and athletic as himself. "Nice elks, dude. I owe you a beer," he says. We tramp to the narrow end of the park where we set up the rain collector on its telescoping pole. The mechanics—thumbing bolts into holes and wrenching clamps on cable—are a bore. The good part is getting to the place and going back, which fortunately take most of our workday. We finish setting up the rain collector and install a clean two-liter bottle.

Since I'm trying to balance Jim's dose of equations and computer programs with a course in the mountains, I ask him to lead the way back. He scrambles down a slope of overlapping moraines, look-alike aspen, and grassy swales. We take giant, downhill steps and wind through the white boles, under new leaves the size of a lamb's ear, through waterleaf and larkspur, green plants leaping up fast in the early heat. "Aspen buds," I say.

"What about them?"

"High-protein. Elk love 'em. Bears eat 'em too, when they wander down from their winter quarters. Very important dietary item."

"What do they taste like?"

"Never tried one. Waterleaf's good, though." I pull some leaves and eat them. He tries a taste. It's a mild flavor, lettucy.

After the long winter, the green is like strong drink. Maybe revolution isn't a flower of the cities. Maybe the whole idea of revolution comes from the northern spring. Let the ice melt. Let the water run. Throw off the old, soggy, brown ways.

"This is great," Jim says. "I hate to go back to the trailer."

"We don't have any dinner," I say, "but we could have spring beauties and elk milk."

"No way. How do you milk an elk?"

"You locate a fresh cow-elk—one with a calf—and stalk her from downwind. Get real close."

"Yeah?"

"Hang a bucket from your belt ... if you're right-handed it hangs on the left."

"Yeah?"

"When the cow runs, you dash up alongside, shove the bucket under her flank, and milk like hell. The trick is to finish before she gets to the thick timber."

His eyes narrow to slits. He ponders it, then wrinkles his nose. "I almost thought it was true. But then I considered the source."

Laughing, we lope down the mountain's green flank, breathing the fecund air, facing into the sun. Jim sees elk sign everywhere, pointing out daybeds under fresh-leaved aspen and firs. Under the matted leaves, the mud and fallen limbs are slick. You have to watch it. Down we go, until he finds the truck, right on.

12

*I*n June, there's the sound of water. In my bed, I could hear it rushing through the willow-bordered ditches along the hill, purling through headgates, flooding the meadows of native grass hay. Even now, at the cinderblock Forest Service warehouse, I can hear Pine Creek, loud and boisterous beyond the chainlink fence, sweet, green water coursing from the highlands, bank-full and racing, clear enough to see the granite cobbles rolling in its bed.

I picture a high lake melting out, a band of opaque turquoise growing between the snowy shore and the white of the lake ice, water filling all the pores, gathering. Another day and swirls appear across the whole surface, shifting from bluish green to greenish blue with cloud cover, a hue which makes the pines look black. Then, pools grow on the ice, sharpening the light. Then, open water appears at the bank, shimmering between floating ice and the eye, dark under the rock buttress, jeweled with last year's willow leaves.

We're going to a high lake. It will be surrounded by snow, perhaps partly covered by ice. It was near freezing in town last night, so the snow should be set hard. The time to travel on spring snowpack is early, from a couple hours before dawn until the shadows grow short. After that, it turns to slush and won't support much weight. We planned to leave at six, but I woke up late. When I crept into the office to sign out, one of the clerks had a sheaf of papers. When I went to my desk—actually a drawing table since the very sight of those gray steel government desks fills me with horror—there were slips of yellow paper, messages from various labs and regulatory agencies.

So at nine, Jim and I are still packing, stuffing the big, red expedition packs with some fairly odd gear. The warehouse faces east, so it's already hot as we lay out our equipment on the loading dock. From the stack of gear we pick each item and cram it into the packs in a semiorganized fashion, as I sing out the names like a short-order cook: "Float-tube, drysuit, rolled and tied, hang a swimfin on the side."

Jim cackles, trying to keep up with the flow of gear. "Footpump, bug jugs, label pens, sample bottles, twenty-five." As the pile on the dock diminishes, our packs grow and tighten. "Plankton net and plankton bottle, formalin and alcohol, two-hundred-meter cable, probe, thermograph, bathing robe . . ."

"Bathing robe? C'mon," Jim says.

"It rhymed. Probe-robe."

He shakes his head. "It's easier to keep track if you don't rhyme."

"That's not what Robert Frost said. Anyhow . . . Surber seine and brush and salt—got it?—breadpan, wetsuit booties, gloves."

"Wait. Where are the neoprene gloves?"

"In your hand."

"Oh. You distracted me." He crams them into his pack, which is now pocket-high and taut as a balloon.

"You take the stove, I'll take the pots. Ringstands, clamps, ten-inch funnel, tubes, all the little hardware for the rain collector."

"You take the poles and I'll carry the tent and fly." As I stuff them in, I can hear the stitches squeak. Just the science gear is a big load, not to mention the Boy Scout Handbook things, like camera, matches, knife, sunscreen, watch, water bottle, toothbrush, and toilet tissue (unscented, since perfume has to weigh something). And of course, food. We each brought two days' worth. Jim doesn't like granola, and some of his choices—Pop-Tarts—don't seem like food to me.

"Any last requests?" I ask.

"How about two Sherpas?" Both packs are waist high, but my waist is higher than Jim's. I have the extra-large size pack, which accommodates nearly eight thousand cubic inches; even so I have to punch my sack of clothes to get the drawstring cinched. The red nylon rings like a snare when I tap it. It looks bigger than usual, with a roll of blue instrument cable, black swimfins, and snowshoes hung on the outside. I'm afraid to weigh it, since I want to maintain the illusion that we can actually carry these loads on snowshoes through a jungle of boulders, deadfalls, and collapsing snowbridges. I hoist it, with a grind of my teeth, and manage to carry it to the truck, trying to hide my grunts under a cheery "not too bad, pretty well-balanced load." Jim tugs at the shoulder straps of his pack with a skeptical frown.

"Wool," he says. This is the sound that issues when he says "well." "Wool, I guess the straps won't rip off. Immediately." He heaves it off the ground and staggers to the truck.

The trip is an experiment in itself, to see if we can get to the lake with the requisite gear by using snowshoes and packs. The lake always thaws and warms before the trail is melted out enough to allow packhorses, which we need to haul our inflatable boat. Samples taken at the peak of the snowmelt are valuable, since most of the acids melt out of the snowpack with the first flush of water. Ice has a regular structure, a lattice of atoms, more open than that of liquid water, with more space in it, so ice floats.

As ice melts, the heated atoms vibrate faster, and the lattice breaks down. Picture a hall full of square-dancers, then a sidewalk full of commuters: the dancers repeat a set of ordered patterns, not bumping, staying in the hall. They are more like ice. The commuters, jostling, crowding, each with an individual mission, form a rush, channeled by buildings and chance into definite currents. They are full of energy, disorganized, more like snowmelt. It is this initial rush that leaches out the acids in the snow.

It occurred to me that we might try a float-tube, used for calm-water fishing, along with a drysuit and layers of long underwear. I managed to borrow a tube and the first big question—will all the gear fit into two packs?—has been answered. The gear is ready to travel. Now we can begin our questioning of the lake itself.

We drive to the east, up the road that climbs 2,500 feet to the trailhead at Elkhart Park. The park is a grassy opening in the head-waters of a small stream. I don't know who Mr. Elkhart was, or if there was one. There's an Elkhart, Indiana. A hart is the male of the European red deer. Elk is also a European word. The North American species is called *wapiti* in Cree, an Algonquian tongue. It means "white rump." I try to remember the Shoshoni words for elk and heart, but can't.

I give Jim an extemporaneous rant on place names as we wheel around the curves, pines tipping by like a train movie. "What kind of name is Elkhart? Let's change it to Elk Heart Park. Or Moose Turd Park. Something damn well indigenous." He nods, somewhat puzzled. "Piss Ant Flat," I intone, "Suicide Lake, Dirty Devil River, Jackass Pass, Crazy Woman Creek, Crowheart, Tensleep, Saddle-string, Burnt Fork, Big Timber, Buffalo, Red Lodge, Mexican Hat. Good names."

"Yeah. Those are good ones."

"Why all this slavish imitation and worse, lickspittle naming of perfectly decent places after politicos and capitalists who've never even seen them? Who wouldn't be caught dead outside a four-star hotel. It's an outrage," I cry, peaks revolving in dizzy array, Jim nodding, until we pull into that oxymoron, the wilderness parking lot.

"You get excited about things I never even thought of," says Jim.

"Too much education. After a BS, it's all downhill."

The trailhead is deserted. Nice view and only a few mosquitos. We snap a few pictures of our outer burdens and then escape into the woods before any curious gringos arrive: merely standing with a pack this heavy is bad enough, let alone having to answer questions about the snowshoes and swimfins.

At the register, Jim suggests that we sign in as Dale Murphy and Wade Boggs. These are not familiar names to me, like Sid Vicious or W. S. Merwin, so he explains that Murphy is a right fielder for the Braves and Boggs a first baseman for the Red Sox. I suppose aloud that I am to be Boggs. "Right," he says.

"Any reason?" He shrugs.

Twenty minutes up the trail we encounter deep drifts and cross the creek to the sunny side of the drainage, where, amidst marsh marigold and pale yellow anemone, I begin to, well, wade bogs. Jim follows, snickering. I invite him to lead. "Wool," he says, "you know the way better. Off the trail, I'd get us lost."

The ground is flowing with snowmelt, plush wet and green as a soaked velvet sofa. In some spots, the yearly growth is such that the buildup of organic soil has raised the surface into a convex delta shape. These spots quiver underfoot with all the water they hold. The growth is intense: mosses, dwarf willows, sedges, bulrush, grasses like deschampsia, flowers that are hydrophytes—water-lovers—like the yellow monkeyflower that will nod here later in the season. There isn't an inch of bare soil visible.

The way the water rests and drains makes a difference. The water regime of the area just uphill suits the pines, which stop at a very well-defined edge, where the soil becomes saturated. The next strip along the slope, one where organic matter has built thick horizons that hold water like a sponge, is suited to the willows and their flowery companions, plus mosses and such. At the base, the fast-draining stream below actually lowers the adjacent water table, so its banks are thickly grassed, with sedges in the overflow spots that are submerged every spring.

The angle of a slope to the sun is also important. North-facing slopes keep their snowpack longer and are dependably watered late into the growing season, but their soil temperatures stay low. A lot of the spruce-fir forest in the central Rockies grows on north- and east-facing slopes. On the north-facing slope, we'd be wading in three-foot drifts.

A friend, ecologist Sherman Jensen, refers to the condition of a place as an expression of its composition and state. I like to think of it as like a facial expression, one slope grinning daisies, another solemn with spruce. Much of what I've learned about moving water comes from editing Sherm's reports: we'd thrash around late at night in a coffee buzz, puzzling over definitions, drawing circles, ellipses, and figure eights, and reach epistemological fusion some-time near dawn, when we'd make Tai Chi–like gestures and howl *Everything Is Everything* at each other. We need more scientists like Sherm.

Jim and I—as Dale and Wade—cross willowed sponges sepa-rated by rivulets. We can't straddle deadfall pines and spruces with these packs, so we hop from tussock to tussock, trying to keep the water below boot-top while I introduce the various flowers to Jim and Jim to the flowers. Having suffered hydrologic equations and engineering classes, he claims to detest the scientific names of plants as bothersome trivia. If I say *Claytonia* he shudders; if I whisper *Pseudotsuga* he moans.

I never took a class in plant taxonomy, but had a series of college roommates who'd trade me sixpacks to drive them around on dirt roads to fill out their plant collections. We'd be careering down some two-track like an outtake from *Thunder Road* when the budding taxonomist would holler, "Whoa, boy. There's a *Potentilla gracilis* over there under that *Populus tremuloides*. Let's bag that sucker." About three roommates and gallons of beer later, I had the basics. As a campjack, I took a plant book into the Salt River Range for three months and checked off a lot of species. I love plants because they stay put, unlike birds which won't hold still, but the names I learned through family tradition and from old ranchers left room for improvement.

One rancher called every conifer except lodgepole pine a "piss fir." Ask him about anything from limber pine through Engelmann spruce and he'd answer "piss fir." Another rancher had three plant categories: trees, feed, and poison. Point to lupine and you'd get "sheep poison," and for larkspur, "cow poison." "Feed" ranged from sunflowers—nothing is more heartbreaking than to watch a herd of sheep devour every wild sunflower in a meadow, like stars winking out—to good old grass. Anything a cow or sheep would eat was feed.

The only thing that gave him pause was willows. They weren't big enough to be trees, but only a moose would eat them with any relish, since a cow or sheep would partake only when starving. He finally decided they were feed, "but damn poor."

Jim and I climb up to drier ground and find spring beauties—*Claytonia* I hiss and he shudders dependably. Across the drainage, the trail runs through big conifers, still three feet under drifts. Only an idiot would hike over there, in sight of dry ground, but there are tracks, several sets in fact.

An elk trail cuts left and we follow the elk up the hill, where long strips of wet ground run between the drifts. The tracks of deer and elk make heart-shaped cups in the ground for water to collect, sheened with the oily resin of pine needles. I notice large trees, mostly lodgepole but a few big spruces, that are freshly fallen, drying mud clotted between the exposed roots. On June 15, Waylon Jennings's birthday, there were high winds which caught the tallest trees with thawed soil soft around their roots and flung them down. The fresh-fallen ones lie along the track of that storm, southwest to northeast, and this happens luckily to be the direction we're going.

Bushwhacking, it's easier to follow the grain of the place than to cut across it: here, the deadfall forms lanes along the prevailing wind. In another place, it may be a hard layer of sandstone that defines a good route. Some Forest Service trails, usually the older ones that followed elk trails, go with the grain of the land, while others, recently engineered, seem to find every late snowdrift, bog, talus slope, and snag patch.

A poor trail may be linked to a fine view or a spring or something worth the effort. More often it results from the action of a well-intentioned bureaucrat who spent four years indoors studying recreation management and most of the time since then in an ill-aired, fluorescent-lit office, drawing lines on maps to meet production quotas. Most of the people who run the Forest Service know very little about the forest as a living thing: they spend the bulk of their lives in an office or at a computer terminal, like the rest of their generation of managers, seldom touching the lives they manipulate. They confuse the Service with the Forest, as if the pines required a bureaucracy to exist.

The best way to work for the Service is to stay out in the woods and get paid enough to buy food so you can stay out in the woods some more. Would a forest supervisor like wading bogs with this pack? Probably not. At the moment, the forest is supervising us.

We meet the trail again as it emerges from a nightmare of drifts, water-filled holes, and hacked-off stumps. I change to plastic mountaineering boots and we don the snowshoes, aluminum framed, with plastic lacing. The wet snow and mud would wreck a wood-framed, rawhide-laced snowshoe, so we strap the high-tech wonders to our feet and waddle off like giant ducks of burden. Clawing up and sliding down, we sound the drifts with ski poles, trying to avoid

pits made by hikers who came in early on the frost and wallowed out after the daily thaw, postholing.

We take the webs off and have lunch where a flowery meadow tops out, hearing water creep out from the edges of drifts, form runnels, gather into freshets, and bound off toward the nearest creek, carrying soil, needles, tumbling the cones of lodgepole and fir, dissolving the scats of squirrel and grouse, deer and elk into their constituent organic parts, collecting in pools to brew up earth tea in the sun. This is where it starts.

A few observant years in the West and one begins to define the country not in terms of state boundaries, which are absurd rectangles (the Four Corners Monument being the *Kaaba* for this particular delusion), nor in terms of roads, county lines, or any of the divisions that derived from the Homestead Act and popular practice in the flatlands of the well-watered Midwest. Such checkerboards can work where the land is uniformly flat and fertile, but they are nonsense where the elevation varies 3,000 feet in the course of a day's walk, with corresponding changes in temperature, rainfall, soils, and vegetation.

The unifying quality of this western landscape is drainage—how the water runs. This is the best way of integrating the landscape into an understandable whole. It was in the bones of the people of the Desert Culture who lived successfully in the arid and beautiful heart of the West. Many of their petroglyphs are maps in which the primary reference is water: seeps, springs, streams, rock tanks, and irrigable pockets in which crops might be seeded. Their routes tend to follow rivers and the canyons carved by streams, or to be quick traverses between them. There is nothing in our civic life comparable to the Pueblo cycle of dance, song, and ceremony linked to the water cycle and seasons.

Major John Wesley Powell, explorer of the labyrinthine canyon systems of the Green and Colorado rivers, proposed political divisions for the West by river drainage, grasping that in the arid lands the flow of water was the great law from which others must be derived. In the 1870s, when the common belief and civil religion of America included Manifest Destiny, such departures stank of heresy. The Homestead Act with its grid-patterned survey based on well-watered one hundred sixty-acre homesteads was a largely ficti-tious opportunity for the common man and his plow. Powell's wis-dom, though adopted by a scientific elite, was devoutly ignored by the public and its lawmakers, a response like that on the natural fire issue today. The fires in Yellowstone were a sad example: the tourist industry squawks, congressmen threaten investigations, and the government promptly forgets fifty years of its own research.

The best way to know this range is to watch how the water goes. Water never follows imaginary lines. Water persists, in its milky issue from glaciers and snowfields in June, its slow boil through the broken substrates of braided streams, its pools and overflows, its gleaming flounces down bouldered stairsteps, its blast over falls, its rest and deepening in lakes, its pulsing, convex roll into the outlet streams, on and down, joining to maintrunk streams like Frémont Creek and Pine Creek, down and on to the foothill rivers—East Fork and New Fork—and then the arteries of the broad valleys and grand canyons, the Green, the Colorado, the Snake, the Bighorn, and the upper Missouri. Water lends not only life, but also direction and meaning to the West.

The Wind River Range is a headwater to all the big internal drainages of the lower continent. At its crest, the Continental Divide defines the flow east, into the upper Missouri and to the internal sink of the Great Divide Basin. West of the Divide, the water slopes into the basin of the Green and Colorado up to Pinyon Ridge, where the streams run north and west to the Snake's headwaters in Jackson Hole and eventually into the Columbia, bound for the gray thunder of the North Pacific.

We devour our cheese and crackers and gnaw our apples to hourglass cores, lolling in the sun. Then we resume the slog, hot even in t-shirts, shorts, and gaiters. Jim tells me my bright blue shorts are cute. I tell him his haircut does a good job of hiding the lobotomy scars.

Miller Park is mostly under snow. We meet the pair who signed out in the trail register for Dinwoody Pass, about twenty miles farther on. They have soaked boots, inadequate gaiters, and two ecstatic black dogs that bound the whole time we talk.

Despite their alpine ambitions, they failed to reckon on the snow and fetched up wet at Miller Lake, four miles in. The dogs seem to have been the chief beneficiaries of the trip, porpoising and splashing in a circle as we talk.

The disappointed pair see our snowshoes and ask if such can be rented in Pinedale. They intend to head to the Cirque of Towers, farther south in the range, hoping for less snow. The more bearded and sunburnt of the two regards my plastic funnel, roll of blue cable, and swimfins with a curious eye for some minutes before he asks what we're up to. "Lake studies," I explain, "snowmelt pulse, Big Science, yodelay-hee-hoo."

"You get *in* the lake?" they ask.

"Yeah."

"But there's ice in the lakes."

"Yeah, probably—I've got a drysuit."

"Drysuit?"

"Like a wetsuit, but dry."

"No shit?"

"Rubber—you wear longjohns under it." I tell them about the air pollution from the power plants and the cities, and being city lads, they tell us about the littered campsites at Miller Lake.

"People around here sure throw a lot of trash," one says in reprisal.

Since they seem, like us, to be traveling later in the day than is smart, I throw in a brief pitch for the alpine start: cruise on the frost, snooze on the thaw. "We never thought of that." They mush off entwined in black dogs, casting dubious glances at the swimfins.

The ski tracks from my trip with John in April are still apparent, slight grooves in the trees where shade holds the snow, and slightly raised ridges across the meadows, their melting slowed by compaction. Climbing the ridge of Photographer's Point we start to flail. It's hot in the sun, even though the air temperature is probably only about 50°F. Through the conifers we have the relief of patchy shade, little gasps of coolness like the shadows of buildings in city heat. Breaking into an open saddle, we feel cooked again. The snow is slushy, collapsing in spots to reveal a few inches of water burbling along the ground. This heat—abnormal temperatures are being logged all over the West—is creating a major pulse of snowmelt.

The acid in the snowpack melts out with the first pulse, when the high lakes are still mostly under ice, open only at their inlets and outlets. Researchers say that 80 percent of the acids concentrate in the first 20 percent of the melt. This is known as an acid shock, and has been posed by researchers like John Harte of Berkeley as a major cause of death for aquatic insects and amphibians. Some mayflies can't emerge from their pupal stage if the pH falls (meaning that the acidity increases) below a certain point, often about 5.3. An acid pulse can wipe out the reproduction of insects in inlet streams, yet be gone or diluted by the time one can hike in on dry ground.

Many researchers claim that it's impossible to monitor these snowmelt pulses except with heavy artillery: fixed installations or helicopter access, both forbidden by the Wilderness Act. A further problem with fixed gear is that the sensors have to be calibrated every few weeks. South of Laramie, researchers from the Forest Service Experiment Station maintained a site at Glacier Lakes, sensitive waters that were not in a declared wilderness. Each week they drove to the site in a large snowcat, like an orange van perched on broad tracks. Aside from a few contretemps, like breaking the snowcat through lake ice, the commute seems to have been enjoyed by all. A snowcat, if you hacked trail for it, could make it to within a couple miles of our lake, but beyond that the terrain is too steep. They'd never get it out of Depression Depression.

The U.S. Geological Survey often gets approval for helicopter use, claiming their equipment is too heavy or delicate to be packed in. Helicopter access to wilderness is a touchy subject, since many outfitters would like to fly clients into wilderness camps rather than horsebacking them in. Helicopters are used for high-budget flyfishing, big-bucks hunting, and backcountry skiing. The flights are obtrusive, noisy, and quick. Landings are often approved for rescue and for firefighting, but if all those who want helicopter access got approval, the wilderness would buzz with more than mosquitos. Helicopters would haul elaborate camp equipment to remote lakes—echoes of the British nobility touring the West with their entourages—and fly-in outfitting would become routine for rich tourists, as it is in vast areas of Alaska and Canada.

Add to that the summer vacation research of universities, Forest Service "administration," scenic flights with high-altitude landings, and a likely increase in rescues and bailouts. Popular wildernesses would become snarls of low-level air traffic, like the Grand Canyon at present.

Viewed in the light of efficiency or expediency, our foot trips are a romantic contrivance: we would easily fly over the lake to see if it is at the proper stage for early sampling and land at the inlet, drag our gear out of the ship, grab our samples, and hoist off in a couple of hours. It would be efficient in the modern manner, that is compressed into a shorter time by using more resources and spending more money. The sampling would be done by higher-paid and more sedentary persons. It would also require a Möbius twist of logic: we sample this lake to preserve its wilderness character, which requires us to violate its wilderness character. If that sounds strange, read up on the Central Intelligence Agency. Rules are never enough to leave a thing alone.

To reformulate the notion, perhaps the way in which we conduct these trips—by informed hunches about weather and conditions, on the ground with muscle, according to rule and restraint, in a manner that we hope will save something precious—is not so much contrived as it is fitting. We suit our methods to the place and what seem to be its inherent values: remoteness, beauty, severity, and a spare order. Maybe we're practicing for the future. I can only hope.

The meadow falls off easily south to Sweeney Lake and hard to the north, into a gorge of polished walls and cataracts. The skyline is jagged with summits, Frémont, Sacajawea, Helen, Woodrow Wilson, Arrowhead. The foreground is a rocky fist, sparsely haired with whitebark pines. At our feet is a slush pool, the melt saturating the snow, filling a low spot which spills to the bowl below, from sponge to stream, chased into snowbanks like a silver inlay.

I'm hoping that under a pair of giant whitebarks at the rim of the bowl there'll be bare ground for our camp. I recall it being clear in other years, a good place for a sunny lunch, a warm boulder for an aching back. We snowshoe down the slope and it's perfect. An island of heat, clear and almost dry. Packs are dropped with great thumps, the tent balloons from its sack, the stove alights on a flat rock, and wet boots slouch, tongues lolling, against a sunny boulder. We are in camp. Pots in hand, I posthole barefoot into the slush and dig a pit into which water flows, clear, snow filtered, cold.

The solstice is tomorrow. The light stays late. We recline, putter with gear, nibble, cook a lazy dinner, take naps. Firmly on my back, I eye the two aged whitebarks, thankful they are still alive, surviving the gusts that brought so many other trees to earth. Such things can be our ancestors if we let them.

The pines stand at the ends of a large boulder, two druids guarding a turtle, the southern tree gnarled and variously branched, bole split and veined like a miner's forearms. The northern pine is fortunate, taller, straighter, nobly proportioned under its shaggy cloak of needles, sheltered by its ragged mate. The southern tree has exposed sapwood etched to grooves and cracked, a weathered, austere gold. The bare wood, an exposed scar that spires up the narrowing trunk, is coated in spots with the mustard of dry pitch and lined with char black, rust, sienna, umber: lightning's print.

The bark is thick, with squarish, brick red or clay-colored scales edged in gray and black. Stout limbs erupt in whorls every yard or so, dropping slightly to diverge in branches and twigs, each terminating in a thickened tip from which spring tufts of needles, sharp and sturdy, bunched in fives like those of cousins, limber pine and bristlecone, trees that love lonesome ridges and windswept elevations.

The needles are triangular in cross-section, like Civil War bayonets, and as long as two finger joints, a moderate green finely striated with yellow, leading to a crisp point. Each is coated with a thin resin, not sticky, that protects it from the wind and sun. In these fibrous leaves, each about the thickness of cotton string, the life of the tree simmers, fixing atmospheric carbon into organic compounds: photosynthesis, life's fundamental note.

Before we could explain this, we had the good sense to use trees as metaphors, to correspond their branching with our generations, their leaves with our brief and repeated existences. *Branch* comes from the Latin *branca*, meaning "paw" or "hand." *Root* comes from the Old Norse; its Latin form, *radix*, became *radish, radical, race,* and *eradicate*.

As twin saplings, these trees were more alive than they have been since. After their first winter dormancy, a new layer of living cells formed under the bark to carry water and nutrients up from the soil to the needles. The last season's layer remained, strong, inert fiber. Trees grow out as well as up. Each new layer—called an annular ring—had a greater surface area. As each relinquished its living role to one of support, the strong, passive heart of the tree grew in proportion to the living layer under the bark.

The earth resembles a tree, the delicate bark of the atmosphere, a thin sapwood of soil and plant and bug and beast, the deepening layers of once-living carbon in the crust, and the bulk of the planet a dark heart where life does not exist. If the cells necessary for the transport of water and nutrients for photosynthesis and growth were scraped off this tree, most of it would remain: when old whitebarks die, they stand for decades, monuments but no longer trees.

These old pines don't have deep roots. There isn't much soil above bedrock. They send a taproot into a joint or crack to collect hidden water, but most of their roots fan out, a shallow anchorage between air and solid rock. After the thaw they are vulnerable to high wind. The last three years, they have also suffered from heat and drought. On the hotter, drier southwest exposures, whitebarks several hundred years old are dead, since the shallow accumulations of groundwater that sustained them have dried up for lack of regular rains. This tells us the seriousness of this drought, the worst in the long lives of these tenacious trees, sufficient to kill many of them. One can also kill them by exposing their shallow roots, by tying a horse up to paw and scuffle or by trenching to drain a tent.

If the usual August crowd of campers had been up here during that June windstorm, someone would have died, crushed in a tent as big trees went down. Senseless, we'd say. Terrible. People, though, kill more trees than the reverse.

Jim rises in the low light while I enjoy the warmth of my bag, the rasp of the stove, the shadows worked into the green fabric of the tent, the scent of moisture, a sense of ripeness, of heaviness in my arms and legs, the beginning rattle of a pot lid over boiling water, then the odor of cocoa and a slight wind sorting through needles above. I can see my breath.

Sunrise. The Divide is a band of old silver, the sky deep and shifting, like pearlshell, bracelets on a woman's wrist. As the sun lifts, the sky flattens to ivory around it. The old whitebarks stretch out in the first warmth and give off incense. The pores along the bundled needles open, breathing in the light.

We step onto firm snow at about seven o'clock. The sun is close to the Divide and we drop quickly into shadow, following old ski tracks toward the outlet of Barbara Lake. There are streams snaking around boulders and roots, lacing through coarse yellow grass and dwarf willow. We climb up the talus-choked corridor to the lake, which is frozen, and look for a snowbridge to cross the outlet creek. I strap on snowshoes and the bridge I choose holds me—four steps and a sigh. I wait for Jim to either get across or need rescue. We can hear the drumming of water sealed under ice and snow, a hollow, muffled boom. Before bridges and cars, getting sucked under stream ice used to be a frequent cause of death.

Jim decides that being lighter, he can make it without webs. He takes a step and falls through—into a shallow side channel. Wet footed and grumbling, he scrambles back and puts on the snowshoes, making it over in my tracks.

The day is cold out of the sun, with a rising fringe of cloud along the west. Light reflects between the clouds and the snow, diffusing shadows, which sharpen and go black as the sun emerges. On high peaks, south-facing arêtes and wind-scoured faces show gray stone to the sky. We follow the course of the summer trail over the snow, down the shadowed slope where the angle gets intimidating. Noticing the roundness of Jim's eyes, I give a course in steep shoeing— point the toes uphill, raise the heels to hack the aluminum claws in, keep the weight centered over the feet. Don't lean uphill. I fall in order to self-arrest with my single ski pole. It would have been nice to give Jim some training beforehand, but you can't show someone how to handle steep snow unless you are on it.

He learns fast, tiptoes across a nervous gully and gets round-eyed again as he sees me sitting down for a butt glissade, lifting the snowshoes slightly and steering with the point of the pole—zzzang— the downhill direct. He tries it, though he doesn't quite grasp the steering part and spins as he descends, hooting.

We detour big downed trees and then gliss the long slope into Depression Depression. At the base, we're grinning, sweating, reveling in the indulgence of season and landscape. I have apprehensions about tubing among the ice floes, but I save them.

We climb up a rocky sideslope, snowshoe over a knoll, and see the lake. "Dammit," I say, "too icy." (Good!) We hike over to see if we can take inlet samples and discover that the inlet stream has opened a lead to the deepest part of the lake. Alas. The weird part will go on as scheduled.

Snowbanks dive into the water, which is a dark, metallic blue with the deposition bars at the mouth of the stream thrust out like brown tongues, disappearing into the dark. The edge of the ice curves like an eyelid away from us, varying whites and blues that lower to dove grays as the sun clouds over. Across the ice are whitish lines, like the Martian canals, and I realize that they are old ski tracks.

The tracks we left in April are visible two and a half months later, plain on the melting ice. I feel haunted by my earlier presence. Jim can't decide where I'm focused. "Those lines on the ice," I say. "Ski tracks. John and me." He gazes at the dark water under the icy lip and looks worried.

I pull the float-tube rustling out of my pack and find the foot-pump. As Jim inflates the tube, I fill two sets of bottles from the inlet stream, feeling the cold of the water drill the bones of my arm. Do I look forward to this? No, but backing out would be shameful after we've packed these brute loads in. So I shrug into two layers of long underwear and slip the black drysuit gaskets over my ankles, just as if I intend to get into the water. The sun burns clean and the lake ice is pretty, like slabs of turquoise floating in coconut milk. The open water is black.

Jim finishes pumping the tube as I pull on wetsuit booties and the oversized fins. The suit is tight around my wrists and ankles; the neck gasket feels like a noose. I gag as Jim zips me across the back. "Okay?" he asks.

"Too tight at the neck. I feel like throwing up." While I still don't intend to get *in* the lake, I wonder idly what it would be like. Even choked by the neck of the suit, I like it here on the bank. *If luck is with thee, why hurry? And again, if luck is against thee, why hurry?* The Afghanis say that.

After several winters of skiing across lake ice and dreading the water underneath, I'm uneasy about going into it. This is the summer solstice, but it's not summer under the ice. The water is about

one degree above freezing. Any second I'll say that the weather looks
chancy or the suit doesn't fit or find something to forestall this. I
look at Jim. He looks confident, nothing out of the ordinary.

I drag a stocking cap over my hair and load sample bottles, a
water thermometer to which the coil of blue cable belongs, a plankton net, a plankton bottle and formalin, and a coil of nylon line.
The final touch is wetsuit gloves.

Jim has what is usually called a shit-eating grin. I realize that I
look foolish, holding the tube hula-hoopwise about my hips and
trying to balance all the stuff tied to and resting along the rim. On
my head is a pink and baby blue cap, gotten for free from an
outdoor shop unable to sell it: female colors in a male size, said the
owner. My hair sticks out Bozo-esque over my ears and the drysuit,
red from the chest up and white below, adds to the clownishness.
In neoprene gloves, my fingers have a frankfurter bulge, like cartoon
digits. At the bottom of all this are swimfins. They look huge. The
owner explained that they need to be big, because you can't kick
well sitting in the tube. "Just walk backward into the lake," he
advised. Obvious.

I walk forward, toward the lake. The fins either flap on the snow
or slice into it, causing me to trip. Jim stifles his first laugh. Walk
backward into the lake, the owner said. How do you walk backward, in swimfins, down a snowbank? Jim chokes and finally lets
the laugh fly out. "You shouldn't laugh at someone who's about to
die," I say.

He ties a safety line to the tube, and I try again to walk backward
down the snowbank. Galoot, galoot, galoot. It doesn't work with all
the government property attached to the tube. I've got to face the
water. Stalking forward on my heels, rubber fins flopping in the air,
I manage to enter the inlet stream, which is moving smartly toward
the black depths of the lake. As a compromise, I try walking backward down the stream, which has Jim near hysteria. "Stop laughing
and breathe," I yell, not wanting him to pass out and drop the
safety line. I'm counting on him to drag me from the icy current
when I pass out. I reel and curse, fins grinding in icy gravel, until
I simply fall in and am swept away from shore. Flushed, as it were.

I wait for the icy chomp of the water on my thighs, the deathly
grip of cramps, and the wonder of hallucinations, but except for a

little nip around the ankles it's not bad. The pressure of the water glues the suit to my legs and puffs up the chest. Jim brings it to my attention by jumping and howling incoherently while stabbing a finger at my pneumatic bosom. "You look like, like, Dolly Parton." Hurt, I tug at the neck and let the excess air out. I wonder if Dolly ever wishes she could. Then I paddle around, look at the shifting blue of the lake ice, the cloud-rimmed sky, the peaks. Jim hiccups into silence.

Truth is, I like this. Like ice climbing, it's fun partly because it's so improbable: this is not a place a human being ought to be. But . . . *"Banzai! Hoka-hey! ¡Muy Torcido!"* I yell. Jim's head snaps up. "I'm the olive in God's martini. Stirred, but not shaken!" I untie the safety line and paddle out to the deeps. I spin around and Jim looks vaguely alarmed. Mental impairment, he's thinking, rehearsing his testimony for the inquest. First he untied the safety line, then he started revolving. Yelling in Spanish or something. I couldn't understand a word. Except he said he was an olive.

I try the thermometer, which doesn't work, reading 13°C. That's about 55°F. It's a safe guess that a lake still 90 percent frozen is not that warm. "The stupid thermometer doesn't work," I yell.

"Drop it in the lake," Jim yells back, "so we won't have to carry it out." I'd say this water is somewhere between one and three degrees. Thus, I need only a surface sample, which I collect, bottle caps awkward in my cartoon fingers.

As the novelty of my situation wears off, I notice that I seem to be sitting low in the tube, which has a fabric seat presently at my back, while a narrow nylon strap supports my entire weight by the crotch. I fumble blindly with the strap before giving up. I can't feel much in these gloves and would rather not disengage the buckle by mistake. Pretty black down below. I shiver hard. Looking down isn't a good idea.

The sky is clouding heavily. A wind springs up, and I flutter the fins to stay in place near the edge of the ice. I lower the funnel-shaped plankton net, watching white nylon line disappear into the water, red marks winking out each five feet and blue each ten. At forty-five feet, I haul the net back up, piling the wet line on the tube. It appears and I raise it, letting it drain through fine silk mesh. The cylinder at the bottom detaches, though not easily in foam gloves. At its center is a brass plunger. Centering the brass cylinder over a small bottle, I lift the plunger and dark specks of zooplankton—tiny and mysterious lives—flush into the bottle with the last teaspoon of water. I can see them kicking and pulsing, not many after eight months under ice. I rinse with formalin, a preservative that kills the plankton fast. Two repetitions, haul and drain, and the plankton sample is done.

Jim is fishing at the inlet but catching nothing. The water's too cold, I think, and feel pain start up my legs. But *it's not that bad*. Having the water sample and the plankton, I'm done with the science. I flutter the fins, fighting a cramp, and drift over to the edge of the ice.

Against the lake's bottomless black, the ice grades from swan white at the surface to mild grays, a stony green, and several poignant blues. In it are air bubbles and a few rusty pine needles. This is the ice I almost fell through last December, the ice I skied across in February and April. It's thinner than I thought, probably melted quite a bit. There's a lot of water under it. After years of being scared of this, I'm here. Without a drysuit, in full ski kit, with a heavy pack, dragging a loaded sled, I'd be dying. Would the ice look different? By the time I thought about it, I'd be dead.

This triple boundary, water, ice, and air, has a value for the heart that is uneasy in words, so I'll leave it at that: three states of matter touch, with no conclusion. I'm getting a bad chill now. I start to shiver, then shudder, each tremor rising from the root of my spine. To stay longer would be foolish.

I paddle up the current and lurch out of the lake. Fins kicking up chunks of snow, I flap up the snowbank to a reprise of Jim's hysterics followed by a victory handshake and an attack of gut-bucket shivering.

Later, I sit on the tube, eating a bar of chocolate, waiting for the bottles to dry so I can label them. From the woods, a bird calls, *chert, chert, chert, cheert,* in a descending scale. Jim natters about a girl he met. "She's too pretty to talk to," he says. "A biologist." I let the chocolate melt under my tongue and watch clouds ride the high blue, forming and diffusing, new streamers becoming visible as I watch, as the invisible wind climbs these mountains.

Hallelujah. Yes. Amen.

Part V: Rock and Leaf

13

I swear I will never again mention love or death inside a house.

Walt Whitman, *Song of Myself*

*A*fternoon. I sat down to clear my head and it feels so good that I'm thinking one of those office jobs might not be as awful as I thought. A desk, a coffee cup. A padded chair.

But there are two packhorses tied to pines, and Jim is bustling about, arms loaded. I'm his superior officer, so to speak. I could sit here and wave my arms and exhort him to labor for our common good. Tote that barge, lift that bale, drop that bomb. Meanwhile, I'll sum up the capital gains, have a drink, call the club.

Jim is looking at me. In a few seconds, I'll heave myself upright and stride purposefully over to the mound of gear and sort the chaos, saddle the horses, load them with perfect, Parthenon-like packs, bound with diamond hitches.

Yesterday was July 4, the date in 1845 on which Thoreau moved to Walden Pond. Linda and I went to a memorial Mass, the 150th anniversary of Father De Smet's Mass on the Green River, celebrated in the heat by the prickly Cardinal O'Connor. "Father, You are the Lord of History," he said, his skin almost transparent in the harsh light. The only part that meant much to me was hearing the

Lord's Prayer in Shoshoni. The woman, stout and gray, prayed in a low voice and paused at the end of each line for the translation. *As we forgive those who trespass against us . . .* At that point I got tears in my eyes. As we drove home, my volunteer fire department beeper went off, so I called the dispatcher and then drove to a fire.

South of Boulder, near the old Oregon Trail, a lonely house was burning. Boys had shot a hole in the gas line with their .22 rifles, the leak had ignited, and the propane tank, around which the householders had stacked firewood, exploded. This blew a fireball of burning logs and liquid petroleum over the house. The fire drafted under the eaves and began burning between the three layers of roofing. Firemen were reeling from the smoke, one doubled over retching. As I helped connect a hose from a tanker to the pumper, a change in the wind blew the plume across the trucks, and we started to cough and grow dizzy. We saved the house, though the roof had a large hole burnt through and several smaller ones cut to put the fire out. We didn't leave the fire until ten-thirty and didn't get the gear—hoses and pumps and air tanks—cleaned and repacked until after midnight. After packing for the trip, I hit the bed at two.

In this country, the day starts before the sun. We bound out of bed at 5:00 A.M., shave with hatchets, swill a gallon of black coffee, devour bacon, sausage, ham, moose steak, eggs, pancakes, hashbrowns, and toast, then saddle up the GMC and haul blue-jeaned butt. A bit later in the day, though, we are often found sitting on rocks. The untold story.

This morning, Jim and I scooped up the gear for sampling two lakes, drove eighty miles to set up two rain collectors, caught the horses, loaded them, and then drove another sixty miles to this trailhead. It's nearly four o'clock. I'm barely conscious, so low that I'm looking to the lichen and moss on this boulder for intellectual stimulation. *Rest,* they advise. *Don't go. Abide.*

Jim gets desperate enough to put a packsaddle on the bay. Backward. He's trying to figure out what's wrong, squinting first at the confusion of straps and then at me. "Turn the horse around," I want to shout. He's also got the hairpad on top of the saddle pad. On the bright side, he remembers from last year that the pads and saddle go with the horse. On top. In the middle. That's a good start. I get up. It feels terrible.

The only saving grace is that I've done this so many times it's reflex: center the pads, settle the saddles, cinch the cinchas, hoist the panniers, tuck the manty, lash the loads, diamond the hitches, lead the snorting beasts up the trail, pick the sad feet up and smack them down, like a dismal hand of poker, only 17,600 more steps to where we'll camp tonight. I calculated it, once.

In contrast to the northern part of the mountains, where we found three feet of snow and frozen lakes on the solstice, the southern end is dry; the trail gives up dust as we shuffle along tugging at the horses. The grass is lush and alive with moths that seem never to light or rest.

Jim is also weary, from celebrating the Fourth with his new girlfriend, a golden biologist fresh from Yale and the Peace Corps. She works for the Big Piney Ranger District, and her name is Elizabeth. "She's beautiful," he says, "and she's an athlete: she won a cross-country skiing championship."

I give him a scrap of poetry—*"Wine drew me on, Love thrust behind, I was not master of my mind, And when I came I did not cry . . ."*—and he blushes. It's lewd, out of context like that.

"What's that?" he asks.

"Callimachus, from the Greek Anthology."

"Oh."

"Hic, hic, est quem feris urit Amor."

"What's *that*?"

"Latin. From a Fourth-of-July poem by Ovid: 'That's him, there goes Cupid's firework.' " He blushes again.

"Where did you learn that stuff?"

"I only remember the trashy parts." Around us, horseflies dive and attack, nipping pinheads of meat from our wrists and the backs of our knees. Up higher, they'll be reinforced by mosquitos. From now till mid-August, they'll be constant. Along with the bugs, I've distracted him long enough to get the horses packed.

"Let's go." The flies bore in, thick around the horse corrals. My strategy, as a hater of repellent, is to wear shorts and t-shirt, for the coolness, and to walk very fast.

At the trailhead, a horse party from Rock Springs is packing up, tying sloppy loads and sweating in full weekend-cowboy gear, big floppy chaps, fringed vests. We're headed for Black Joe Lake, a favorite spot for catching big cutthroat. Below the lake is a campsite with a meadow for the horses. I fear the horse party is headed the same way. In the narrow defile of the lake, meadows are not just few—this is the only one. I'd like to beat them to it, so we hustle. Mountain etiquette decrees that the first party with horses on a meadow has precedence, and later comers must look elsewhere, since strange horses often get into spats.

We intend to sample two large lakes, collect the sample from a bulk snow tube and dismantle it, and replace it with rain collectors for the summer. It usually takes a full day to sample a lake, but we'll try to do both lakes tomorrow, deal with the collectors Saturday morning, and return to Pinedale for the Saturday night festivities. In Pinedale, Independence Day is a minor holiday compared to Rendezvous, a celebration recalling the yearly meeting of fur-trappers with fur-traders on the Green River. There is immoderate drinking and dancing, and I hope to add my disorderly conduct to that of the throng.

In the broad meadows of glacial outwash, the flowers are mostly brilliant yellow, cinquefoil, buttercup, and several kinds of sunflower, punctuated with the white of bistort and daisies and the purple of lupine and larkspur. We stop briefly to give the horses a nip at the grass, enduring the mosquitos, and make good time up the trail, roller-coastering through lodgepole to Big Sandy Lake. The lake is a fervent blue in its mountain cup, like sapphire tea. We stop and let the horses graze while I change to heavy-duty sandals—river-guide models of nylon webbing—in order to wade the horses across the roaring streams that enter the lake from the north and east. First, Lost Creek, then North Creek, and finally Black Joe Creek, all split and braided through rubble deltas deposited as they exit steep canyons into the gentler grade of the lake basin. As I tighten the sandal-straps, the cavalry detachment from Rock Springs emerges from the woods at our backs. I take the horses and splash ahead, leaving the unsandaled Jim to find hop-crossings on boulders, drier but slower.

The trail to Black Joe is steep and loose, but I manage to get the horses up with only a couple of stops, then wade them across the outlet creek where cold water reaches my thighs. The horses balk but slosh after me at last, snorting and rolling their eyes. In the bed of the stream, golden sand alternates with nests of boulders.

I loosen the hitches and begin to unpack. Jim shows up, having used the boulder jump downcanyon to cross the creek. The riders headed around Big Sandy Lake to the inlet of Clear Creek on the south, so my heroic charge up the gorge through remnant snowbanks in sandals is for naught except pride.

We used to ride in, leading packhorses, four horses in all, but I noticed that we were pounding the meadows where we camp, so last year we began hiking and leading two packhorses. The success of our snowshoe trip to Hobbs Lake—backpacking a lake sample out—has gotten me interested in doing it with a single horse or perhaps llamas. Our rubber boat—a necessity for these big, wind-swept lakes—weighs about sixty pounds, so the weight of that, with camping gear and fifty-five bottles of lake water, twelve bottles of aquatic insects, two bottles of plankton, and all the nets and lines and devil-boxes we use, is beyond two human bodies.

The outlet tumbles down a bouldery channel from the lake, then makes a long curve around this meadow, hugging a low cliff to the south. To the north is a steep zoo of talus, then another cliff, onion-skin slabs of silvery granite, running with water, streaked black. Above is a long slope, steep rubble and slabs; at the top is the Divide. In the riffles, cutthroat trout are mating, some near the length of a forearm, large for this high country. Their steel gray sides are rosy with spawning color. Jim has a flyrod, but as we set up camp and picket the horses, he declares himself too tired to fish.

"Too tired to fish? *Amor!*" I raise a forefinger to heaven. He blushes easily today. Clouds have filled up the west, threatening rain, sending humid gusts whuffing through the talus boulders above the camp. We set up the tent, picket one horse and hobble the other, and set up our stove in the lee of a boulder. The mile-long wall of Haystack Peak begins to glow like a calendar photo of the Great Pyramid, and I climb up stacks of big granite cubes cracked from the flank of the Divide to watch.

The cloud has flushed from a nasty gray to apricot, streaked violet by the shadows of peaks, Bunion and Warbonnet. In shadow, the rock has gone blue, and the snowfields are immodest scarlets and pinks, shades for which a painter would be called cheap. Out here, back of beyond, it all fits. Haystack, polished and implacable, vibrates with blood and oranges. The fractured nordwand of Temple Peak shivers at the head of its cirque like a drowned rose, caught in a slower current of the fading light. I look down at the boulder where I sit, quartz, feldspar, biotite, hornblende, a mass of welded crystals, each facet giving back a different gleam, like the eyes of a crowd. The air darkens and we finally converge at the tent.

We cook and eat in the growing dark. My tiredness rolls over me. We crawl into the tent and murmur goodnights. Craving sleep, I don't get much. P. J., the comely bay horse who replaced our old, plodding Sam, is a pet. He likes me, nuzzling my hand, sniffing my back, watching me between bites of grass. He is hobbled rather than tied to a picket stake, since I've been told that he's not picket trained, and is wearing a bell to help us locate him if he strays.

He does the opposite of stray: he thunders around the tent, somehow locates my head, and sounds his bell. Then he breathes heavily a few inches from my ear, causing an unpleasant dream, set in a cathedral, featuring large reptiles in clerical garb. *Father, You are the Lord of Hisss-tory,* one says. I wake up in a very bad mood.

I whack the tent and the horse retreats, but comes back to breathe ardently next to my ear, pulling me from uneasy sleep. The clapper of his bell is muffled with duct tape—my innovation—but at six inches it sounds like Big Ben. My dreams are from Bosch, clangs and screams and groaning sinners. Jim sleeps through it.

Why I never think to step out, remove the bell, and tie the horse to a tree, I don't know. He comes closer and I sucker-punch him in the rubbery nose, right through the tent. He bongs and thunders off. Jim wakes up and compliments me, in a sleepy murmur, on my swearing. "Jeez, you're good at that," he says and goes back to sleep. P. J. returns. Bong. Wiffle-waffle-wuffle. Bong. *You daft, gelded, bastard get of a spavined banshee!* Whack! He thunders off, tolling the lost hours.

Against all odds, I rise at five, start the stove, and assemble breakfast, tossing murderous looks at P. J., who nickers and starts over to wish good morning. "Your name is Mud-squared, horse."

Jim, chuckling at my grouchiness, is more or less normal. I totter around heaving packsaddles, ropes, and infernal machines into the air, and, somehow, they end up lashed to the back of the mannerly Buck, a buckskin dun whose zombielike calm I now value. If I tied him to this tree and left, I might return in a year to find his skeleton standing and yawning, unaware of any great change. P. J.— Purgatory Junior—is haltered to accompany us up to the lake. If left alone he's likely to throw a fit and strangle himself in his rope, maybe not such a bad idea. But then we'd have to carry his load out.

And so, in a trance rather than entranced, I stagger up to the lake, climbing the rough trail over the rockfill dam that was built early in the century to hold irrigation water. Weathered logs are cribbed into a headgate, twelve feet high, probably hewn by Norwegians from the straightness of the strokes and the fit of the joints, through which the water funnels in a jet that blasts white into the outlet stream and tumbles into a boulder-heaped thicket of willows.

Black Joe Lake is in a glacier-carved hollow in bedrock at 10,258 feet. The silvery granite bedrock is striped with whitish bands of pegmatite crystals and dikes of black diabase, rusty black, and mafic rock, light green with white spots. To the north, the Continental Divide crests around 12,000 feet, sloping east to a broad plateau remnant. Southeast is Wind River Peak, the seldom-visited high point at this end of the range.

The lake, one and a third miles long, is narrow and shadowed by the slick walls of Haystack on the south. It holds 2,590 acre-feet of magically pure water, with a deep spot of 85 feet. At the head of the drainage are small glaciers and permanent snowfields. Most of its water flows over rock before entering the lake or the inlet streams: 42 percent. Less, about 29 percent, finds soil on its way. About 24 percent encounters both soil and vegetation. The remaining 5 percent lands directly on the lake's surface. Much of the lake's water never interacts with soil, the main way in which acid rain is buffered. The granite and grit around the lake have about the same capacity to neutralize acid as broken glass.

We skirt the rocky shore to the south, following a faint trail to a sandy point, that is, there's some sand between the rocks. I unload the gear and tether the horses while Jim pumps the boat. We load up and push off, him rowing and me starting to feel human again, glad at our early start. The sun has barely touched the lake, a narrow fiord that snakes for over a mile between steep walls, the inlet hidden by a rocky point, the water green and cold.

The morning wind is in our favor, scooting us up the lake. Later in the day, it will grow stronger. The hard part in sampling these high lakes is to hold the boat in place over our lines as we take temperatures and seine plankton. Stretching the line at an angle gives false results: where the depth marker reads fifty feet, the slanted line only reaches down to thirty. On the other side of the range, they have permanent buoys anchored to hold them still, but our handlers have decreed such means inconsistent with wilderness, so we row instead. Consistently. Holding a small rubber boat in place under high winds is hard. Despite the coolness of the air and the following wind, Jim's face shows a sheen of sweat. As he strokes and puffs, I lower the thermometer cable.

The sun's heat is the main variable in the changing temperature of lakes. At this latitude, when the sun is high and the days are long, the lakes heat up. The water absorbs heat, with greatest potential heating at the surface. As light penetrates the water, it is scattered. The shorter wavelengths are scattered more easily, so lakes appear blue to us; if the longer waves scattered more easily, they would look red. Imagine that.

Anything suspended in the water changes the behavior of light. Algae and cyanobacteria add a distinct green. Fine particles of clay can turn the water yellow or brown. Lakes in limestone have large amounts of calcium carbonate, which shifts their scattering index toward the greens. Lakes under active glaciers often have a greenish opacity due to finely ground rock flour called till. Above Black Joe are smaller lakes, which catch most of the till. One of them is called Jesus H. Christ Lake, in memory of my attempt to take a swim in it. In July, when the ice recedes, Black Joe Lake is a deep, steely blue. As the surface warms and the plankton populations explode, Black Joe shifts a bit toward green, richer, but never a friendly color.

When the ice goes out, the lake is isothermal—all the same temperature. The sun heats the surface layers, but the warmest wavelengths don't penetrate far, so the deeper waters stay cold. Hobbs Lake is a smaller, sunnier body of water. It forms distinct strata, with a surface temperature of 18°C (64°F) or more, sometimes warming almost to the bottom. Black Joe is shaded, so it doesn't get as much direct heat, the surface seldom getting warmer than 15°C (or 59°F). It's also windy, with the gusts fetching along the lake from end to end. The lack of heat and the strong winds keep Black Joe from forming strong temperature strata.

When layers of water have different temperatures, they don't mix. Each layer circulates within itself, isolated from the warmer layer above or the colder layer below. A difference of one degree will create a physical barrier to mixing. If you swim down into a mountain lake, you can feel these layers. As the sun heats up the surface in the long days of July and August, the stratification gets stronger. Going down, the temperature drops layer by layer until the thermocline is reached. The resistance to mixing is strongest here, where an abrupt temperature drop holds the water in the bottom of the lake separate from the surface layers.

By late August, if there is not much wind, the upper layers may range from 15°C in one-degree drops down to 12°C. Then there will be a sharp drop in less than a meter, from 12°C down to 8°C or less. This is the thermocline. The water above it is called the epilimnion, the water below the hypolimnion. For all practical purposes, temperature separates them into two bodies of water. They will have different oxygen levels, different chemistries, and harbor different species of plankton.

I hold the pencil in my teeth, noting the temperature every five feet. So far, the lake isn't stratified. The temperatures grade slowly from 6°C to 5°C over forty feet. The warming of the lake depends on the length of the days and the angle of the sun, but it lags behind the solar year: turn on the burner and the kettle takes a while to boil. These lakes don't reach peak temperatures until about a month and a half after the summer solstice. Then they cool. The shortening of the days and the big fall storms lower the surface temperature until it is the same as that of the layer below. As the temperature difference disappears, the stratification collapses and the two layers mix. This progresses from the top down, until the epilimnion is mixed. As it cools further, the thermocline disappears, and the lake becomes one again.

I haul up the plankton net, and the catch-cup throbs with little monsters, red and brown and black, daphnia, copepods, cyclops-eyed wiggles, that die as the formalin washes them into the bottle.

Requiescat in Pacem. Along the north shore of the lake are several springs, which ooze through sloping bogs, the water carrying nutrients that the water coming directly off the rock lacks. Thus the plankton populations are far more robust than in nearby Deep Lake, which gets more of its water off bald granite.

A cubic meter of water is 264 gallons. One species, *Daphnia rosea* (daffy roses), increases from 100 per cubic meter now, in July, to 2,500 in August and to 10,000 in September. In my samples they are the largest species, reddish ovals, beating visibly like little hearts.

Cyclops bicuspidatus (one-eyed Jacks) are copepods, little shrimpy things, which circle the catch bottle at a fast twitch. They survive well under ice and explode earlier in the year, with 8,000 per cubic meter in July, 13,000 in August, and 18,000 by September. By early September, the lake will hold about 32 billion daffy roses and 57 billion one-eyed Jacks, each carrying on its tiny dance.

During the summer, the trout devour flying insects and aquatic larva, like stoneflies, mayflies, and caddises. When the lake is under ice, which is usually from late October to late June, about eight months, the trout depend on zooplankton. High lakes with sparse or small zooplankton can't winter big trout.

Think of this: we could split into two groups of walkers. Between here and Denver, each person in one group would get a Big Mac every five miles; each person in the other group would get one peanut. The Big Mac eaters would get fat while the peanut eaters would starve. The trout in Black Joe Lake are like the first group. The trout in Deep Lake are like the second.

Acid pollution kills some species of plankton before others so the balance of different species is a clue to impact. The same holds true for the aquatic insects we collect in the inlet and outlet streams. A pristine stream may hold mayflies and stoneflies; acidified, it may hold certain tough caddises and hordes of blackfly larvae. Plankton and aquatic insects respond to pollution before its effects can be seen in trout, plus they are easier to collect.

The wind gusts and the boat pitches. Rolling up my sleeve, I fill six bottles, two white ones with black caps, one white one with a red cap, a brown one with a black cap, a little glass one with a green cap, and a clear teflon one with a clear teflon cap. My hand goes numb in the cold water. Everything's done. Jim looks worn, so

I shout *Amor!* and point to the rocky shore. He blushes, nods, and swings us around. We've bagged the deep spot. Let's get off before we have to swim.

We beach in a nest of huge rocks. There is calm in their shelter, the lake water clear over the sharp gravel. The gravel is fresh, faceted, and glinty. It takes a long journey downstream and a lot of pummeling to make rocks round. Up here, the edges are still sharp. Wading a creek in bare feet is like walking on broken cinderblock. We find the gear for the inlet stream and shove it into daypacks. I put a boulder in the boat to ballast it. The wind isn't strong enough to steal it now, but things happen quickly up here.

Right here, years ago, the wind picked up this boat and spun it on the rope like a cheap kite. We had just leaped out onto the shore, chased off the lake by a combination gale, blizzard, and lightning storm. As the boat lifted off, our samples and gear went into the lake. We reeled the boat in, dumped some rocks into it, and then jumped in after the gear. The water was painfully cold. Then, we sat between two big pines and shivered until the lightning quit. After that, my partner, Bill, let me row back alone while he hiked the shoreline. He'd been surprised once too often.

Not many people come this far. Most are stopped by cliffs and talus near the outlet, but in the woods just below timberline are old camps where the dambuilders roistered and fed as they cut the pines from the shoreline and floated them down to crib the dam. In the bushes are gallon syrup tins and constellations of rusting evaporated milk cans.

Out of the woods, buffeted by the wind, we hike a gravelly crescent to the inlet. There we see big cutthroats lined up to discharge eggs and sperm, tails flashing in the clean gravel, water roaring down from the confusion of rock and snow above: big scoops of dirty white snow surmounted by walls, spikes, spears, gendarmes, arêtes, cirques.

These are the headwaters, but you could call them skywaters. There's not much between us and heaven. Up here, the racing clouds tear open on the Divide, lowering to the surface of the lake to scatter rain and snow, a river that comes out of the sky. We are here because the river is not as pure as it once was. The river is not as pure as it once was because we are here.

I watch the trout shy from Jim's wetsuit booties as he wades over, then shoot back to their gravel beds, cutthroat, native to the region but not the lake, which is isolated by a steep outlet stream. They have silver flanks darkening to a steely overtone at the back, with spots of deep black. Below the gills, they have a streak of gold, orange or deep crimson, which brightens on spawning males. There weren't many native trout in the high lakes of this range. The outlets are too steep, cascades and waterfalls. Trout couldn't ascend to the headwaters. In the early part of this century, dude outfitters began to guide fishing trips into the range and stocked many of the lakes. They caught fish lower down and horse-packed them up in milkcans. Finis Mitchell, who ran a dude camp at Big Sandy Opening, tells of packing trout to high lakes and dumping fresh water in the milkcans at each stream crossing. He probably stocked this lake.

The thousand or so high lakes lacking native trout made the Wind Rivers a *tabula rasa* for the fever of transplanting and importing that followed. Many lakes are isolated even from others in the same basin, so there is a patchwork of species. Kayo Robertson, an old friend, tells of a flyfishing trip up the East Fork drainage on which he caught six species: brown, brook, rainbow, golden, mackinaw, and cutthroat.

The first generations of transplanted trout grew huge—oldtime guides show tattered photos of lunkers—but the population explosion is not ours alone. After twenty or thirty generations, the number of trout outstripped the food supply in many lakes. Where food is plentiful and spawning limited, there are still monster trout. Where spawning is easy, there are scrawny, big-mouthed multitudes, snakeheads as the old men call them. In some lakes, like Deep, where neither food nor spawning comes easy, the trout remain small and few in number.

There have been more generations of trout in this lake than of Anglo-Europeans on this continent. The cutthroats are good, hardy, rugged, sturdy, steady, pink-fleshed citizens, not easily hooked. They swim up to a fly cautiously. When they get mad, they face off deliberately, flaring their gill covers out to flash red before taking a nip. Rainbow trout, also spring spawners, are more nervy and pugnacious than cutthroat. Studies suggest that rainbows literally drive cutthroat from their spawning grounds by their greater aggressiveness, that male cutthroat can be stressed to death in a day.

The wind is kicking whitecaps off the lake. The stream is so cold that my arms ache, dipping the bottles. Big trout shy away, charging up and down the current like bumper cars. More than two thousand eggs in every prospective mama trout. The males pick gravelly spots where the water tumbles, oxygenated. As females swim upstream, the males shoulder over and deliver marriage proposals. If they're lucky, a trout-woman stops and threshes her tail, making a rough nest called a redd. Then she shivers, loosing pearly eggs into the

current. The male, flanking her downstream, jets a whitish cloud of sperm into the water as the eggs tumble into the interstices of the gravel. Fish in Love.

The trout look good, stout and sleek after their winter under the lake ice. Jim is absorbed in thought. He scrubs bugs off the rocks with a brush into a silk net and then offers them up, net flopping in the wind. I pick and sort, filling plastic bottles, killing stoneflies with grain alcohol. This is descriptive science. We take samples. We are objective observers. Audubon shot birds. We kill bugs.

One of our indicator species is the mayfly, *Ephemerella doddsii.* I have a mental image of a parched Victorian belle, flouncing her petticoats up the steps as the maid's voice carries through the door: "Please, Miss. Ephemerella Doddsey is here."

The Forest Service Aquatic Ecology Lab at Brigham Young University has a forty-year record of stream insects in waters from pristine to foul. The impact of such insults as mine drainage, paper mills, urban sewage, and other modern miracles on aquatic insects is well documented.

So far, the insects are holding their own. A change in species composition will tell us of a problem, but perhaps only when it is too far advanced to be helped. If *Ephemerella* fails to reproduce for two years, then what do we do? Get on the phone and ask them to turn off L.A., Las Vegas, Salt Lake City, the natural gas fields, a half-dozen coal-fired power plants, and a couple of smelters? Stop commuting, folks, shut down the works and pumps, click off the lights and heat and TV. Our mayflies died.

It's a conundrum. We're up here in beauty's lap, carefully monitoring her potential death by poison. Kiss, kiss. Be bones, be dust. Fall in love, buy a car, buy a house. Join the plague dance. The Free Market. Thieves' Road. Trail of Tears. Bosque Redondo. Wounded Knee.

The cursed Economy. Eco-gnomy . . . Maybe I'm an Eco-gnome. An Eco-gnostic. I'll stay up here and live under a big boulder and make up haiku. Catch trout with my hands. Lure brown-skinned mountain girls with my voice.

I eat a few leaves of grass. Good stuff. Makes the elk fat and horny. Or antlerish. I lean over and pick a different grass. *Deschampsia caespitosa.* Grassy tasting. Leaves of Grass. *All truths wait in all things.* Walt Whitman wrote that. The taste of grass calms me. This place looks good. It looks better than good. It looks like heaven.

But heaven's windy. A gust almost blows the bug pan out of my hand. I finish tweezing caddises and moss into the third bottle. Jim looks cold, nostrils pinched, bluish around the lips. We'd better get back to the boat. Whitecaps are marching up the lake, pale stripes on a jade tiger. We pack up our bottles and hike fast.

At the boat, it's calmer. I decide to row back, while Jim hikes the shoreline. Rowing a loaded inflatable is tough against a high wind, tougher with two. I cast out onto the tattered surface and pull, hup, hup, hup, as he strolls easily west through the pines, looking for cutthroat spawners in the inlet creeks. This effort is what I need, steady when the wind relents, then a sprint against the gusts. Unequivocal. The world and the flesh. I dig deep and throw my back almost level as the wind sheets spray over the low bow.

Rowing, I shout out lines from Whitman: *I say the whole earth and all the stars in the sky are for religion's sake.* One and two, three and four. *The friendly and flowing savage, who is he? Is he waiting for civilization, or past it . . . ?*

I row hard and find myself moving faster than Jim walks. He hears me yelling poetry and looks across the lake. I'm not trying to show off, so I slacken my stroke, but there is a rocky point to clear against the wind, and the twin rhythms compel me, Whitman and waves. *I think I could turn and live with the animals, they are so placid and self-contain'd. I stand and look at them long and long.* One and two, three and four. The right oar is four inches shorter than the left— we broke one of the originals—so pulling evenly I get across the wind. The strongest gusts blow a bit harder than I can row. The shoreline flows backward, then forward, then back.

Between huddled pines, the lake is scaly with wind, twisting between great rock walls, writhing under slides of talus. The boat pitches up at each wave, dishing icy water onto the back of my neck. Around me, peaks waltz to the wind's drum.

Cold hands on the oars. Waves slap the rubberized fabric, but I'm getting near the west end of the lake and the fetch, the distance over which the lake is exposed to the wind, is less. The rollers diminish. Jim hikes dutifully through the whitebarks, probably glad to be where he is but also feeling left out of the main chance. He's an ideal partner, plucky, steady, bright, considerate. He'd take on almost anything I asked, but it's my turn. It feels good. I beach and pick him up before the barrier cliff. At the lake's west end, the wind relents, and we have a dreamy row under a little waterfall that drafts off a granite brow into dark water, waving like pale hair.

It's noon when we get back to camp. Since Deep Lake is above timberline, there's not much to hold a lively horse. We leave P. J., or Puke Jam as Jim now calls him, tied up near camp. I wade the creek in my sandals, towing Buck, as Jim circles down to the jump crossing. Plastic Jesus cuts didoes around the little tree, bugling and pawing. At the spine of the ridge, I watch him and decide that he will raise considerable hell but is too smart for self-injury. So we drop down an old sheepherders' trail to Clear Lake and find the wet path that will take us up to Deep Lake.

The sheep have been moved farther north, with no grazing in this drainage for the last seven years or so. Some of the broadleaf plants are coming back. We wind through the whitebarks, through a sparse groundcover of grouse whortleberry and into a south-sloping, flowery meadow. Where the meadow levels, the main trail is a muddy rut, with well-trodden campsites evident. An ill-considered article in *Outside* has funneled campers here the last two years. There aren't many level campsites, except near the trail and the lake.

The trail dives into forest and then wanders onto bedrock. The stream cascades over slabs and rests in gorgeous pools. Little cairns built by hikers decorate the way up, between polished walls of granite: not a tough route to find. In level spots, a few inches of soil cling precariously.

When a basin gets more water than it can hold, it spills over. Some of the lakes in the Wind Rivers have more than one potential outlet, since ice will follow more than one way down, but only an extraordinary influx, heavy rain on melting snow, will bring both outlets into play.

Water may leave a lake in ways other than a stream. Broken or porous rock beneath a lake may carry water out below the ground. Lakes on faults may lose water down the cracks and seams. Below Deep Lake, there is a crack in the bedrock that surfaces along a great slab below the outlet and runs cold and strong when the surface channel above is almost dry.

The other way water leaves without flowing over the ground is by evaporation. In the Great Basin, lakebeds occupy the lowest points in a landscape with no outlet to the sea. Despite its singular name, the Great Basin comprises many isolated watersheds.

With no surface outlets, sealed in their beds by great depths of fine sediments, these Great Basin lakes rise and fall according to the climate. During hot, dry times, they shrink, flowing back into the heat-whitened sky. When there is more precipitation, or the summers cool, they grow. The futility of the tremendous pumps installed by the state of Utah during the last rise of the Great Salt Lake can be seen by looking at a map of prehistoric Lake Bonneville, which lapped the mountain fronts for more than two hundred miles. The elevation of the Great Salt Lake will tell us how the climate is tending. The pumps will be of use only during times of indecision.

We come out of ragged forest to a crossing, where an overlap of big slabs lets the horse step dry-footed across the creek. From there, we wander up through rock overlaps toward the lip that confines Deep Lake. There are only two ways to get a horse up and we take the less exciting. When I scouted a week ago, the lake was still bank-to-bank ice. The heat has opened it, I hope, to let us out in the boat for an early sample.

Deep Lake is one of the sublimest landscapes in the Rockies, kept by stunning winds and lightning from being merely picturesque. The lake is shaped like the hind quarter of a deer, and surrounded by bare and breast-polished rock, a steep world of walls and spikes and domes, streaked with oxide blacks, solid as the foundation of the earth, which it is. This rock is more than two billion years old. It will last, even if we wipe out the mayflies, kill the trout, foul the skies, wear gas masks, and devour each other in jungles of terrible cement. Through Cataclysm, Catastrophe, Apocalypse, or Armageddon, this rock will stand.

We level out on the boulder-strewn shelf from which the outlet spills. There is a thin shield of ice near the shore, but the lake is open. Buck, dour and hungry, gets looped to a rock. Jim pumps up the boat as I sort the jumble of variously shaped and colored bottles.

The teflon bottles cost thirty-five dollars each. Half a day's pay for us. We load and cast out, Jim rowing toward the deepest point, which I identify by lining up a confusion of broken boulders on the east shore and an ice-cave high to the west.

The wind blows from several points of the compass in rotation, slamming us with gusts, whitening the surface to lace, skimming the boat like a leaf. Jim pumps the oars as I lower the lines, taking the temperature—3.5°C. Still mixed. I dip the surface samples, the cold twisting my bones like spaghetti. I groan. "Why don't you wear your neoprene gloves?" Jim asks.

"I like to touch the water." He looks incredulous. We labor through the plankton hauls—not much life in this pure water, like seining the depths of space. Then, on to the inlet, my favorite place on earth, still, on July 6, under a shield of snow and ice. We pull into a rocky cove and meet ice floes, white as the neck of a nun, bobbing in the emerald swells.

The floes guard the shoreline at our landing spot. I have to crawl out of the boat onto one, sandaled feet ticking with the cold. "Why didn't you wear your booties?" Jim asks.

"Life is suffering." The truth is, they're too tight—size 10. Surplus gear from the EPA Lake Survey. I shift my weight from foot to foot, tipping the ice cake as Jim stares at my sandaled feet and makes fish mouths. My feet don't feel as bad to me as they look to Jim. With scientific composure, I drag the boat onto the ice, the floe dipping under the weight. Jim scrambles out. "Glad To Be Here," I hoot, "Mississippi John Hurt said that." We drag the boat over the bobbing ice.

I leap onto the shoreline snow. The ice floe is thrust away from the landing, but I have the rope. With it, I haul the floe, boat, and Jim to shore. Jim, wearing his farmer-style leather boots, clambers out onto the rock with relief. We tie up and pack the inlet gear over a low gap, but the stream is still hidden under ice and drifts.

What now? No inlet sample? Unthinkable. Jim proposes digging down to the creek. We could use the oars, I think, but I see a run of open water flashing against a rock ledge. I take the bag of bottles and crabwalk across boulders and hard snow. I can hear water rushing not far below. Suddenly, I feel like a dumbshit.

Bloop. I plunge crotch-deep in snow, both feet in the creek, icy slush circulating nicely around my toes in the current.

"YOWOOOWOOOWOWOOO," I yell. A raid on the inarticulate.

Jim is rapt. He makes no move toward rescue. Instead, he starts to giggle. "You're, you're COLD," he yelps. "COLD! You're FREEZING YOUR ASS." He regards it as divine justice. I've been hiking on snow and ice in my goddamn sandals without a peep, after floating in an inner tube in icy lakes, and have been inhumanly, indecently happy about it all. He's been waiting for this. "COLD!" he sings. *"COLD!"*

I don't find it amusing, feet washed by the coldest water in the galaxy, toes packed in ice, but I grit my teeth. I struggle out onto my knees and crawl onto a lone, flat rock, standing up to stomp the ice from between my toes. "COLD!" The little bastard keeps repeating the word, until I want to attack. Instead, I fill the inlet bottles, bare handed, with immense dignity. "COLD!" Snort, snort, snort. He has to stop and take deep breaths.

Bottles bagged, I wallow back across the snow, plunging into the water with involuntary shrieks. Sometime after the millennium, I join Jim on his dry and sunny boulder. He snickers.

"Well," I say, "you're up, Rocky. Time to catch some bugs." He looks across the snow imprinted with my suffering. "Over there where it's open." In the stillness I can hear the wind fluting through pinnacles on East Temple.

He looks at me with such sincere horror that I repent. "I forgot my booties," he says in a tiny voice. He points down, mystified, at his leather boots that cover up his pale, bare feet. "Booties. Forgot."

Revenge consummated, I wave a hand. "Oh, well. Probably not much *biological development* up here. Too . . . mmmmmm . . . *cold.*" He exhales and laughs. He knew I was fooling. We wander back to the boat. The silver walls catch the sun and kick it in all directions. In a brief calm, the lake is a great prism, accepting the flood of light and giving back opal and aquamarine, turquoise and amethyst. There are colors here that know your life story, colors that, if you look long enough, make you cry.

We load the boat and lift it onto the ice, then shove it into the lake. Jim flops into the stern with a sigh. I climb into the bow and take the oars. "I'll row," I say. "You just look around."

We're tired. We struggle through outlet samples and then return to camp. P. J.'s glad to see us and wants to stick his nose in my armpit, but I picket him on some good grass and he seems content. Against another stormy sunset, I watch the narrow profiles of solitary firs, blasted by the wind. If all things have souls, they could teach us endurance. Here at timberline, they never grow beyond this first, slow, thrust. They may never set cones or produce seed, yet they have a lean, specific beauty. They could teach us relinquishment. How to live without swarming. I leave the horsebell hanging on a pine.

I fall asleep, dreaming in sound. The coooosh of boots in melting snow. Stepping on a willow hummock: scritch, thoonk. Snowmelt dripping and pooling: ti-thock . . . pi-took. The deranged yammer of a Steller's jay. Blood-bay horse sighing, warm, moist, into my cupped palm. Pump-pack. Pack-pump. Pump-pack-pack-pack: gusts hitting a nylon tent. Hoofbeats, a wave of rain, a lull. A horsebell softly struck. A change in the wind note as the gust sheers out of the forest and onto the talus. Sliding naked into a sleeping bag: sheeeeeeee.

The next morning we rise, take down the snow collector tube, set up the funnels of the rain collectors, and then rush down the mountain, elated by having gotten it all done, and done well. It's a long way out. At the trailhead, we heave the panniers into the truck, boom the horses into the trailer, and dust off for the U.S.A.

We make it to town around five-thirty, having to dodge our truck and horsetrailer around the Rendezvous Parade, modern-day mountain men and fake Indians in Tandy buckskins, drunk as ministers, ping-ponging up Pine Street on disgruntled-looking horses. We unload the gear and get our samples into the refrigerator.

The town is heating up with music and frenzy as we hit the showers and then the streets. Jim finds Elizabeth—and they disappear. I catch Bella Linda striding like a pocket empress down Pine Street and claim a huge kiss, leaning into her salvation, back again, among my kind.

14

I placed a jar in Tennessee,
and round it was, upon a hill.
It made the slovenly wilderness
Surround that hill.

Wallace Stevens, "Anecdote of the Jar"

After leaving the trailhead, I hike past newly dumped gravel and freshly scraped waterbars. At a bend I stop, seeing a man in the shade, heavily tattooed, a revolver at his belt. After a second, I focus on another man, smirking, leaning on a shovel. It looks like a scene from *Cool Hand Luke*. I walk up humming, so the guard notices me. The man with the shovel stops and looks, his mouth slack. He wears highwater jeans and a blue workshirt. He looks at me with the same flat-eyed gaze that he uses on the guard. We're one side, he's the other. Then he goes back to a desultory poking of the dirt, staying in motion but not accomplishing much. Looking at the guard, a slouch-bellied man whose jaw moves in a constant, measured gnaw, I was just thinking the same about him and the prisoner. I'm one side, they're the other. Fifty feet ahead is another pair, almost identical though the armed guard lacks tattoos. The guard nods and the prisoner ignores me.

It's a trail crew from the Wyoming Honor Farm, a prison. There are several men farther on, heaving deadfall logs out of their beds and lining them up along the trail, then a few more digging out waterbars. Looking at faces it's hard to distinguish the prisoners from the guards, but the guards all have massive pistols and some have whistles around their necks. The prisoners, in their posture, in the way they move through the pine shade, are more relaxed.

I walk fast through the shade-striped woods, sweating. There are backpackers ahead, dressed for visibility, a walking fluorescence, so I catch a side trail and pass unnoticed. Across Miller Park, there's a breeze jigging the grasses, long leaves shooting up but no seedheads forming yet. Three weeks ago, Jim and I were on snowshoes here, crossing the bright expanse. Now, on July 10, the trail wears a half inch of dust. In the unusual heat, the snow has melted fast, the last drifts outlined by spring beauties. The streams that rose fast in June now recede as the high country assumes its deepest green.

The pack is bothersome, about seventy pounds, loaded with steel ringstands and assorted parts for rain collectors which I'm setting up in the wilderness. Jim is working on a fish habitat project this week, dumping boulders in a creek, which the fisheries biologist calls something else. This is a job I've done each season, mostly walking, mostly alone. I have to take down the snow collectors and collect a final sample from them, then replace them with rain collectors.

Each collector is a ten-inch plastic lab funnel with a loop of tubing below, feeding into a bottle of inert plastic. The bottle's cap has two holes drilled for plastic nipples, one for the tube leading from the funnel and the other for a vent tube. Both funnel and bottle are supported by a lab ringstand with a steel base, two rings, and a burette clamp to clasp the small end of the funnel.

The collectors were designed at Hubbard Brook, New Hampshire, where scientists Gene Likens and Herbert Bormann started work on the water and nutrient cycles of a single watershed. Likens and his partner Bormann, a Harvard ecologist, used these collectors to catch rain in the sixties, when little work had been done on the effects of air pollution. They noticed high acidity in New England rainfall and set out further collectors in the surrounding area. This revealed patterns of acidity, which corresponded with prevailing winds and sources of heavy sulfur emissions in the Midwest. In 1972 they published their findings in *Environment*, and in 1974 in *Science*. Likens may have introduced "acid rain" as a popular phrase. When the press broke the story, it was greeted by a storm of disbelief and outright abuse.

Utility companies and coal interests sent up a barrage of canned editorials and brutal cartoons. They hired experts, many of them aimed square at Likens's personal character. Their reaction followed a well-worn template. Over a century earlier, newspaper articles about the sickening pall of smoke from the mills in Cleveland were greeted with a similar blast, assaulting the patriotism and morals of anyone so foolish as to stand between the "legitimate interests" and a dollar.

An 1855 editorial reads, "We have now in and about our city scores of chimney stacks, that pour out clouds of smoke and soot, producing a great amount of discomfort." There were laws passed, without effect. In 1860 a mill that produced iron was indicted for excessive and unhealthful discharges of smoke, but nothing came of the charge, of which another writer said, "The idea of striking a blow at the industry and prosperity of the infant iron manufactories of Cleveland . . . is an act that should and will be reprobated by the whole community."

This sounds, with a sad diminution of style, like the statement of a Wyoming official in 1990: "We feel sincerely that free-market economics will protect the environment without locking up our resources and destroying the lifestyles of Wyoming citizens."

The studies by Likens and Bormann sparked further research, changing the pivot point of the scientific community even as they were lambasted in the popular press. Twenty years later, their findings were doctrine. Other researchers have been similarly served, from Stanford population biologists Paul and Anne Ehrlich to Miami University ecologist Orie Loucks, who demonstrated the first ecological models for DDT contamination and acid deposition. All have been relentlessly savaged by industry and bureaucrats for trying to find out how the world actually works, and for telling us that our acts have consequences.

Once, while I was hiking in to set up a rain collector, a gringo asked me why I had a funnel tied on my pack. Rather than disturb his wilderness jaunt with a talk on air pollution, I told him I slept out in rainstorms with the funnel in my mouth to rehydrate. "It's lighter than a quart of water," I explained. "No risk of *Giardia*."

Persisting, he finally got the awful truth. "I'm measuring air pollution," I said.

"Great," he said.

"Great?" I must have looked stricken.

"It's great that somebody's doing something about it."

"But I'm not doing anything. I'm only *measuring it*."

"That's better than nothing," he said, and walked away.

I cut off the main trail through a bloom of yellow, cinquefoil and mountain dandelion, following the original path up through a chain of narrow glades hedged by whitebarks and Engelmann spruce. The woods are still wet up here. There are not many tracks on the cut-off: one horse and one man hiking with a heavy pack. It doesn't take a mystically gifted tracker to decide that a size 13 boot sunk an inch into the mud is probably not on a female foot, or at least not a human female foot.

A trick for walking these woods when they are soft and moist is to step on the high spots, mostly exposed rocks. There are usually plenty of rocks, and they are usually solid. What seems like toil at first becomes natural, an exercise in balance and rhythm. I'll add that you ought to walk regularly first to strengthen your ankles and then practice with loads lighter than the average backpack. Most of the rescues and evacuations up here owe to sprained or broken ankles.

But enough caution. I'm not being cautious at all, just walking. Under my big pack, rangy legs poking from my shorts, I resemble a sandhill crane. Storking from stone to stone, I often pause but never quite stop, since there is a whizzing cloud of horseflies, mosquitos, and nostril-chompers in my slipstream, darting in to land at the slightest halt. Walk fast or bleed.

I cross the main trail and see two couples trudging along in full Everest-summit gear, Gore-texed from head to foot, flapping their hands at the bugs and sweating like draft horses. They have a little dog, spinning and snapping at the bugs under a fancy nylon dog pack. I wave but don't stop. They goggle at me from under their hoods, sweat popping out on red cheeks, and I'm gone into the trees.

I worry for persons who are uncomfortable, nervous, scared, and overequipped. I mourn for those who read too many wilderness books promising ecstasy, delight, and mystical oneness. I suffer for those on four-day trips who await the flick of the Divine Finger and instead stagger back to the parking lot dappled with welts and bruises.

I grieve when I hear that there are not enough trail signs, that the camping spots have rocks and branches in them. I am shame-faced when told that the fish aren't biting, as if they should be eager to be hauled up on a hook, and when I hear: Why aren't there elk, like in the photo book we bought in Jackson? We're climbing Gannett; is there supposed to be this much snow? When we called the Forest Service office, they told us that . . .

I struggle for kindness, but only so far. At heart, I'm a curmudgeon. A tinker. A ragamuffin, vagabond, hillbilly, bush-wolf, dharma-bum, skid. I'm up here because I need to be, and I pay in poverty for that privilege. This place is my vocation, not my vacation.

In the wild, I will hide, walk fast, pretend to speak only Spanish, Navajo, or Chinese, camp in remote, brushy crannies and otherwise seek with my utmost diligence to enhance your illusion of solitude. At such times, I can begin in the mildest way to appreciate the feelings of Geronimo and Crazy Horse, of Wovoka and Captain Jack. I realize that what right-minded Anglos call paranoia on Indian reservations or in the mountain villages of New Mexico or in enclaves of Palestinians may be in fact good sense. If you catch me flatfooted, stuck on the main trail, I will endeavor to be a Good Host. "Where are they biting?" you ask.

"Deep," I will reply. "Way deep."

In my notebook, I write a heading. July bloom: bistort, buttercup, early arnica, cinquefoil, clover, dandelion, yarrow, silky phacelia. Parry's primrose. Green, the sedge and bulrush, green the wheatgrass and bluegrass and timothy. Higher, under whitebark and spruce, there's a little, heartbreaking, pink, seven-petaled beauty that looks like a tiny bitterroot.

In the summer, I place bottles and funnels on the heights at four sites in the wilderness. Most of my time is spent getting to each and coming back. The sum of the week's mileage is between fifty and sixty: maybe not as much as a waitress. But I like to walk. I'm made to walk.

I'm a primate evolved for foraging the African savannah. My basics—legs, eyes, hands—are suited to light scavenging. My eyes are good at picking up quick movement, the flop of vultures from a lion kill or the scuttle of rabbits into brush. My hands are good for wrenching the joints of carcasses, prizing roots from the earth, plucking leaves and berries. Like my hands, my digestion is able to handle a wide variety of things.

Walking has changed my body. My upper trunk is modest, except for a knotty set of forearms from building log fences for some years. Below the waist, I'm a different creature. My thighs have a long outward arc down to a distinctive bulge above the knee. I'm often asked if I race bicycles. Jeans that fit my waist are always too tight in the thighs. My knees are bony and well scarred by rocks, sharp ice, and youthful sports. My calves are stringy and tapered down to thin ankles. A friend who makes cowboy boots said that I have strong feet, with the spread and spatulate toes of a Balti porter.

Walking, along with grasping and talking, is a human birthright, but few of us do it well. Listen to the way your foot meets the earth. Is there noise? Set aside the lore about walking silently, since we are not sneaking up on sabertooths, and consider the physics. We walk by rolling the body's weight forward and falling slightly, then swinging a leg out to arrest the fall, placing a foot on the ground. Any sound, slapping, scuffing, sliding, thumping, means that there is energy being wasted. Your foot should descend softly and kiss the earth. Scuffing means your foot is being dragged. If it slides back as you launch, you may be taking overlong strides, leaning forward too much. Make clean, sharp tracks.

In my teens, I was duckfooted. Now, my feet lie straight, parallel to the direction of travel. While this has been enforced by the strict parallels of cross-country skiing, it is also the yield of many thousand miles on dry ground.

Half of walking is falling. Without falling, without the pull of gravity, walking would be a very different process, as the goofy bound of astronauts in the lunar dust shows. But one must fall with grace. Many hikers pound each foot into the ground: a contact sport. Shock-absorbing insoles can help if the habit stays. If your foot meets the earth too soon, it pounds and scuffs. The beneficent pull of gravity has been thwarted. If too late, in a high jog, it shocks the knees and back. It's a pleasure to watch the relaxed walk of someone who is good at it. It's no coincidence that the military mind loves to pervert this essential act into a stiff march, a tight-sphinctered strut, or the jerky goose step of the Nazi legions.

I don't march. I don't wear a uniform. I just walk, 1,760 steps per mile, and this trip, to the highest collector and back, is one of over 53,000 steps. Each one is important. Small ills multiplied are grand maladies.

Legs take care of themselves: walking develops the muscles for walking. The only care is to stretch the hamstrings and thighs. Before and after a walk, stretch your hamstrings with an exaggerated forward stride, rear foot flat on the ground. For the thighs, do a slow squat and rest on your heels until the tension eases. You might also want to rise on your toes: walking maintenance. It's simpler than changing the oil, lubricating the chassis, waxing the finish, and vacuuming the leather interior.

Walking with a pack changes things. With a heavy backpack, the center of gravity rises from a point below the bellybutton to the solar plexus. This complicates the reflexes of balance. In level walking, the difference is not as evident as when hopping rocks to cross a stream or balancing up a spooky ridge. Remember—any angular motion will be exaggerated. In jumping streams or rocks, try to land at the deadpoint, which is where the forces balance. Too much momentum and you flop forward. Too little and you fall back—splash. Sideways falls are also common, and they sprain ankles.

Mental readiness will not suffice. You are more than a brain. After summoning helicopters for those who tried to go from sedentary, financially rewarding lives to grunting sixty pounds over the slippery cobbles of alpine streams, I counsel you to prepare. Riding horseback with a broken ankle is bad—you can't put one foot in the stirrup, which is rough on the crotch.

But here's the hidden cost in becoming a long-haul walker. Once you get used to it, you will require it. Most of us get sore from long hikes. I get sore without them. During periods of sitdown labor, I develop a sore back, stiff ankles, and cramps in my legs. A dayhike takes care of the pain. My body has ripened to constant movement, making scholarship more painful than snowshoeing.

The best pace is one that can be maintained without stopping, except for short rests on the steepest parts. Most of us hike fast, get tired, then stop to rest: the rhythm of city traffic. Breaking habits is hard, but one way is to keep walking, no matter what. If you are tired, slow to a snail's pace, one step to every breath or even every two breaths. Pretend you're near the summit of K-2. As you recover, you will gradually quicken the beat; when you grow tired, slow down again, but don't stop. Try to lessen the difference between your fast pace and your resting pace. In the course of a backpacking trip, you should notice a difference. After you settle on your natural pace, it's more tiring to break it than it is to maintain the beat.

Walking also helps the flow of thought. Have you ever spent the whole day walking and thinking? I've waded and snowshoed and postholed and dusted and skied these trails and shortcuts until they are familiar. My feet are intimate with every loose block and awkward step, so I don't have to guide them in their work.

Instead, I look around, smell the air, listen hard, feel my breath coming and going. I see the changes in the flowers, the birds, the weather, see the tracks of boots and hooves and clawed feet, but note them all almost unconsciously. When I walk, my hands touch nothing but my pockets, my pack-straps, the air. Walking, I'm perfectly free to think.

Reaching Hobbs Lake, eight miles in, I'm trailed by a cloud of mosquitos. Bushwhacking around the east shore, I raise them from the willows in gusts. When I reach the snow collector, they settle in for a fiesta. I put on windpants and an anorak to preserve my scientific demeanor. The bugs land on my eyelids and chew on the lashes. They organize skating parties on the inner surface of my glasses.

I erect the ringstands, wiring them to sections of steel fenceposts. I level the funnels and rinse them with distilled water. Every joint and angle is checked and tightened. I uncap the bottles and fix them in place. If a raindrop falls, it will be monitored.

In this ragged splendor, it's a shame to care so much about the ten-inch diameter of a white Nalgene funnel, but I do. A yard above the earth, it gathers the rain and all that accompanies it. Nitrate, sulfate, blessings: the evidence we confront. After years of setting these up and taking them down, carrying empty bottles in and full bottles out, after compassing my hikes to converge at this spot, I've made it something other than a place. It's become a reference, topographic, practical, moral, for my life.

Wallace Stevens is my favorite poet, until further notice. Does the wilderness sprawl, toothless, around the maw of this ten-inch funnel? Hardly. It's an operation of the mind, a distortion of the field. The dance of nature and mind is what fascinated Stevens. He would have smoked out, up here.

The wilderness is immense, green, insistent, flowing with water.

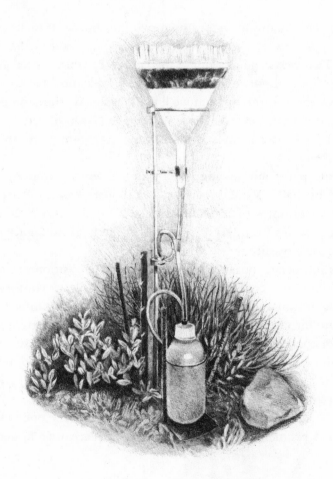

The white plastic funnel is an artifact, a trap for the rain, slick and blind. It is compounded to change nothing, to remain aloof. In this hidden pocket, it will stand and witness the fall. My pact with this nation is to give it truth for lies: evidence, precise and accurate. Others can testify to the spirits they encounter here. I'll watch the sky and count the losses.

The snow collector looms over me. If it is full, then this will be hard. Picture a garbage can half full of water balanced on top of two other cans. Getting the sample to earth is a tricky proposition with two. Alone, it is wildly problematical. I unbolt the flange and tip the upper sections. Slosh. They feel light. I heft them and they are reasonably heftable, so I unclamp the guy cable and set them on the bedrock. Much of the sample has evaporated in the sudden heat.

I drain the remaining water into a two-liter bottle. It looks soupy and cloudy, showing a high rate of evaporation. The heat has been unusual. Two years ago, I painted the collectors white. After asking the science guys about it (mmmumble we'll look into that) and the policy guys about it (grrm-grrm we'll contact the Washington office) I waited patiently. I never heard from anyone. Tired of getting poor samples, I packed in primer and select-quality white paint and did the right thing.

Since the paint job, spring evaporation from the collectors has decreased by half. Winter melting has almost ceased. Where we used to find samples of stratified ice, showing intense melt-freeze cycles, we now get fresh, crystalline snow. The bags no longer burst from freezing pressure.

This is important because our estimates of deposition are based on two things: the concentration of chemicals in the samples and the volume of rain and snow. In theory, an evaporated sample would compensate for decreased volume by increased concentration, so an estimate of total deposition would be correct in either case. But if the melt-thaw cycle ruptured the plastic bags or a high wind blew the collector down or a snowslide overrode it, then there is no sample to analyze.

There is a gulf between the standards of laboratory poodles and the physical problem of collecting data in a place that humans—

over ages—chanced only during brief summers and never dared in winter.

I'm grateful for the knuckle-gnawing lab techs, who are compulsive about quality control and decimal places. But I couldn't be one. The numbers are symbols for the things I love. I'll suffer to catch rain, but I don't feel much at heart for a Pearson Correlation Coefficient. It doesn't have to make sense, but I must be near it.

Over the years, I've beaten avalanche-squashed snow collectors round with rocks, replaced cheap guy lines with aircraft control cable, grommeted cable holes so the sharp edges no longer saw through as the wind shakes the collector, replaced puny half-inch stakes with sections of steel fencepost or expansion bolts drilled into rock, and installed heavy-duty clamps and turnbuckles to take the strain of a settling snowpack. The supplies came from hardware counters in Pinedale or my kit of climbing gear: low tech, way cheap. I'm a bargain for taxpayers.

After six seasons, the collectors no longer blow over or jerk their anchors from thawing soil or blow their bags or cook samples or disappear under sliding snow or any of the other circumstances that denied us. It's good to find everything in place.

The mosquitos increase by squares, and tiny flies cheer them on, like high school coaches. I pack the sample, bag the tools, and squelch away through the pines to set up my tiny tent, a glorified bivouac sack, eighteen inches high at the ridge. I heat some soup and from it pluck drowning insects, give up, then retreat into the tent, struggling out of my windpants and anorak, which are slick with sweat inside. The tent is stuffy as a bus station phone booth, so, bugs be damned, I unzip and wander west. I sneak around the predictable campsites, then look back to find no tents in them, despite the hikers I passed. They must have taken the Miller Lake off ramp.

I sit on the precipice, looking down to where the outlet streams of Hobbs and Seneca lakes join in a frothy twelve-hundred-foot drop, meltwater, gleaming off a ledge like a torn steel hem, spreading white into the sun's glare, present and gone in a roar. There's not a breath of wind. *Schatzo.* I was hoping for wind on this exposed edge. Spinning around the bowls of my ears, the mosquitos hum Steve Reich's greatest hits. I try to distract myself by looking at the rock and the lichens on it.

Lichens. Lime. Chartreuse. Rust. Iron. Sienna. These frescoes are alive. They need nothing but rock, water, and light. An alga and a fungus make a strange little marriage called a lichen. Neither can live apart from the embrace. I have a liking for them. They make the rocks look less random, less like shattered rubble. They feel rough, yet with a slight polish, like the scabs I got falling off my bike. I put my tongue to one—not much taste. I spit out flecks of grit.

The bugs are too much. I scramble from the rim and charge up to the outlet pond, warmer than the lake. On a flat rock, I drop sweated shorts and shirt quickly, then take a flat dive into my own reflection, seeing white fire as I hit. Ahh, Christ, cold. I breast-stroke the symbol for infinity into the water twice and then succumb. Floosh, back onto the rock. I smell more like the pond than like myself. The bugs are confused, so I hop and squeegee and whirl my arms, uttering grunts of satisfaction, hoping my groin dries before the bugs get a fix.

They win the race. That may be one of our great truths: the bugs win. Reclothed, I watch the trout I spooked start to feed, lipping flies through the sheen, leaving behind little shivering moons. Then I hear a wonderful bellow, human, and hope that a bear has arrived to conduct camp inspection.

I sneak up into the pines, where a peek reveals another bather, erupting from the somewhat cooler waters of the lake. He's big and pale pink, probably Mr. Vibram Sole, 13D. He dances and flaps a white towel at the bugs and doesn't notice me. I contour out of sight, toward my camp, hearing the gulp and rustle of water, looking over the banks of columbine.

Columbines look like a sculpture of moonlight. The blooms are intricate without giving up chastity. Below the flowers, the leaves are modest and proudly held. Columbines are the prime indicator species of my vital habitat. They are the finest vegetative work of the North American continent, what I want to be when I grow up.

Dark. Mosquitos in a frenzy on the netting three inches from my nose keep me awake at first. In sedge-lined tarns, frogs strike woodblocks and copper bells, then cease all at once. An unknown bird sings, away in the heavy dark of pines, one breathy fall of notes that

I try to recall the moment after and can't. Uncommon sweet and sad, that single melody.

Night sounds—a pair of deer curious about my tent, the sniff and rustle of a carnivore in the duff (coyote? fox? pine marten?), and then the baritone flute of a great horned owl, west, between me and the lake—lift me out of sleep. In winter, night noises are witless, wind or flakes on the tent. In summer, the woods wake up and speak.

The late moon, three days past full, wakes me again. Around the tent, spruces take on a tarnished gleam as the light picks out each tufted limb. East, a line of whitebarks limp, backed by the moon's gleam on glacier polish, as the white disc drifts free and shows its black belly to earth.

I hope to beat the mosquitos by starting early, but they rally to the tent zipper, congregate over the pocket stove, and poke their mean little snouts into my circulatory system. I load a daypack with bottles and tools, tying my ice ax to it, hopping and slapping until the tea is made. Then, I take to my heels with a Texaco Food-Mart mug in one hand and a Sue's Breadbox Locally-Owned-and-Operated Granola Bar in the other. In my vest pocket is a handful of dried pear halves: a juggler's breakfast.

The grouse whortleberry is green, tiny leaves catching early sun under the pines. It blooms discreetly, with tiny flowers you have to kneel to see. On the margin of each pond the first pink bells dot the resilient, evergreen mountain heath and its deciduous cousin, alpine laurel. Ponds that catch snowmelt and hold it in dips and pocks cut by glacial ice are plentiful on this upland. At the low point of each basin is a lake, set in a diadem of wetland and tarn. I skirt a bog, an old pond that caught sediment and grew sedges and willows until it filled itself with a mat of organic soil, slightly above the water table. Crossing it would be like stepping into a sponge.

The names of plants are beautiful when said aloud: arctic willow, drummond willow, eastwood willow, grayleaf willow, planeleaf willow, netleaf willow, scouler willow, tweedy willow. Big-flower groundsmoke. Shootingstar, lambstongue, bellflower. Littleleaf blue-eyed Mary.

I circle a large pond in which I often swim, the surface green and still as tourmaline set in a ring of stone. This pond gives into a near-vertical outlet stream that joins the outlets of Hobbs and Seneca lakes almost in midair, so no trout have migrated into it despite the fact that one could almost throw a rock from here into the lake. Instead, grooving the periphytic scum are two kinds of caddises, one with cases of whitish, cemented grit and the other rolled like cigars in blackened leaves. Bronzy water beetles ping-pong between the surface and the hunting grounds below. Later, at the pond's surface, warm like broth, there will be clouds of plankton and freshwater shrimp and tiny black leeches. This is a prehistoric pond, the native fauna before the invasion of planted trout.

Last June, I spent an hour here, retrieving the white roses of tissue left by winter campers, plucking them with a pair of pine twigs from the heath and willows, unplastering them from boulders, and leaning out over the pond with a long stick to fish disintegrating wads of white muck from the surface. From the volume of tissue, it was either a big group or a sick one.

I join the main trail, stepping over wet spots. The sky is an excellent blue, cloudless, jetless, thoughtless. Seneca Creek roars white, dodging between massive jags of rock that hedge its drop down this gorge, tossing vapor ghosts into the morning air. From here to the lake's outlet it's a good scramble.

I descend in the shadow of a rock face to the ford and fill my water bottle. The logs heaved by hikers into the ford are slick and black: fool's road. I climb upstream through talus to the hop-crossing, a scary but easy step above a waterfall. There's no one on the trail this early and there are few footprints. Turning from the trail, I follow my best shortcut up narrow slots in the bedrock, where the glacier lapped over a dome. Emerging from a steep V full of rattly cobble, I step across the crest and look down. In its drowned canyon, Seneca Lake is grave and still, like green lacquer over black, bottomless as the hood of a chauffeured Bentley.

Up here the evergreen heath is luxuriant, lush as anything gets this high. Where snowmelt percolates through broken rock, there are shoots of cow parsnip, hemlock's cousin. In the drier rocky spots there are phacelia blooms with lavender corollas and long, dark purple stamens, tipped with yellow. There is also a striking little plant with silvery blue leaves in a rosette at the base of a single stem headed by a cluster of creamy flowers with stamens the color of old burgundy. I think it's a saxifrage. The name diamondleaf pops into my head. Diamondleaf saxifrage? The name has an epic beat to it, a double dactyl. I stop and sketch the plant in my notebook next to a question mark.

It's a morning to die for. To hell with all money in banks and the gas in the tanks and bombs in the bellies of B-52s. None of it is worth a day like this, a cold night followed by flawless sun, good flower-opening weather.

Flowers are my favorite glance of summer. I can get in close, because they hold still. I reached fifth grade in a blur of undiagnosed myopia, having learned to prod my right eye with my finger to focus and to memorize the eyechart used for our annual exams. Tests, I learned, were better passed than failed. I learned to read blackboard English as a set of smudgy ideograms and made fair grades, but I had trouble recognizing friends and caught softballs with my face.

The landscape was a mystery: the mountains could as well have been far-off thunderstorms, and the trees might have grown translucent fuzz instead of leaves. I often climbed an elm behind our house to look at leaves up close. I could memorize them and then, looking at the tree from a distance, imagine endless repetitions of serrate edges and etched veins instead of the shimmering fog I saw.

Birds were atmospheric sparks, voices without bodies. My friends shot sparrows with air rifles, but I could never see birds well enough to hit one. I spent a lot of time on my knees, alone in the desert, peering under old boards and newspapers, tracking snakes and centipedes along the dunes, catching soft milk-and-cinnamon-colored geckos to hear them squeak, to watch as they froze in disbelief— uneaten—and escaped my open hand. After wanderings and homework, I read feverishly. Words painted the world in detail, a world that I saw as tides of color.

I clean my glasses with a faded red bandanna and trade them for dark ones. The landscape is wallowing in light. The sun pumps its torrent onto every surface. I shed a sweater and head out, before the mosquitos can form more than a thin cloud.

Along the trail, shouldered between bright rock and the lake's plunge, are camps: a light blue dome between rock fingers, a wedge of killer orange strung between stunted pines, a hemisphere of arcs and panels, like the Sydney Opera House miniaturized in buff and plum. Outside the last tent are unscratched ice axes and crampons stacked for visibility, glinting their code—We Climb. I go quietly so as not to wake them.

Around the head of the lake—miracle—the Boy Scout Bog is empty. It's one of the few spots large enough for more than one tent, and the Boy Scouts always crowd in, tromping the green into a poxy muck.

Once I rounded this hillock as gunfire echoed ahead. Had mosquitos and diarrhea shoved some heavily armed geek over the brink? I was tempted to slouch behind a convenient boulder and sit out the fun, whatever it was. Duty, dammit, I thought, and stepped out.

There were three men trotting toward me on horseback, teamroper saddles slung with half-furled sleeping bags and lumpy duffles. All were barechested, body-builder pectorals bulging like the tits on a Barbie doll. They had bandannas around their heads and were reeling in their saddles, waving revolvers and taking random shots at marmots and trail signs. I am not making this up.

I wanted to evaporate, even as I stood in the middle of the trail. They jerked the long-suffering horses to a halt and rested their pistols on their thighs. We had a talk. I watched the guns twitch in their hands. I could smell the bourbon.

I looked calm, but didn't feel it. I said that freedom of the hills didn't include busting caps in a place where people camp behind almost every rock. "I know you feel good," I said, "but you'll feel bad when you blow the back off some high school girl's head with a ricochet." I stood there blocking the way until, one by one, they stowed their pistols in the messes behind their saddles.

"Fuck you in the fucking mouth," one of them replied as they rode by.

I loop around a series of lakes, ascending the drainage, leaving gentle country behind. Exposed rock occupies more of the view than anything except the sky. I work through willows, then onto talus, then up a steep gully between rock faces, then onto a narrow bench. The bushy grass is pale between late-lying drifts, its roots needled with frost. In the low spots are hairgrass, sheep fescue, and scaled sedge. On hummocks the first leaves of alpine avens are fingering out, soon to be followed by yellow blossoms. The growing season here is mid-July to the second week of September. There is no frost-free month.

Farther up, there are firm tongues of snow, shadowed by cliffs. The head of the ice ax warms slowly in my hand. I kick up the frozen crust of a gully, feeling insecure in light hiking boots, checking each step, planting the pick for balance. It steepens under the cornice and I can touch the snow at breast height with a flat hand. Four years ago, after a heavy winter, the snow was even steeper. I fell here and slid back, headfirst, porpoising around a boulder that lurched up at my face. It would save weight to leave the ice ax home. I could third-class the rocky arêtes that flank the gully. But I'm attached to this ax and don't get to use it as much as I did. It's like walking an old dog.

The snow at the top is rolled like a quilt by the northwest wind. The surface is hard, sun-cupped, starting its daily melt. Against the rocks are concealed voids, so I take a long step onto bedrock, not wanting to drop through into a moat. The commonest issue of such falls is striking your knee, elbow, or chin on the rock. Moats can be good belay spots on couloir climbs, protection from chunks of rock and ice that come skating down. But in a couloir no place is safe. Years ago, I was belaying a partner on a frozen waterfall pitch, from a moat in the couloir just below. I had a helmet. He loosened a head-size chunk of ice that caromed off both walls, spraying stars, popped into the moat, and shattered, pieces whacking me on the ear under the rim of my helmet. I yelled so loud that he almost fell off. Blood. Back in town, I had to soak it out of the rope.

To either side of the snow saddle are broken summits, shaggy with knee-high spruce. The rock is split and planed into steps. Not far, now. It's a fun scramble. I take a different way each trip, easy or hard. I traverse narrow ramps and toe up shallow cracks until there is no farther up to go. My pack clanks down on a rock platform, and I scan a skyline as familiar as my own face.

Northwest, the upper valley of the Green gives way to forest blue, which gives way to rock peaks: my friends, Glover, Oeneis, Stroud Peak, cutting the wind above Shannon Pass, Bow Mountain, and the sharp ridge of Arrowhead. The toothy masses of Buchtel and Henderson dipping to Knapsack Col. This part of the range, folded of blocky migmatite and gneiss, holds the highest peaks, while the monolithic south end is known for sheer, glittering walls.

It's a High Gothic landscape, arched, strong, full of light. Past the Col, my eye traverses Twin Peak, Woodrow Wilson, and the Sphinx, all above 13,000 feet, their summits crowding toward Dinwoody Pass where climbers draw labored breath as they exit Titcomb Basin en route to Gannett Peak. Rising southeast are Dinwoody, Doublet, and Mt. Warren, then the faceted spire of Helen flanked by couloirs and a glacier, then Mt. Sacajawea.

The topographic pairing of her peak, spelled with a *g* on the map rather than the preferable *j*, with Frémont's has led to a romantic but mistaken association between them in the minds of visitors. If she met Frémont on his trip in 1842, she was a formidable, fiftyish matriarch.

A captured Shoshoni whose name means Bird Woman, she was bought, one of two teenage wives for Toussaint Charbonneau, a borderer who took her west—babe in arms—with Lewis and Clark in 1804. Having helped the epic along and been justly admired by the explorers, she dumped Charbonneau. One version has it that she died at Fort Manuel Lisa in present-day South Dakota about 1812. Another version has her joining the Comanches, speaking-cousins to her tribe, and bearing other children before returning to the Shoshoni. She found her people camped in the Bridger Valley and went with them onto the Wind River Reservation, where she is said to have died in 1884. Since she was born about 1788, this would mean she had ninety-six years. There is a grave at Fort Washakie marked with her name.

The whale-backed peak south of Sacajawea is named for John C. Frémont, who climbed it in 1842 by scrambling the southwest buttress with members of his expedition: Descoteaux, Janisse, Lajeunesse, Lambert, and Preuss. He thought it the highest summit in the Rockies. This is a natural judgment, under the grand west face with its frightening architecture of walls, aprons, funnels, and minarets.

Frémont makes me frown. The Byronic son-in-law of a powerful senator, he sniffed out the trails set by others. He numbered what they knew in latitude and longitude, then imposed his choice of names, often those of persons he wished to cultivate. His reports read like tracts for Manifest Destiny, embellished with the daring of their author. He served the national craving for a comprehensible hero. Preuss was the mapmaker of his expedition. From his moody diary it seems that he came to hate Frémont, calling him, among other things, a "childishly passionate man."

Titcomb Basin, the long blue shadow under Frémont Peak, was named for the jovial brothers, Charles and Harold, who climbed there in 1901. (They also climbed a summit in the south of the range and named it Pabst Peak, for the beer they guzzled at the summit: my kind of explorers.) Fifty-nine years earlier, in 1842, Frémont's party were perhaps the first Americans to enter the high basin, calling it "a defile of the most rugged mountains known."

Guided by John Enos, a cat-faced Shoshoni, they saw from the valley a hulking skyline peak, which was "decided to be the highest in the range." After an interminable approach, a bout of altitude sickness, and a desperate scramble on all fours, Frémont, in his own words, ". . . sprang upon the summit. . . . another step would have precipitated me into an immense snow field five hundred feet below." It is not a summit on which anyone, especially in moccasins, does much springing.

The peak was later found to be the second highest in the range— Gannett Peak, about five miles northwest, is fifty-nine feet higher— but fine distinctions are elusive in such country. "Around us," Preuss reported, "the whole scene had one main striking feature, which was that of a terrible convulsion. . . . A stillness the most profound and a terrible solitude forced themselves constantly on the mind as the great features of the place."

The solitude no longer seems as profound, though if I had broken a leg in the snow gully it might become so. A few years back, a solitary climber spent a week belly-crawling out of an isolated high valley to the south, picking maggots from his compound fractures. Strangely, being alone in rough terrain eventually lends a feeling of security.

Everyone screws up. Objective hazard makes it more costly. The key is not to screw up when it matters. I've poured coffee into my cereal, lost my car keys in snowdrifts, and bashed my head on doorframes. Out here I keep my screws tight and hope the angels don't strike when I'm strung out between ledges.

I try not to fabricate dangers when I don't feel them. Right now I feel safe, but I'm at the top of a peak, at the high point of the quest. In structural terms, there should be some kind of *deus ex machina*. I wait a bit, hoping for something, eagle, lightning bolt, whatever. A compelling event.

The wind lifts and settles back. The mountains are patient but stubborn. What kind of climax could an overeducated, deconstructed neo-Druid expect, what sort of manifestation? A glowing Madonna or a fiery wheel?

Maybe I'll see a 737 strike the face of Frémont Peak, a cascade of flame and shocked alloys, a rain of flesh and metal whistling down into Titcomb Basin. That's believable, likely to happen in America, an excess of *machina* and not much *deus*. Crashes are more common than angels. I wait.

I look around at the big, quiet mountains and they remain: big, quiet mountains. A singer named Donovan Leitch once stole a lyric from a dead Zen master: *First there is a mountain, then there is no mountain, then there is.* I look, close my eyes, and look again. I can feel them, even with my eyes shut.

Rock and sky. One and all. *Nada más.*

I tip my pack and the ironware clanks onto a flat rock, stands, rings, and burette clamps. I fix the funnels, level the rims, loop the plastic tubes, settle the bottles, and whirl the wingnuts: the high drama of environmental monitoring. In the stacked boulders, the wind makes a soft *hooooooooooo*.

Visible on a shelf below is the snow collector, holding snowmelt six feet off the ground. I'll glissade the snow gully, unbolt the bolts, and hide the steel sections in a heap of talus. Cradling the taut plastic bag, I'll draw a liter of water into a clean plastic bottle and measure the rest, record the volume, pour the meltwater on the pale grass where it belongs, and watch it soak in. I come to take the world's pulse, not to bear false witness.

I'm trying to do my best for all of us. If you come here, you'd be wise to believe that grace, like the landscape, is rocky and spare, thin air and harsh light. No Renaissance angels. It will be sky, wind, rock, lichen, grit, tough grasses—until it becomes memory. Then the mountains may disappear, and you'll sink. There will be no mountain left on the entire earth.

15

. . . the world is at some kind of border; if it is crossed, everything will turn to madness. . . . And it will take very little for the glass to overflow, perhaps just one drop: perhaps just one car too many, or one person, or one decibel.

Milan Kundera, *Immortality*

*M*orning. August. The southern sky is white with haze, layers of diminishing contrast that swallow mountains along the horizon. The blue Wyoming Range fades into muddy gray at Deadline Ridge. South of the border, in Utah, the high Uinta crest looks like a drift of cigarette smoke.

Cheryl is worried about the bear. A small black bear has been scrounging food from campers at Big Sandy Lake. On my last trip, I talked with two women who showed me a claw-torn backpack. The bear, quite practiced, simply unzipped the nylon fabric with a judicious clawstroke and extracted the edibles.

Cheryl's my boss, a hydrologist who herself reminds me of a bear, talking a blue streak as she hikes and I lead two packhorses. She's wearing black lycra running tights that squeech with every step, and her head is covered with shaggy blonde hair. She comes from a Rock Springs family of "coal miners and asskickers," immigrants from Eastern Europe who got their stake in America below ground level.

Cheryl is pinkish, blondish, and bearish. She has that same rolling stride, that same happy engagement with her surroundings. I

251

like bears. They're quieter than backpackers and more fun to watch. They have a good attitude. They have a lot of fun without much in the way of recreational equipment. They are covered with all-natural fibers.

The little bear is causing quite a fuss. There were pages of bear notes in the trail register. *The bear ate our freeze-dried bouillabaisse. The bear wouldn't go away, even when we yelled. It ate our apricot-carob power bars and left the wrappers. It stuck its face into the door of our tent.*

I seized the pen and wrote my own entry: *The human staked out an ugly orange tent next to my favorite berry patch and then took a crap in it. Unreal! The Bear.*

Another woman told a wilderness ranger that she saw the bear diving into a nook in the talus after it bore her daypack off. She— the camper, not the bear—talked a neighboring camper into crawling into the lair. He found a nicely stocked den: water bottles, daypacks, fanny-packs, sunglasses, and a couple of unmatched running shoes.

The campers, having read the bear notes, could camp someplace else, but they like to adhere strictly to plan. If they decided, back in Consumer Falls, Illinois, to hike 6.6 miles on Friday, August 10, and camp on the west shore of Big Sandy Lake, then it is so ordained. Anything else will make them nervous.

August. Summer is physically easy, mentally hard. It doesn't freeze at night. I could sleep out on the ground under my jacket, like a gypsy fiddler. But the roads fill up, parking lots are packed, trails are beaten, elk spooked, and forest fires out of control. The far mountain ranges are brown smears against the sky as the horizon is lost, occupied, tarnished. I gather battles from the air, wars from the fall of dust. The concentrations will be measured, checked, and printed out. I have the care of filters and vacuum pumps, must see to the aiming of cameras and light beams, must stagger through endless, repetitive, numbing detail. I collect rain samples exhausted, with a fifteen-mile hike still to finish, trying to check myself against error: did I wash enough bottles for tomorrow's trip; did I order the filters for the lake samples; did I pack the set of field blanks? My patience frays.

My field assistant, Jim, is in heavy demand as a firefighter. He got shipped off to Idaho, was back for a few days, and then got jerked someplace else. I do his work along with mine, coming back to the office after dark to find my drawing table stuck with "could you do me a favor" notes from others sent to forest fires. I drag home from work to hoe, water, weed, harvest, shell, blanch, freeze, and can. Linda is in charge of a trail crew in the neighboring range, gone for eight days at a time, so my love for our garden is tempered by my slave status. Each morning, I spend an hour bucketing water or crawling in the dirt before driving to work.

I feel like a thin rope, strung tight. My moral fiber is frayed. Tap me on the shoulder and I'll go four feet off the ground. But the mountains are still there, my love and my book, what I wish my soul could be, high and spacious, life and water cupped in their rocky palms. It's good to be here.

Cheryl worries aloud. "What if the bear comes into camp?"

"You sing. I'll ask it to dance. Unless it's really ugly."

"No, really, what will we do?"

"Be scared, throw things, make loud noises, toss it the foodsack. We'll think of something."

"I'll die."

"The horses'll give us an early bear warning. They always raise hell when a bear's around. No sweat. Nothing will happen."

"No, I'll die." She leafs through her catalog of anxieties. Her boss has committed outrages A, B, C, and D. Her husband is guilty of sins E and F. How can we ever afford a house in Jackson? If we have a baby, we can't get a house. If we get a house, we can't afford a baby. Somehow, I don't mind listening. Even her laments are bearish and good-natured.

The trail is crowded: blue persons with orange packs, orange persons with blue packs, crimson persons on certified wilderness experiences, purple persons who are petulant for not having had theirs on schedule. I shy from trailhead carnivals, ranked minivans, and suburban four-wheel-drives; flee from the supple gleam of lycra and the sheen of new bikes; shudder at unscratched kayaks racked on the roofs of Volvos, like Sidewinders on the wings of F-15s. I cringe from glossy couples in rainbow-lensed glasses, with matching knickers and plum-colored berets, brandishing costly cameras that buzz and extrude black-muzzled lenses.

"What's in the packs on the horses?" A fortyish consultant-type

in puce nylon shorts pins me with disapproval. A woman in matching togs looks at me with embarrassment. "Horses damage trails
and cause pollution."

What's in the packs? I want to say something disturbing. *Rock
cocaine. Nuclear waste.* Cheryl can see my look. She purses her lips
and gently shakes her head. So I zen back and give him a list.

"Avon two-person raft, Van Dorn bottle, Michigan plankton net,
a hundred meters of nylon rope, formalin, alcohol, modified Surber
seine, sixty high-density polyethylene bottles, a battery-operated an-
alog marine thermometer . . ." He interrupts me. His thighs look
like defrosted chicken.

"Why do you need so much stuff? You could carry backpacks,
like us."

I'm carrying a backpack, but he doesn't seem to see it. "We're
sampling the lakes. It's a long-term monitoring project."

"Are they okay to drink from? I mean, horses don't help, you know."

I wanted to punch this geek. Cheryl can tell. She shakes her head
and tries not to laugh. His wife shares her look: she's been through
this before. I suffer from punch-lust. *Sir,* I'd like to say, once he was
on the ground, able to concentrate, *Sir, I am a dedicated Public Ser-
vant, protecting our water resources for future generations. As part of our
new Biodiversity-in-Hiring program, these horses are my field assistants. I'm
doing a survey. May I ask how far you drove in your hydrocarbon-spewing
luxury sedan to plague me and these innocent beasts?* But, of course, I
don't say that. Nor have I punched anyone since high school, alas.

"We're doing air pollution chemistry, not sampling for *Giardia.*"

"There's no pollution here. This is a Wilderness."

I'm beginning to sputter. Cheryl swoops in and extricates me.
The good citizen and his unfortunate spouse march stiffly west, and
we continue east, toward the big peaks. Cheryl snickers, then snorts,
then guffaws. "Californians. Sahara Clubbers, probably. Doesn't it
make you wanna commit murder?" she asks.

"I can't afford to kill a conservation voter. Theoretically, we're
on the same side. Ugh. So much for common ground."

We keep walking, smiling fixedly at the backpackers, horsepackers, dayhikers, climbers, and flyfishers. In return, we get dirty looks
from the backpackers for our horses and dirty looks from the
horsepackers for leading them on foot. Pale bodies in various stages

of fluorescence jiggle by, nursing their blisters on the way to the parking lot. I gag at expensive panniers draped over exclusive little dogs. The dogs, never amiable, are offended at being treated as common beasts. They have strict notions of privacy and personal space, defending their bit of trail to the death.

"He won't *bite* you," says the lady in cavalry twill. "The pack just makes him *nervous*. His name is Brightwaters Lama. This is his First Wilderness Experience. We just moved to *Santa Fe*."

I slink onward, plotting the fall of Western Civilization.

Cheryl's on a different mental track. She loves malls, so a crowded trail doesn't bother her in the least, but she's getting red in the face, talking about what she'd like to do to her boss, who torpedoed her during a meeting last week.

It was the Big Data Powwow. We were in a stuffy room in Jackson. I was wearing my good shirt, pure cotton, Robin Hood green. It was the day after Iraq invaded Kuwait. The Exxon vice-president was huddled with a phone in the corner, hand cupped over the receiver.

We were there to review the figures that Cheryl and I got from our raw data on the rain and snow samples. We hoped to agree on a data set, a plausible hell of numbers from which the DEQ, Exxon, Chevron, and our humble selves could proceed to unravel the atmospheric affairs of the Wind River Mountains.

When the corporations proposed dehydration and sweetening plants for natural gas, they had to get a permit from the state. In turn, the state had to consult with the Forest Service about the effect on Class I wilderness air. As a condition of the permit, Exxon and Chevron agreed to contribute to an air pollution monitoring effort, which the Forest Service undertook. There were conferences and symposiums. I missed out on the festive beginnings. The resulting documents were marvelous in scope and detail but the next phase, field sampling, started haphazardly.

We are accosted again and lectured about horses. "Our gear is heavy," I sigh. I try to explain that I'm not collecting lake water to find out whether we can drink it. They seem surprised that I would collect it for anything else. Isn't that water quality? Whether you can drink it? Is there *Giardia*? Do we need to boil it?

Boil it, *please*. Dump raw iodine in it, then boil it till it evaporates. Do *I* boil it? No, I mix it with whiskey and chant over it. I have this prototype .000003-micron superfilter that runs on twelve lithium AA cells, that'll suck the growth rings out of a stump. Put mule piss in and it gives you Saratoga Water. A prototype. What? Around $14,000. No, there are no beaver at this elevation. Everybody wants to camp by the lakes. When you gotta go . . .

I try to stay out of these blighted moods, but it's like trying not to probe a toothache with your tongue. I try to think of the annual invasion as a visit from a hundred thousand close friends, but it never works. Instead, I slouch through the woods, snarling like a Problem Bear.

"Cheryl, I've gotta get off this trail, quick. I'm gonna bite a taxpayer."

Cheryl ignores me and goes on about the meeting and her boss, whom she calls Squirt. In the meeting, Cheryl began by explaining her methods for boiling the raw figures on deposition and chemical concentration down to monthly and annual values. The state regulators responded with caution, the corporados with mannerly skepticism.

There was a tension in the room, to which the veteran regulators and corporados seemed accustomed. I'm not. I have trouble sliding into that polite, adversarial stance. I am used to thinking of my enemies as a faceless aggregate—developers, fascists, coyote-poisoners—and granting the powers of reason and goodness to those individuals I can see. I never quite believe that anyone I've met, whose name I know, can be bad. Irritating, stupid, difficult—all those, but not bad.

There was strain between industry and government: we were trying to build a case for our data set and they were trying to lay a foundation for doubt. Such doubts may involve vast sums and often end up in court. The Exxon vice-president, a courteously taciturn man, made notes on a yellow pad. His suit spoke softly of time more precious than our own.

Another tension had to do with jockeying between the State and the Feds. The DEQ man was concerned that the upcoming Clean Air Act revision could compromise the powers of the state of Wyoming to regulate (or deregulate) its sovereign air. He had the look of a man used to guarding his back, and his front.

Another level of tension smoldered among the Forest crew, all of us accustomed to budget raids and cross purposes, lacking the unity of big money. I'm the feet of the project, Cheryl the fingers, Papa Al the brains, and Squirt, it seemed, was the mouth. He detected sins against higher statistics. He puffed out his chest. He cited his mathematical excellence as a trained biologist. "I am thoroughly familiar with statistics," he said.

"No," Cheryl countered, "you're talking about the statistics of *populations* as opposed to the statistics of *data sets*." Daggers were whizzing above my head.

Squirt kept taking potshots, breaking the pace of Cheryl's argument, turning the attention to himself. She fumed. Her fists balled up. Her face got red. She is big and active, not saintly and all-forgiving. She could be very dangerous. If Cheryl has a motto, it might be: Speak loud, carry a big stick, *and* keep a .357 Mag under the seat.

Cheryl spat nails. Squirt ducked and sniped again. The Exxon engineer, a porcine chap with a gimlet eye who looked like he'd relish a mixed grill of regulators and environmentalists, proved to be a crisp cookie. He looked hard at Squirt, then he quietly scribbled columns of figures on a pad and announced, in a no-more-bullshit tone, that it didn't make one whole hell of a lot of difference whether it was figured Squirt's way or Cheryl's. Exxon to the rescue.

As a rock-ribbed environmentalist, I should automatically despise corporados, but I can't. They refine the gas for my little truck, the propane that cooks my beans back home. I try not to use much of either, but I still need some. Of course, in turn they overcharge, build huge, ugly summer homes, and subvert legislators. I hate it, but those are national failings rather than personal ones.

America gets things done: dig holes, find gold, pipe gas. These men are functionaries of a society that demands gas and oil. Like bomber pilots, they are practical operators. They have the leverage of popular demand.

Wanting to be outside, on the lawn, anywhere but in a meeting, I zoned out. Someday, things might break up badly. I pictured myself crouching in the talus at 11,000 feet, sniping like a tribesman as oil-company gunships wheel down to fire rockets. With me are guerilla wilderness rangers and renegade mountaineers. Our flag curls from a timberline spruce, with Blue Sky Republic in gold letters and a silver coyote on an azure field. Liberty or Death. The rocket's red glare, the bombs bursting in air. I shouldn't daydream in meetings.

Still, there is tension between the world I know and the numerical world in which rules are spun, permits drafted, and penalties assessed. Such things as collection efficiencies are half numbers and half pure observation. I argued that my field notes should stay with the data. Squirt scowled and savaged me again for averaging percentages. Papa Al, who looks and talks like an Anglican bishop, soothed the turmoil, elicited agreements, and gently shook hands all around. After the meeting broke up, I had to talk Cheryl out of hunting Squirt down and beating him to a pulp.

The open slopes along the trail are filled in with needle grass, *Stipa lettermannii*, which marks longtime, heavy sheepgrazing. Sheep prefer small broad-leaved annuals and consume them year after year, until so few produce seed that they disappear. The bare soil is then taken over by tough perennial grasses, so the sheepherders must range their herds higher in search of prime feed, up onto the rocky slopes where there are still broadleaf plant communities. The higher meadows, under greater temperature and moisture stress, are more vulnerable to heavy grazing, so after a span of years they may become barren.

The herds are too big, often 4,000 to 5,000 ewes and lambs. This saves the owners money—sheepherders get around $700 a month and good ones are hard to find—but is tough on the land. Economies of scale—increasing unit production to decrease monetary cost—are ecologically inefficient. When I was a range rider, I asked the herders, Basque, Mexican, and Peruvian, what they thought was wrong up here, and almost all of them said too many sheep. I remember their names: *Carlos Acuturi. Daniel Acuturi. Vidal from Sonora. Nestor and Alcibiades. Javier Segura. Pablo Duran. Eugénio Duran. Leandro Duran. Juan Garmendia.* Too many *borregas* in a band for proper herding in this rough country. *Mucho trabajo en estas montañas.*

There is a place on a high, windswept shoulder north of here called the Sheep Desert, where trailing herds rest and feed after climbing out of a steep canyon. Much of it is bare, mineral soil, washing out, leaving boulders perched on bedrock like balls on a pool table. Too much, too many.

On we tramp, hooves thwocking behind us, getting sleepy in the midafternoon heat. Around us, horseflies vector and spin. Cheryl has exhausted her grievances and I'm tired of being outraged at tourists. We wander around Big Sandy Lake, kicking up dust, yawning. I wonder why I stay with this. It probably won't make any difference. The rain won't look much different, falling out of the air to wash the rock and soil, dirty or not. But water is like blood. So is the air. I think of what I do as a blood test. A blood test isn't simply about blood, but about the body. The air is a medium, circulating, dissolving, transporting. The body is the earth.

Forty years ago, such things were not studied much. The air was a void, and we lived and died and knew not. Comedians joked about the L.A. smog. *Smog* was a new word: it sounded funny. Now, we have densitometry, chromatography, and scattering index. At conferences, we talk about airshed loading and Standard Visual Range. We can demonstrate the niceties of emission, long-range transport, and deposition. We can run the TAPAS model on a sulfate plume and define its vector and spread. We monitor microequivalents-per-liter and parts-per-billion. Postdoctoral consultants beat the electronic drums for the ritual dances of NEPA, EA, EIS, FONSI, and PSD, jockeying the inputs and matrices to equal No Problem, No Sweat, No Significant Impact.

Money circulates, too, lighter than water, but heavier than air. It dissolves and dilutes. It permeates our way of doing the simplest thing. *I can't afford to worry. Think of it as an investment. The bottom line is . . .*

Numbers. Cheryl and I have been drowning in them. Sheet after sheet of printout. Hobbs Lake Bulk Deposition, July 1989, in milligrams per square meter: $Ca = 33.203$; $Mg = 4.35$; $K = 8.08$; $Na = 9.71$; $NH_4 = 4.07$; $NO_3 = 66.54$; $Cl = 14.26$; $SO_4 = 57.72$; $PO_4 = 0$; $H+ = 5.648e\text{-}004$; total precipitation $= 6.79$ cm. That's what was in last month's rain, besides water.

What does this mean? Take SO_4, sulfate, the stuff that turns into sulfuric acid in the rain. In July, one month, 0.058 grams fell on the square meter around the collector. Multiplied, this is 0.58 kilograms of sulfate per hectare. The metric system is great for this, but since these units may not mean much, let's convert to pounds and acres. A kilogram is 2.2 pounds, so we'll multiply again: 1.3 pounds per hectare. A hectare is 2.47 acres, so we'll divide: 0.51 pounds per acre.

Following the same process for nitrate, NO_3, which becomes nitric acid, we come up with 0.59 pounds per acre, last month. The rain collectors are about 90 to 95 percent efficient—they catch ninety to ninety-five raindrops of every hundred—so these figures are conservative. A little of that sulfate and nitrate, about 10 or 15 percent, is natural, what we call background. The rest is the effect, of which we are the cause.

The south end of the range, where we are today, is closer to the sources and gets heavier loads. Let's calculate last month's deposition for Black Joe Lake. Sulfate, SO_4 = 88.79 milligrams per square meter. That yields 0.88 kilograms per hectare, or 0.79 pounds per acre. Nitrate, NO_3 = 111.13 mg/m². That comes out to 0.99 pounds per acre. This collector gets stronger winds, so it's probably 5 to 10 percent less efficient than the one at Hobbs Lake, thus we could correct our monthly deposition to a little more than one pound per acre.

When I first calculated these values, I started with grams instead of milligrams, because that's what Cheryl had mistakenly entered above the columns. So I came up with 887.9 kilos per hectare, or almost a half ton per acre. This upset me. "Holy Sebastian," I raved on the phone to Cheryl. "Either the units are wrong or the backpackers are going to melt next time it rains. We'll have a slew of Wrongful-Death-by-Melting lawsuits. Jeez Louise, at this level the lakes should be about pH 2. Vinegar is only 3.5."

Cheryl called Papa Al. "The units are wrong," he said. "Should be milligrams: divide by a thousand."

It was a relief. But when you start multiplying that one pound per acre by the number of acres, 428,169, in the Bridger Wilderness, you get 428,169 pounds of sulfate deposited in the month of July: 214 tons, a good bit. Of course it's not that simple. The amount of deposition changes with altitude and aspect and wind direction. The worst air comes from the south and southwest, having passed over Los Angeles, Las Vegas, Salt Lake City, and everything in between.

On mornings in August, I see the oncoming haze, a shroud of yellow and gray. Salt Lake City wakes up, eats, groans, locks the door, starts the car, and rolls up the ramp onto I-15. In the mid-eighties, the three urban counties in northern Utah sent up an average of 80,500 tons of SO_2 and 58,356 tons of NO_x each year, a lot of which rides northeast in summer clouds, our way.

The emissions are probably higher now: more people, more cars. August heat. The old woman lurches from her bed and gropes for the air conditioner. The foreman of the coke plant checks his gauges. The broker flips a rocker switch and gazes into the green glare of his terminal. I-15 glints like a dragon, with rainbow scales and a hundred thousand glass eyes, wavering in the heat. From the body electric, the numeric grid, the teeming avenues, exhaust rises like hot, gray breath.

From coal, the burnt sulfur rises mostly as sulfur dioxide, SO_2. The Naughton Power Plant, near Kemmerer, Wyoming, is fueled by an open-pit mine, a mile long, a half mile wide, and a thousand feet deep. The coal burned by the plant, 2.5 million tons a year, is fairly high in sulfur. The state is leaning hard on the plant to reduce its SO_2 emissions. It has a permit for 25,820 tons a year and sends out twice that, or more, along with at least 21,980 tons of NO_x. The larger Jim Bridger Plant, southeast of Rock Springs, was putting out about 65,000 tons a year of SO_2 and a similar amount of NO_x in 1985. With state-mandated scrubbers, the sulfur has been halved, to about 31,000 tons a year.

The flies are bad today, thick as consultants. I could probably get a consulting job, but columns of numbers have a way of staring me down. So, I'd rather be up here, dragging two packhorses, staying poor, listening to Cheryl's woes taper off as she gets breathless with the climb. Like Saint Brendan said: "A pox on poxy fughing meetings." I'm having a good meeting now, between my feet and the earth. No reason to doubt this place. A granite boulder doesn't claim to be limestone. Engelmann spruces don't hatch plots to oust the subalpine firs. Nobody sues a lightning bolt.

We chug up toward the high lake and camp where I don't think a bear would want to go, wading a fast creek and finding a strong-hold in the rocks. Cheryl is still nervous, so I pile some bear-discouraging cobbles to fling during the night and put a horsebell in the tent. "It's a black bear, probably a yearling. You weigh more than it does." She huffs and glares at me. "Not only that—you're more ferocious."

"I'll die." She rolls her eyes, so I dance around and yell some random swearwords in Navajo, telling her it's the Anti-Bear Chant. *Shash* means "bear." I holler the words for beer, meat, bullshit, pickup, sheep, horse, snake, dog, crazy, mountain, and whis-key, sticking in an occasional *Shash* and random conjunctions. To wind up, I shriek *Na' nizhoozhi!* which means "Gallup, New Mex-ico." That's it. Never failed yet, I say. She's reassured. We roll out sleeping bags and cook. After dinner, I tell her a bear story.

I had a friend, Hazardous Joe, a walking statistic. When we'd go climbing, he'd see a girl someplace, trip over the rope, and fall off the belay ledge. He was famous for sudden forty-foot leader falls, always zipping at least two pieces and flipping head down. When we went ice-climbing, he got clocked in the forehead by falling ice and sprayed a big rising sun of blood on the frozen waterfall. I tied him off, rappelled, butterfly-bandaged the gash, climbed back up to my anchor, and got ready to belay him up. Instead of climbing, he dug for his camera to get a picture of his own blood-spatter. *Bad* instincts.

But about the bear. Joe, seeking an adventure of broader dimen-sions than falling off belay ledges, went to Alaska. One afternoon he was hiking, pockets stuffed with munchies, and met a bear. Since it was Alaska, the bear should have been a mighty brown, but it wasn't. It was a lowly black bear, although one of good size and weight. The difference is significant in light of what followed.

The bear growled at Hazardous Joe and sniffed in his direction. He had heard, someplace, that the only way to survive a grizzly attack was to roll in a ball and play dead. The bear growled again, so Hazardous Joe prostrated himself and curled into a politically correct ball. The bear had not attacked, nor was it a grizzly.

The bear, curious, strode over and sniffed this oddity: a healthy male human being acting like a baby rabbit. Hmmmm. The bear sniffed the munchies in Joe's pocket. Joe, drawing on his reserves of Inner Zen, remained rock still. The moment stretched.

Then the bear bit Joe's pocket, hooking a tooth in his thigh. Joe abandoned Inner Zen. *Fucker!* he howled and punched the bear on the rubbery nose. The bear jumped up and ran off.

Joe was bleeding, but not dangerously. His leg hurt like hell. Unwilling to risk another encounter with the bear, he made his escape by limping to the nearby river and leaping in, following which he almost drowned. He told me the tale himself, without a hint of irony.

Cheryl doesn't like the story. Too much falling and biting. I wander away from camp to watch the sunset. Stony blues hide under the peaks, inlaid with steep remnant snow. Under an approaching storm, the light is a milky, roseate orange, rippled with blue shadows, fading to turbulent, purple-shot grays. Thunder and lightning tonight. I go back and tell Cheryl about the approaching storm. "Great," she says. "We'll get hit by lightning, and the bear will devour our roasted bodies. I can't wait." We zip up and tuck in.

The chant works. No bear arrives in the dark. The horses behave. I actually get some sleep between storms, and the storms are fine ones, with roaring gusts, big booms, and scary flashes.

There are large, shallow deposits of low-sulfur gas hemmed by the Wind River Range, the Wyoming Range to the west, and the Uintas and Bear River ranges to the south. In the 1960s, natural gas was found in a deep geologic structure, at 14,000 to 18,000 feet, east of the overthrust that forms the Wyoming Range. The reserves are estimated to be 20 to 30 trillion cubic feet of low-grade, or sour, gas. Sour as in sulfuric acid.

In the early 1980s several corporations proposed drilling and processing the sour gas, but only Exxon followed through, building about a quarter of the total capacity first proposed. The depth of the deposit required the use of heavy-duty, deephole rigs and considerable manpower. The mid-eighties saw the upper Green in a boom of trailer hookups, prefab motels, and convenience stores. A lesser boom occurred when a drilling rig blew out west of Big Piney, gassing a herd of antelope with hydrogen sulfide. Investigation revealed that the oilfield contractor had installed the costly, high-tech blowout preventer upside down.

High times and wild nights. We even had hookers, one of whom gained local fame for transiting nightspots in nothing but stockings, heels, and a black leather coat. When the drilling was done, the froth ran back down the hill while high-interest loans chewed up the survivors. It was like watching an avalanche melt out, leaving a stack of broken pines.

The state of Wyoming and the Forest Service put a requirement in the industrial siting permit to move the gas processing plant south, which aimed the plume at the southern end of the Wind Rivers rather than at their heart. If you drive north from Kemmerer, you can see the plant, like a goblin castle, east of the lonely road. At night, its lights are a strident yellow.

Sour gas contains 67 percent carbon dioxide, 20 percent methane, 8 percent nitrogen, 4 percent hydrogen sulfide, 1 percent helium, and water vapor. To reduce this to marketable natural gas takes several stages of processing. The initial stage is dehydration, which gets the water vapor out. Before dehydration, sour gas eats the inside of pipelines "like mother-fucking atomic termites," said an inside source, after nine beers.

After dehydration, the gas is shoved inside massive pipes to the main processing plant. The whole smack—CO_2, CH_4, N_2, H_2S, and He—goes into the "sweetener." The "sweet" gas, CH_4, N_2, and He, is what results from pizza and beer (not sweet to anyone but Exxon). This goes to the nitrogen rejection unit, which kicks the nitrogen and helium into the air, yielding 97 percent pure methane. The leftovers, CO_2 and H_2S, go to the sulfur recovery unit. Carbon dioxide, one of the gases-of-concern in global warming, is vented in the millions of tons. Legally, it's not considered air pollution. Exxon somehow manages to get huge tax exemptions in the process. The remaining murk goes to a tail-gas clean-up unit and then to an incinerator which emits more CO_2 and also a few big whacks of SO_2. Despite this, natural gas is a clean fuel compared to coal or oil. And the plant is clean, too, compared to the coal-fired power plants and cities upwind.

On a map of Wyoming, if you center your right palm on the Continental Divide, the Naughton Plant will be just off the base of your thumb, and the Bridger Plant close to your wristbone on the other side. Under the ball of your thumb are huge natural gas fields and processing plants.

Starting up a gas field is dirty. At the start, 1983, Chevron's Carter Creek Plant sent up 29,779 tons of SO_2. Now it produces 1,350 tons a year. Amoco's Whitney Canyon Plant, starting that same year, emitted 18,910 tons of SO_2. Now it puts out 6,400 tons. Exxon's Shute Creek Plant, the one that caused the furor that got this project started, began in 1986 with 8,500 tons of SO_2. Now it releases about 1,500. Added up, these three gas plants emit less than a third the sulfur of either coal-fired power plant.

There are also soda ash plants, phosphate plants, coking plants, the towns of Evanston, Green River, Rock Springs, and Kemmerer, and the constant traffic of I-80. The total permitted emissions for southwest Wyoming—permitted means from large, stationary, regulated sources—are 96,856 tons per year of SO_2 and 106,862 tons of NO_x. If the Clean Air Act is reauthorized, a likely result will be to drive industrial air pollution out of urban zones and into sparsely populated and politically conservative areas like southwest Wyoming. This is the view from the wilderness, looking into the prevailing wind.

Rising sun. The ground is wet with night rain, the lake black under its cliff, burnished by silence. I hold a breath, four beats, and let it go. A dawn wind lifts my hair, brushes the lake with silver. I look back at Temple's north face, blue in a glancing light: shins and thighs of rock, skirted by hanging ice gardens under a choppy ridge, like a pyramid hacked by giants. Thunderstorms have cleared the air. Remoteness has a smell. Not whitebarks or rockfall or melting snow or bear den or any single scent that can be named.

I walk back to camp and start the stove. Cheryl wakes up as the wind rises, and we sit around camp eating and watching the pines pitch in the gusts. We hike up to the lake, and it's too choppy to put the boat out. The wind whirs in the pinetops and tears spray off the lake. We wait. Finally, I decide not to risk it. Cheryl gets nervous in a small boat in a high wind and drops things into the lake. Last time she dropped the cap for the formalin bottle. I get nervous, thinking she might want to row the boat again. Her last try was memorable for both of us. "Let's skip the lake," I say. "Jim will be back from the forest fires next week, and we'll come up and try then." She agrees, relieved. The part of our work—numbers, budgets, agency politics—that threatens me is her preferred realm. She's bright: she'll do well.

We hike over and change the bottles on the rain collector. "Wonder what we got this time," she says, peering at the water in the plastic jug.

"Disposable diapers and wads of bubblegum. We'll send it in and find out."

It's hard to get poetry out of your system. I found a lovely line in a scientific report: *In the Greenland ice, man-caused emission swamps all natural sources of sulfate.* That has a Whitman-esque lope. What would he say, Old Walt? *Sulfur dioxide! Rude phytotoxin! Acid precursor! Fuming and mastering the interminable, sweet-aired plateaus.* When you slice an onion, sulfur compounds are released. When they are deposited in your eye, they react to form H_2SO_4: sulfuric acid. That's what makes your eyes burn.

Once, from an airliner leaving Salt Lake City, I watched heat trailing from the black turbines on takeoff, the flaps wheezing into the wing, the falling profile of low hills and the net of highways. I saw the air itself passing over the city, brown as unwatered grass, simmering under the grand facade of the Wasatch, lapping over passes, Emigration, Parleys, Echo Summit, eddying like mustard gas round the blue Uinta shoulder. As the plane rose east, so did the air, thickening over the mines and dynamos of southwest Wyoming, lifting plumes of construction dust and dust from the soda ash plants, dust from the phosphate plants, fingering north and east like a hand to touch the Wind River Range.

I was flying to New York City to read my work at the National Arts Club. I had a written itinerary and a handler named Frazier, a black-jacketed artguy with wit, charm, complexes, and towering hair. Linda had a new black dress. The reservations were all made, the tables booked. I've never had the courage to calculate the impact in gallons-per-poem. From New York, we flew to Minneapolis, then Cincinnati. There were major and minor contacts, ephemeral regards, a welter of intention and ambition. I was curiosity-of-the-week.

Nitrogen is common stuff. Most of what we call air is nitrogen. When it passes through a flame, some of it oxidizes. It can become nitrous oxide—NO, laughing gas—or NO_2, nitrogen dioxide. These oxides of nitrogen are called NO_x, Nox, the source of many obnoxious puns. If SO_2 is the fell right hand of acid rain, then NO_x is the left.

Strike a match. Smell it discreetly; don't suck the flame up your nose. The first puff is high in sulfur, and after that there's NO_x. The biggest source is cars. It can travel long distances from the source, diffusing as it goes, before coming to earth. When water vapor condenses, NO_x droppeth as the gentle rain from heaven, becoming HNO_3, nitric acid. The evidence says this is the prime culprit in forest death. It destroys the nutrient cycle in soil and kills trees.

Twenty years ago, it was just Gene Likens and Herbert Bormann squeaking valiantly about acid rain, along with a pack of gloomy Norwegians. By now we've had baseline studies and studies of the studies and analyses of the studies and assessments of the analyses. We're getting smart: we can almost define what's going on in the air, why it's frightening and terrible, and what consequences here may be, all nicely graphed in one-year increments.

So, we have Air Quality conferences and Air Quality training sessions. We sign out official cars to drive to Denver where we produce lists of AQRVs leading to LACs for PSD management of our CAA Class I airsheds. The Grand Wizard always wraps up with a speech underlining the need for more funds. Then, with wads of phone numbers, hungover, and coffee'd out, we fill up with gas and drive back home.

It's good to be here, even as the sulfate and nitrate rain down. So far, the acids are somehow buffered in the scanty soil, and the lakes have not died. This is the miracle. Not that wilderness boundaries can hope to preserve this remnant, but that the earth is so muscular, so impervious, so surly and contrary and rude.

So, I'd rather be up here, looking at mountains. I have my favorite parts of this hard-ass, unproductive, high-elevation wasteland, like the parabolic stoop of the east wall of Ambush. The tapered Egyptian column of East Temple Spire. Such names, as if we'd built these peaks: Steeple, Rampart, Pedestal, Bastion, Monolith, Sphinx. Weep, architect, weep. I remember the Gothic east buttress of Haystack, which you can see from where we take inlet samples at the head of the windy lake, a heavy, polished crescent of stone, conifers gathering below like a festival crowd.

We stuff the panniers and pack the horses. The outlet creek, cascading down its narrow gullet of rock, roars and fades in the gusts as we contour down the ridge. It's a cool walk, down the rain-wet trail under big spruce and fir. From Big Sandy Lake onward, we hear bear tales. The bear tore into an empty tent and ate a can of Skoal. It shamelessly devoured a package of jerky and wouldn't run away.

Two years ago, hiking up the narrow ridge to Black Joe Lake, I saw a speck of yellow in a pine off the trail. It was a burst balloon, snagged on a branch. With a fallen limb, I hooked it down. Tied to it was a plastic-coated card. On one side was a teacher's name and the address of an elementary school in Sandy, Utah, south of Salt Lake City. It had been released the day before. I taught in Sandy, as a Poet-in-the-Schools, classes of pretty, suburban children. Sandy is just south of Big Cottonwood Canyon, where my great-great-grandfather staked out his ranch in the 1850s. On the other side of the card were names, the loops and scrawls of a kindergarten class.

Brooke. Beth. Lori. Vivian. Nathan. Cory. Nicole. Esther. Joshua. Laura. Brian. Kati. Suzie. Galvin. Tabitha. Travis. Mort. I can picture them, ritually solemn, laboriously signing their names. This is the hard part. To see all sides, children's faces and air pollution in tons-per-year. As long as I can see faces, I understand. Everything I've been told makes perfect sense, why we live this way, why the process must go on.

But when I get out here, when a solitaire cries at the edge of the pines, I lose the words. I can't think of a word for the way light comes under a cloud or the color of shadow under a cliff. Words make no sense at all. Being here does.

Part VI: Rain's Face, Snow's Mind

16

Water is water's only truth.

Dogen (1200–1253)

*A*lone, in a gray boat on a black lake, cold water cupped in bed-rock above ten thousand feet. No moon, no wind. A sky of high, thin clouds and scattered stars. The Milky Way is an arch, north to south. The water is motionless. Each breath seems like a shout. I row with short, even strokes, trying not to splash, and the boat rises and dips with each thrust of the oars. My marker light, a candle lantern on a shoreline boulder, throws cat-eyes in the wake. I pull the left oar, turn the boat south. The flame diminishes from a leaf to an eye to a wavering dot. I round the point and then it's gone.

Rowing into the dark seems wrong, something not to be done, like backing up to the edge of a cliff. Straining to look over my right shoulder, then my left, I realize there's not much here for the eyes. When I pause between strokes I feel an uneasy silence.

Darkness pales around the granite outcrops and gathers in the pines. It echoes the shape of high ridges and opens at the sharp horizon into stars. In the lake, the deepest black of all, the stars swim with an ominous, flat glint. The surface seems less like a mirror than like a window. I stop rowing and look down. The window opens on a galaxy beneath, a membrane between two facing

270

voids. There is no up or down, only out. The night listens, leaning in. I start to row and miss a stroke and the splash licks my face with chill.

I should be near the deepest spot, east of center between a white cliff and a silver snag of dead pine. Peering into the dark, I try to make them out. The muscles behind my eyes strain with the effort. There's the cliff. The dead pine must be about . . . there, even if I can't be sure. This feels right. I ship the oars and drift into quiet. Little, cold feet walk up my back. The hardest thing to do is nothing: to sit and let my eyes develop that slight, empty ache that comes when there is nowhere for the gaze to rest. The water settles around the raft, with pats and murmurs.

A lake has distinct edges, a bed in which it rests and a skin of surface tension. It is bound to the rest of the world in more ways than we know: inflow, outflow, groundwater, gas exchange, thermal balance, growth, death, decomposition, sediment, beauty.

I know this lake in daylight. I have a name for it and a sheaf of numbers: elevation, 10,069 feet; depth, 58 feet; surface area, 20 acres; volume, 680 acre feet. Its alkalinity—acid-buffering capacity—ranges from around 50 μeq/l to 134 μeq/l, compared to alkalinities around 2,000 μeq/l for lakes in the limestone of the nearby Gros Ventre Range. We're sampling every four hours to find the variation in the lake's chemistry during a single day and night. Otherwise, we might mistake a change as coming from air pollution, when it results from one sample being dipped at 8:00 A.M. and the next at 5:00 P.M.

At sunrise, the phytoplankton start work, the cyanobacteria begin photosynthesis, and some zooplankton dive for the dark while others rise into the light. At night, the photosynthesizers rest while the grazers and predators roam in the millions, perhaps billions. Their life processes change the chemistry of the water in cycles, adding oxygen, then consuming it; taking carbon from gases and fixing it in organic compounds. A lake changes as much between sleep and waking as we do, maybe more. But a lake is not a sum of separate measurements: it should be thought of as a single, living body, its organisms not so much like persons as like cells. The study of any part—like that of the brain or the heart—must be linked to the functioning of the whole.

I've come here before to catch this water in bottles, subject it to a pH meter and the slow drip of acid titration, to take its temperature and seine it for plankton. I've labeled it, packed it out of the mountains, filtered it, preserved it, and shipped it to far-off labs where people I've never met run detailed assays: aluminum, calcium, carbon, chloride, fluoride, iron, lead, magnesium, manganese, ammonium, nitrate, phosphate, potassium, silica, sulfate.

I've touched this water, tasted it. I've caught and eaten its trout, scooped it into pots for coffee, mixed it with my blood, taught it to walk and tell lies, and pissed it back steaming onto the ground. This lake and I have more than a casual acquaintance, yet in the dark it seems not to know me. I can't see my reflection. The water that has claimed a part of my life now holds me in a star-flecked indifference.

To be unrecognized is often to be afraid. So much of our existence is based on recognitions, gestures of longing and belonging, kisses, nations, companies, handgrips, families, clans, and classes. Do we have real selves or do we collect the visions of others, bundle them, and call the sum a self? We go our way in groups and are comforted by it more than we are oppressed: most of us fear solitude more than punishment.

In that, at least, we are not alone. Elk form into bands, cattle into herds. We need to touch each other. Untouched infants fail to grow and thrive; they may even suffer brain damage. Lacking the scent and touch of one's own kind prefigures death. The nudge of fear creates forms as diverse as wolfpacks and universities.

I'm rationalizing, but I'm still afraid. No reason to doubt the boat, a tight, compact Avon inflatable that could float a small elephant. The weather is a threat up here, where sudden winds can tear down trees, where it can snow in any month. But from the sky, I have little to fear. Apart from mild night breezes, it will stay open and calm above tattered clouds.

I could fear my own error: Li Po, the Old Wine Genius of Chinese poetry, is said to have died while drunk, leaning from a boat to embrace the moon's reflection. He fell through the white dazzle and drowned.

I have neither wine nor moon, though either would be welcome. I don't have the absolute clumsiness it would take to fall from a rubber boat on a glassy lake, yet I have a palpable sense of threat. As the boat ceases to drift, the silence hovers, sheer and inhuman.

Beyond our lives, as Roosevelt said, looms fear itself. He paraphrased Thoreau, who wrote "Nothing is so much to be feared as fear." Thoreau may have borrowed from Francis Bacon, "Nothing is terrible except fear itself."

Given the state of the world, there are few places safer than the center of an alpine lake on a fine, black night. Graver by far to be an overweight investor, asleep in a redwood house atop the San Andreas Fault. If the promised earthquake holds off through the night and his heart keeps its weary rhythm, he'll commute up the iron flood of Route 101, dependent on the collective judgment of all within crashing range, all workers having bad days, the radial belts in his tires, the pilots lifting and landing 747s at the airport, the wiring of safety sirens in chemical plants, the pressured engineers who planned the freeway bridges and the contractors who poured them, and every pissed-off laborer who tied steel or grouted the joints.

I breathe the air. It tastes of night, of water and altitude. I pet the slick rubber of the boat. I slip my right hand into the lake's shifting black. Cold, but no monster rises and gapes. Just cold. Just darkness. I hold it under until the chill needles, puckers, reaches the bone.

I take my hand from the lake and hold it between my thighs until it's warm. I find a bottle, uncap it, and hold it under. Three rinses. I count them to myself. Then I plunge the bottle a half meter— about twenty inches—under the surface and let it fill. This is our protocol. Distorted by the water, the white bottle looks strange in my pale hand, like a ghost, open mouthed, in the arms of another. My left hand holds the cap and turns it tight after the last bubble rises. This is the sample from the upper layer, the epilimnion.

I grope for the Van Dorn bottle—every scientific device seems to be burdened with the name of its creator—and find it, round, hard, and improbable: a plexiglas tube, stoppered at each end by caps held by a fingerthick rubber cord. The caps are held open by loops swaged in thin steel cable, each hooked to the trigger bar.

Now I need light. I find the flashlight and snap it on and feel the whole galaxy miss a breath. I find the gray box of the temperature gauge and lower the probe on its squeaky blue cable, stopping every five feet to read the meter. The surface is two degrees colder than it was at ten o'clock, but below the surface the temperatures have not changed. I raise the probe, coil the cable, and stow the gauge. In the spot of light, I center the notebook and log the temperature. I clamp the flashlight in my teeth, needing both hands to cock the Van Dorn bottle.

I hoist it over the tube of the raft and lower it on white nylon line, counting blue marks for tens and red for fives, to the hypolimnion, where cold water rests through the short summer as the shallower layers warm. I watch the marks on the rope, four blues, then a red. The bottle is halfway between the thermocline and the lakebed.

I find the messenger, a cylindrical brass weight that slips down the rope to trigger the closing of the bottle. I slot it over the rope, let the collar snap shut, and drop it. Then I wait, snapping the light off as I feel a faint *chunk* vibrating up the rope. I haul it back. The loaded bottle is heavy. This feels different than catching a fish, hooking into that live resistance, that slippery potential. This feels inert, like a dead cat. The weight of evidence. My pupils bloom to admit starlight as I raise the bottle and plop it into the boat.

The gift of this work, low paid and seasonal, is partly in its being chosen. There is no place, according to my loyalties, where I can do more good; no place where I will do less harm. A gifted nurse works for each patient rather than for the hospital. The finest painters are rarely loyal to art, but instead attend to a naked body, a blue chair, a passing light.

In the Forest Service, one may choose to work instead for the forest: to follow a deeper grain. You won't achieve high rank, but you may get to know the woods. Your dream will be attacked from all sides: you will be counseled to sacrifice your sense of right and wrong to a career. In the bar, a derrickhand will accuse you of being an enemy of working people, of locking up resources for the rich. The rich, who wish to preserve this beauty for their amusement, will look narrowly at you as an agent of the great unwashed.

A close friend, who works as a carpenter in Jackson Hole, will call you an enemy of the earth, a Fuckin' Freddy. Quit the bastards, he will urge. But there are not many ways to live in the woods.

You can help cut them down. Erect summer cabins. You can write a guidebook, or lead overlarge groups on climbs or nature walks. You can barter nine months in a classroom for three up here. What will you have gained?

A passing acquaintance, a visit, an affair. *The marriage of people to a place may be close and considerate, and it may be hardly more than sanctioned rape.* Wallace Stegner wrote that.

What do I have, besides these instruments, this boat, this task? Little enough. This night. This darkness, surrounded by water. Thoughts that stretch for miles and days.

I want to know my proper work and attend to it. There are moments I owe to this marriage, visions possible in only one intersection of water and light. There are wonders that happen only once in a life. If imagination alone doesn't demand this night alone, then I'm grateful for the task that does, even in the bitterness of it.

Because we turn on our lights this night, as all nights. Because we drive to work, board aircraft, depend on electricity as on a heartbeat. I carry a double image of wilderness: as the nest of some marvelous, inviolate, eternal beast, and as a last refuge, dwindling, tainted, forlorn. I don't know how you think of it. But it doesn't help to confuse my ideas with where I am: this place is not my thought.

I decided it would be best to read the land as my book of life. I've read Emerson, Jeffers, Han Shan. I try to read Thoreau. I flunked a class, Thoreau's Prose Writings, because I hitchhiked south to spend a month walking in the redrock canyons, never taking the final exam. It wasn't the best way to get through school. Or maybe it was.

It's hard to tell what part of my feelings come from books and legends. It's hard to say what I know of the place itself, rock, water, air. I can't drift forever. Sooner or later I'll come to shore. Lakes change. Ice melts. Surface layers warm and cool, wind mixes them. Zooplankton rise and fall in the water column. Nymphs in inlet streams emerge from gargoyle skins to fly like dandelion fluff. Trout feed on them or doze, flicking their tails and dreaming with open

eyes, their muscular pink flesh silked and papered into rooms as delicate as Japanese houses.

In camp, my partner sleeps uneasily. Jim, John, Marty, Bill, Tuck, Piers, Enkidu, whatever he's called. He was tossing and groaning as I left. Under an old Engelmann spruce are meters and flasks. Soon, I'll row back with the water. I'll climb out onto the rock with full bottles in a white net sack. Soon, in a weak circle of light, primed with a chemical indicator, the water will change color according to the measured drip of acid.

I'll record numbers for each act, create analogues for what I see, abstract-impressionist renderings of this lake and its life. The numbers will be sorted, crunched, regressed, tested, and distilled. They have been brought into being, they exist. What about visions? If I saw an angel drifting above the lake, who would believe me, even though we look for omens, clues to this lake's future and by extension, human fate?

But we burn no sage, consult no gods. Sometimes, camped up here, I hear owls call from the dark. If I spoke a question and an owl called back, there would be nothing in it for a computer to digest. What can an owl give to me? An acknowledgment? A warning? A cry of hunger in the dark?

I gather fragments. From broken pieces, archaeologists may reconstruct pots, urns, *ollas*. By means of computer-aided topography, they may plot from a single piece the shape of a pot that was shattered in anger twenty centuries ago. Its outline may be traced, its use inferred. Theories may be posed to account for its form, its constituents, its location, and its abandonment. Yet a pot can be made only once. A broken pot has become something else: sherds, fragments, data. The idea remains, but it won't hold water.

This lake holds water. I listen to its mild, measured pat on rubberized fabric. Cool, clear, etc. Water that you can drink, our essence. In woman, water, and darkness, so are we made. *E' í yá' át' ééh*, it is good. Up here in the bright granite, it hangs near-distilled, almost pure, holy as anything on this whole scalped continent.

Rain gathers here, and snowmelt. Spattering and gathering, from rock into rivulet, fall, brook, creek, cascade, over ledge and talus, sheepshead and wall, gathering to this one lake. Here it rests, carrying life in its body. Then it proceeds, threading boulders to the outlet pond, tumbling a thousand feet down to Gorge Lake, Suicide Lake, Long Lake, Frémont Lake, Pine Creek, the New Fork River, the Green, the Colorado, and perhaps the sea, if it hasn't been evaporated from a reservoir or the cooling towers of a power plant, hasn't been ditched or piped for alfalfa, thirsty cattle, or thirstier cities.

No doubt these waters are tainted—or significantly affected as a scientist would prefer to say. The question is one of degree. The increments of distress are not immediately visible, the water still almost pure, yet, a year or a decade farther on, will a certain species of daphnia cease to exist in this lake, or a pH-sensitive mayfly fail to reproduce in the inlet stream? Will there be X percent mortality of trout as a result? Will anyone sue? Will mining jobs be lost in Kemmerer? Will alarm bells clang in the New York Stock Exchange? Will a famous tenor become hoarse?

At what threshold of contamination does wilderness become, in our minds, something else, a wasteland with rocks and trees? What if after due argument and interpretation the studies read: *measurable though not necessarily significant degradation of water-resource quality, given present concentrations of airborne acid precursors, and assuming no significant augmentation or spatial redistribution of point-sources or load-levels.*

Will that move you to action, that Byzantine chant?

Scientists swarm through these peaks, taking cores from lakebeds and glaciers, clipping foliage and scraping lichens, carrying bits and pieces back to labs from Maine to California, whispering and hunkering at conferences, avoiding the obvious. Their conclusions will differ, though it's probably safe to say no one will claim beneficial effects on alpine ecosystems from airborne pollutants. Probably.

Thoughts remove you from a place. I take a breath and look around at the night's sparse evidence. In the open darkness, I feel safe, even loved. After my thoughts, the lake and the sky seem clean and perfect, without contradiction. My hands are cold. I should have worn my rubber gloves. I reach for the oars. They pivot smoothly in their locks, with faint squeaks, but I'm not ready to go yet, to clamber back onto the rock of the world, to bow to my meters and flasks, to admit to numbers and names, duties and debts, tents to be folded and horses to catch.

I like this silence, in which there is hunger but no greed. I feel the urge that drew Li Po out of the boat into the moon's reflection, an image which offered nothing yet contained all. The reflection of light on water has no measurable depth. Even so, stars wink at me from the lake.

This change, from fear to calm, has come over me many times, but it doesn't take. It is as real as the water and the night, but it is nothing I can teach. It burns like beauty in the bones. It comes and goes. It will not abide.

I feel the air on my face, the cloth against my neck and the backs of my arms, the weight of my arms in my shoulders. The oars in my hands. I dip and pull. The blades enter the lake almost without sound. The stars turn, the world turns. I check and pull and the boat surges, rounding the invisible rocky point.

I stop and look. Ahead, the candle in its tiny lantern still burns, warmer and closer than stars. The path of dancing light has no depth, but I see it. I steer along it, the bow of the raft swallowing the glancing flames, and when I pass, it's gone.

Ahead, between the boat and the shore, it wavers and runs true. Surrounded by the cool stars, it floats, gold as willow leaves, and on it I return.

17

How to speak of life and death?
We could just talk about water and ice . . .

Han Shan, *Cold Mountain Poems*

*I*t's late September, snowing at Black Joe Lake, but the snow is half rain, half soft, white pellets, the yield of turbulence in the upper air. We have inflated the raft and turned it upside down on the south shore over the pile of gear. The wind hoots over the abandoned rockfill dam. We retreat into ragged spruces to wait it out, watching black rollers form and leave, east, up the long lake.

No two lakes are identical, but there are resemblances. What comes, in our bodies, from genotype proceeds in lakes from geology, climate, and elevation. Lakes are born. They age and die. The lake that claims a basin carved in granite when a glacier retreats is an infant, vigorous and clean. Black Joe Lake fills a glacial canyon, a steep-sided trough. The ridge of Haystack Peak cuts off sunlight for much of the year, so this glacier probably melted later than the surrounding ones. The peak's shadow still keeps the lake cool. Black Joe Lake is young. A lake that has accepted spring floods with their burdens of mud and corpses, their cascades of black soil and leaves, a lake that has received the spoil and bounty of a watershed for millennia, each year's deposit laid down on the lakebed like a quilt until the stack reaches the ceiling: this lake is old. It holds more earth than water, more memory than life.

The wind has been rising, the cloudcap lowering. Jim forgot half the lunch. I asked him to pack *the* lunch, but he packed *his* lunch. *The* lunch feeds two. This is my custom, and John's and Marty's, but not yet Jim's. I try not to watch him eat, but it's hard. He finally gets guilty enough to give me half, with a joke to cover the awkwardness: half of a pressed-meat sandwich, half a Pop-Tart, half an apple, half a handful of gummy candy, molded into dinosaur shapes. Food is important, but his gesture means more. Not even conscious of a test, he has passed.

With a glance, I welcome him into the clan. He feels something, but doesn't know what it is. He's bewildered by love. He and Elizabeth are together the whole time he's out of the mountains. He's quieter, deeper, calmer: more mature than at the beginning of summer. The moment lingers, then the wind blows it east, over the Divide. We watch the lake and the storm. In this narrow throat of stone, each day the shadows grow and the lake is colder. In a month it will freeze.

A lake is like a living body. There is no single part that can exist alone. Each organ contributes to the entirety and draws life from it. We, too, are mostly water, existing in a distinct shape, exchanging solid, liquid, and gaseous substances with our surroundings. A lake is not just water any more than we are the water in our cells.

Water has much to do with the way the world looks to us, smells to us, how it supports our lives. One H and two Os. The hydrogen atom and the two oxygen atoms it attracts form a triangular bond. It isn't a strong bond, but its geometry and electric properties make it unique. Every molecule of water has a kind of social instinct: it forms a set of hydrogen bonds to the nearest four water molecules. In ice, this is a fairly stable structure, an open lattice of triangles that form regular tetrahedrons. The space within this lattice is what makes ice float.

What if ice didn't float? The lakes in the Wind Rivers would all freeze from the bottom up, and the trout would die. Water couldn't stay liquid beneath ice.

In the terms we call physics, it is hard to change the temperature of water. Only liquid ammonia, liquid hydrogen, and molten lithium have a higher specific heat than water. It takes one calorie to heat up one cc (or gram) of water one degree centigrade. For a one-degree rise, liquid ammonia absorbs 1.23 calories and liquid hydrogen 3.4. In comparison, the average rock has a specific heat of 0.2 calories. This means that water can absorb a lot of heat without changing its state, a property called thermal inertia. Bodies of water absorb heat from the summer sun and hold it. This is why the coasts are protected from the great temperature ranges of the continental interior. It's why peach trees do well in northern Utah, along the steep mountain front east of the Great Salt Lake. It's why a lake steams on cold mornings.

Another quirk of water is that it resists changes in state: from solid to liquid to vapor. This is why our highest lakes stay frozen until mid-July, past the solstice. A gram of ice on the point of melting will absorb eighty calories *before* warming up that one degree, to become a droplet. This is called the latent heat of fusion. In turn, when water changes back to ice, it gives up all that heat, which is why our lakes steam and circulate, sending vapor to the sky as they lose heat in the cold fall nights.

The storm breaks, but there are reefs of cloud to the west, gray banners flying from the peaks. We hurry to get on the lake. Jim rows the boat. I sit and look at the heaving water, then at him: goatskin gloves, hairy wrists poking out of his new anorak, orange life vest with white piping, whiskers on his unshaven chin. I lean far back in the raft and aim the camera. He arranges his mouth, suppressing the tiny grunts he makes with each pull of the oars. In the left lens of his sunglasses, I see my blue windbreaker, a jutting elbow, a red cap, water, the far shore. Around his head is a blue bandanna, rolled and knotted. His brown hair catches wind under his hood, ruffed like a colt's mane. He and Elizabeth are as inseparable as two people working in different ranges of mountains can be. He has assumed a new state, larger and darker in my eyes. Such is the gravity in our flesh.

One of the prevailing mysteries of our bodies is circulation. Medieval doctors saw this as a balance of four humors: blood, phlegm, choler, and bile. These echoed the four elements: earth, air, fire, and water. Health and character both proceeded from the relative amounts of the humors. Bleeding and purging were attempts to restore them to a proper balance. In China, physicians drew maps of vital currents, which they saw as electrical or magnetic. Systems of massage and acupuncture came from attempts to stimulate or direct these flows.

Water circulates over the earth. From the headwaters to the veins of streams to the great rivers into the oceanic heart. The sky is the artery by which the water flows out, diffuses, spreads to the body in its entirety. The rain and snow collect in lakes. Each lake has a circulatory system. The circulation of a lake depends on where it is. Lakes in the Antarctic, iced over for thousands of years, have subtle currents that change in a yearly cycle: a six-month day, a six-month night.

The plainest circulation is from the inlets to the outlet. Water flows in until the basin spills over. The physical path of the water, drawn down by gravity, forms currents. A lake has more inlets than outlets. Some lakes—the Great Salt Lake or the Dead Sea—have no outlet at all, except the sky.

A more mysterious circulation comes from the properties of water itself. We said that ice is lighter than water. Water is heaviest at 4°C, a point not far above freezing. Why? Because the orderly, square-dancing structure of ice collapses with heat. Think again of dancers neatly spread out in a hall, moving in rhythm. When somebody yells "Fire," they all dash for the door, crowding together: they become denser. This is what happens to water molecules upon melting, occurring most intensely at 4°. For water, 4°C is the crowded door.

As water warms above 4°C, it grows less dense, so it rises to the surface while the 4° water sinks. But colder water, between four degrees and freezing, is also lighter, which explains the circulation of these high lakes. As the solar heat lessens and the air grows cold, the surface water chills to 4°C and sinks, displacing the less-dense water below. That water rises, and in turn is cooled to 4° and sinks. It does this whether it is warming to 4° after melting out, or cooling to 4° in the frosts of September. A windstorm or a heavy snowfall hastens the cooling process. Driven by the energy released as the temperature gradients lessen, the lake mixes, becoming one again.

So our lakes circulate twice a year, once after thawing and again before freezing up. For years I heard talk about the lakes turning over, but I never knew the story until I found out about thermal stratification and density change, about hydrogen atoms, water molecules, and the latent heat of fusion. Molecular structure and thermodynamics are keys to great realms of understanding.

In my mind, the grace of science is in description, not in manipulation. It's like an intricate, evolving legend that is marvelous and yet visible, tangible, present. I have never seen angels, but I watch the lakes turn over every fall. If science is good for anything, in the longest run, it is this: we can tell beautiful stories that are also true.

Jim rows the boat. The wind sweeps us down the lake, clouds dropping again. I look up at the peaks that will look much the same when the next hundred generations have passed, if there are that many. There are gray halberds, cleavers, great granite chopping blocks, joined by crenellated walls. There are spiked gendarmes carving the clouds, and onionskin slabs, planed and polished, resisting the light. I look at the walls above us—the mark of the glacier is clear—the ice came so high. The steep walls loom, huge as fear. Above, there are gentler angles, furtive greens seen through breaks in the storm, a lost, high plateau of *felsenmeer*, "sea of rocks" in German. There are broad, lonely plateaus east of the Divide, paved with rock, plane enough that they haven't been subjected to the violent erosion of ice and snowmelt. There were bighorns up there, seen until about 1960, but no more. Hunted out? It's more likely they caught pinkeye from their domestic cousins and died, like the Mandan, the Blackfeet, and the Shoshoni, of epidemic disease.

We gain the deepest part of the lake. I line us up between a huge boulder to the north and a spring that blackens the talus on the south. I lower the thermocouple and note the temperature—8°C at the surface, 8°C at ten feet and for the next forty feet, and the same to sixty feet, where the thermocline is breaking down. Then 6°C, 5.5°C, 4.5°C. The lake is not fully mixed, not quite cold enough to circulate. I have to take a deep sample. I lower the Van Dorn bottle, slot the brass messenger over the rope, let it go, feel the distant click as the bottle seals. Jim rows hard to keep us vertical, over the line. The wind plucks at us, then climbs a wall, the cloud forming a hundred yards above our heads, the snow beginning again.

As air rises, it cools: this is known as the adiabatic lapse rate. It cools about 3.5°F for every thousand feet. This owes to the lapse in pressure, which is why an aerosol can feels cold soon after losing its contents.

Cold air holds less moisture. Rising from the sea up the west slope of the Sierra, it sleets and hails, brushing the sugar pines, rattling the leaves of manzanita. Clearing the crest, it snows hard, in big, moist flakes, sometimes several feet in a single storm. Dropping from the Sierra crest into the Great Basin, the air is pressurized and it warms. It holds its moisture until the next range of mountains pushes it up. Each range of mountains casts a zone of dryness to the lee, known as a rainshadow. The heart of Nevada is tiger striped with ranges of mountains, each standing above a rainshadow desert to the east.

Since the Great Basin is hedged with north-south ranges, the air rises and falls repeatedly before it gets to the high interior and breasts the Rockies. The successive ranges comb water from the sky until little remains. Still, the Wind Rivers collect five to ten times the water that falls in the valleys at their base, casting a broad rainshadow over the Great Divide Basin and Wind River Valley.

I drop the plankton net and haul it back. Once, twice, again. Jim's face thins out, with the discipline of oars and storm. It's getting colder. I try to make every move count, to keep the pencil in my freezing fingers, not to drop the bottle caps into the lake. The snow thickens until the slopes above the inlet fade out.

On these Divide peaks, most of the year's water comes as snow and is held high against gravity's insistence. The combined temperature and elevation at which snow accumulates faster than it melts is called the firn line. Much of the Wind River crest is above this line, accounting for the active glaciers under the Divide, which lately are receding faster than they build. Below the firn line, the meltwater forms streams and lakes.

I finish the deep samples, letting the spurt of water from the Van Dorn sampler rinse each bottle, then fill it. Jim hauls for the shore as I fill the surface bottles, rinsing each one three times, holding it a half meter down for the final draw, hands throbbing with the cold.

"Why don't you wear your wetsuit gloves?" he asks.

"I like to touch the water." He nods, a spark in his eye. At first, he saw me as crazy. Now, he sees something else, feels, I hope, the elemental tug.

We haul the boat up, stack head-size rocks in it against the wind, and hike for the inlet. Snow melts on the rocks as it touches, soft pellets not sticking yet. The ground is still warmer than the air. The water runs from every rock, every leaf, through every porous gravel vein, through every mossy cup, hurrying toward the lake.

The inlet creek is broad and boulder-strewn. Jim crosses, seine flying like a flag, hopping rocks above the clear water. I watch him, teal anorak, camera-strap angled like a priest's brocade, blue wetsuit boots, colors sharp against the somber landscape. The cutthroats have retreated into the lake. Those left in the inlet hide in deep holes next to boulders. Jim leaves wet, black prints on the water-rounded stone. Above the stream there's a narrow band of green, going dark yellow and blood brown—short grass, heath, arctic willow, changing in the hard frost. Above them spreads an infinity of rock. Waterfalls of fractured, frost-wedged stone, between clean buttresses with a pewter shine, the glint and flattening of cloudy light off quartz, feldspar, mica. Colluvium. Rivers of broken rock, unstable, uneasy, fallen by chance into mutual support. The inlet stream is low, the water clear. As Jim seines insects, scrubbing the rocks, the snow begins to stick on the slopes above.

We gather our wet gear, cold seeping into our legs, and trudge around the rough shoreline to the boat. Above us the clouds rise and drop, as flurries of graupel tap our shoulders and then subside. We load the raft and Jim volunteers to row back.

"Thanks, but I need to get the kinks out. I'll pick you up at the usual place."

He hikes west along the edge, then into the fringe of pines. I pull out into the lake, watching the water turn steel gray as the light lowers, as the snow begins again.

Gray rubber boat, sturdy, like a swimming baby elephant, you've been good company these years, on these high lakes. Flow gently, sweet Avon. Curtains of snow waver in the changing winds, flaring and relaxing, each white pellet losing itself in a slight impact, gone into the windy lake, alone no more. I don't mind the cold and wet. By dark I will be warm again. We have a stove and a tent and grain for the packhorses. Another hour or two and I can rest, eat, sleep,

dream. This wind is a fall wind. You can smell the turn of the year in it.

In the next moon, ice forms in the shallows, then in floating plates. When the lake is close to freezing, one still, cold night will ice it thinly from bank to bank. As the sun retreats and the air gets colder, day by day, the thick ice creeps toward the center, altering the lake's color from chilly blue to solemn gray to pure, blind white.

Ice is a membrane between the cold air and the warmer water. It freezes from the top down. In winter, the trout leave the streams for the lakes. The ice cracks, and water wells up through the cracks and freezes. Intense cold penetrates the ice, capturing more water, thickening the ice from underneath. When the ice is thick enough to contain the lake's heat, a snowpack builds above.

In warmer places, some lakes circulate all winter. Black Joe probably has a weak stratification under the ice. I'll never know for sure. I've skied on the lake ice, but what happens under it is a mystery I have no intention of solving. The trout know. Let it be their secret.

A lake is like a living body. Sometimes it looks up, seeing the bright sky and the peaks like a wide, blue eye. Sometimes it rolls and writhes under the wind, furry with spray, roaring in the granite boulders. Sometimes, when the air is quiet, it reflects the stars and holds the full moon like a white thought.

Water curls in its bed like a perfect mother animal, layering its heat, feeding inner multitudes. In September, it turns inward, cooling and circulating as the sun falls, feeling the approach of sleep, reaching a dark equilibrium in every part.

18

As we cross the long meadow of Miller Park, the wind is cutting despite occasional sun. Last night there was a slight fall of snow. Jim and I finished the two lakes in the south end of the range. Today, a week later, Linda hikes with us, leading two llamas packed with our sampling gear. We left the horses in their pasture, nipping the frosted grass. Though there are hunters in the lower country to the south and west, we have heard no shots. I hope that a llama with packs and a blaze orange vest tied over the load can be distinguished from an elk. Years back, a hunter with a moose permit shot and tagged a brown mule without noticing the shod hooves until they were pointed out by a warden. So we stick to the main trail.

The llamas look strange to me, like walking furniture. I can't read them like I can read a horse. They're camelids, distant relatives of the Middle Eastern breeds and perhaps ancestral to them, but adapted to the grassy high elevations and wind on the altiplano of South America. They have been bred for perhaps four thousand years to carry packs. Their wild forebears are smaller, slimmer beasts called *guanacos*. The pattern of their coats, thick and double layered

289

on top, thin on the lower limbs and belly, seemed odd until I saw them lying down.

After a slow folding of front legs, then back ones, their thick hair touches the ground, and they are protected as warmly as in a down sleeping bag. Long hair on the legs would be an impediment in long grasses and thorny scrub. So when they get cold, they fold. But the head, all nostrils, eyes, and ears on a long, well-insulated neck, stays high above the grass and bushes, a conning tower. Jim says that lying down they look like hairy submarines. Natural selection trumps Picasso, as it should.

"Shall we say Lomma or Yomma?" I ask. Linda just finished her BA, with a minor in Spanish.

"Yomma!" Jim insists.

"You get weird looks on your faces when you say Yomma. It's easier to call them Lommas."

Jim and I trot out a few predictable puns. "I've heard those," she sighs, "more than once." As trail-crew boss in the Wyoming Range, she has been using the llamas all summer to pack tools and camping gear.

They are docile but not friendly. They resist being caught and dislike being touched. The more scornful of the two is Jasper, with the eyes of a British diplomat and a profile like a '49 Hudson. They didn't bite or kick or roll when we packed them, but they let out a peevish hum, the two notes wavering at frequencies near but not quite the same. When we pause, Jasper hums again. "Stroke his throat," says Bella Linda, my llama-packing wife.

I do and he stops. His banana-shaped ears ascend. I try rubbing gently under the halter, and his eyes assume the glaze of samadhi. "Don't pet the backs of their necks or the tops of their heads," says Linda as I do both. Jasper jerks away and reverts to displeasure, ears flat, hmmmm, hmmmm.

Bandolero, the larger and calmer of the pair, has a cocoa brown rump and sports a dark patch over his face, which causes him to look like a stretched raccoon. He is tall and lithe compared to Jasper. Linda says he weighs between four and five hundred pounds, while Jasper, dirty white except for a chocolate tail, bulks about three hundred and change. I look at Bandolero. What does he remind me of? Something in a dream? He looks like Anubis. The jackal-headed god of Egyptian tomb-paintings, long ears erect on a strangely upright head. Linda leads them away as I watch, then fall in behind.

From the rear, Jasper resembles an ostrich: he has a bowlegged stance and two-clawed feet that are deeply cloven but not hoofed. Ostrich feet. The hair extends forward on each toe, and the claws are long and polished, while the base of the foot is a divided pad. His tail is fluffy and about a foot long, curling forward as if its main purpose were to tickle. It must protect the tender part from fierce winds.

Catching up, I mention the ostrich idea to Linda, and she tells me that she has also worked with ostriches, which I have never seen except on film. Bella Linda is a woman of unlikely experience. She says that the ostriches were on a game farm in upstate New York where she worked. They could run faster than their keepers and moved their heads quicker than a blink. They had an unerring sense of where your lunch was, in pocket or sack, and would dart their beaks into that place to snaffle the eats.

"Lord preserve us from the Ostrich and the Infidel," I say.

Besides the usual jobs—cooking, waitressing—that women suffer through, Linda worked as a surveyor for a French oil-exploration company. At work, she rode in helicopters, snowshoed, and rappelled off cliffs, which paid well enough to get her nearly through college.

Last night's snow is disappearing fast. The grass has cured to straw gold and the broad-leaved plants have assumed deep gold, russet, sienna, and clove brown: hawk-feather shades. In the timber, the leaves of whortleberry have gone a clear yellow, losing leaves to the mat of pine needles, keeping a few shriveled berries to be plucked by wintering grouse. The dwarf blueberries are a frosty purple, near black, hidden in foliage that has gone from a modest green to a rich burgundy. Tiny blots of purple stain the boulders and weathered stumps, evidence of a berry feast. Berries are seldom abundant in this range, but this year they flourished: whortleberries, blackcurrants, gooseberries, dwarf and bog blueberries. All have done well except the wild raspberries.

We pick and taste as we walk, the clouds racing over us and the wind still cold as the sun nears its height. At Photographer's Point,

we stop and look into the heart of the range, big Divide peaks under a cloudy swell that tells of stronger winds not too far above our heads. I smell the restless air and hope for two good days. Linda hands me the lead and I take the beasts, which are quiet walkers. They lead easily and respond to the slightest pull on the rope, resisting so little that when I turn away, I might be leading two clouds.

We hike through scatters of pine and spruce, feathered with sub-alpine fir, and through rocky glens beside small lakes, green and silver in the shifting wind. Past deserted campsites we make tracks through fresh snow beneath the pines, bright in a shaft of sun. From Barbara Lake, we take the switchbacks down, stepping slowly down the icy gouge of trail, down the shaded slope into the palm of the drainage to cross meadows patched with frost, golden with weathered grass and sedge. We rest and Linda takes the beasts and then we climb contours, winding on a balcony trail through talus, each boulder mixed and swirled with black and gray. There are pikas scrambling in the rocks, speckled round-eared rabbity things, cutting plants for their hidden stacks of hay, carrying sheaves in their distended mouths. One drops its mouthful of grass and buzzes, their alarm call. The llamas jump. Our boots crunch on loose rock until we level off, gaining the heights again.

Leading the procession, I stop and look back. Jim looks grim in sunglasses, that long-jawed, shortstop gaze: anything could happen underneath that brown mask. His red pack frames a turquoise turtleneck and a flowery scarf, which I think may be a token of love. Ragg sweater, camera-strap, limp gloves tucked in his waist belt, then blue shorts and stout jock thighs add up to Jim, pumping up the hill in navy longjohns and good leather boots, a bit wet at the toes.

Leading the beasts, Linda hikes in a green wool logger-check and faded olive pants, the rude pink swooshes on her Nikes leaping out a step beyond her feet. The breast-strap of her pack is black above her breasts. Seeing that I've stopped, Jim stops. He looks up, waiting. She tips her head to see past him. At her back, Bandolero tilts his at the same angle, looking over her shoulder, long ears flicking at every note of wind or pine, every pika's warning bleat.

Over the years, I've worked to shave weight on these trips. My ideal is the coyote, or the red fox: nothing but the body and the senses. Of course we'll never get that far. But the more weight, the more we are tied to vehicles and horses. Little nips and tucks—putting the salt for treating insect samples into the collection bottles rather than into a separate jar, leaving the big green two-burner stove for a lightweight one, finding a tiny digital head to read lake temperatures—each change eases the physical burden of getting in and out. I've been using a float-tube, ten pounds against the sixty for the raft, to take the samples on this lake, which is sheltered and calm compared to the southern ones, where I'd be blown about like a bubble.

The llamas are a try-out, too. I've worked with horses for sixteen years, cowboying, packing, wrangling, rangering, but problems have emerged. Three times each season we return to the same high lakes, where meadows are few. If the horses are tied up, even on a rope highline, they paw. Grazing is so central to their ways that they need to do it, even if they have enough pellet or grain to meet their bodily needs. So I picket them, corkscrewing a metal stake into the soil, on a rope swiveled to a hobble-cuff. They graze around the stake, like center-pivot sprinklers, nipping the grass short to the limit of the rope. I move them two or three times a day, but the meadows get used up fast. Some are starting to show stress.

A horse can carry about 15 percent of its body weight while a llama can easily carry 20 percent or even 25. A llama eats about a third of what a horse does and is more varied in its diet. These two get by on six handfuls of oats a day and discreet browsing— raspberry leaves, a fold of grass, a garnish of willow, and dead pine twigs for dessert. In large herds they would devastate this place, like goats, but in twos and fours they won't. Their unshod feet don't seem to dig pits in wet trails. They can be picketed in open forest or in a small glen. If they tangle, they won't panic and fight like a horse. They'll lie down, mouthing a cud until released. Smaller, neater, and thriftier, they're well adapted to high country.

They're also safer. With fewer ranch kids in the Forest ranks each year, I can't depend on my field assistant knowing horses. Jim tries, but he still can't throw good diamond hitches or predict a bucking spell. Horses are big, with iron-shod feet, and that makes them dangerous. Every season up here there are broken bones— backs, pelvises, thighs—from horsely fits. Lomma, Yomma, whatever. These fuzzballs are safe enough for kids.

The oldtime Forest boys aren't thrilled, since a llama can't be saddled up and ridden. It's not *Western* to walk: not rough and rugged and manly. Instead, you drive the truck to the trailhead, unload the horses, saddle up, and pound off, chaps a-flap. I'm as good at it as anyone.

My great-great-granddad bred fine horses. My great-granddad was known for his love of horses and for his way with them. My grandfather had American Saddlebreds, along with everyday ranch-stock: quarterhorses and big Belgians for feeding cattle with a sled. I have a photo of me at six months, in knitted booties and cap, round-eyed as a baby owl, perched on the glossy back of an American Saddler between my grandpa's huge hands. At four, I'd toss grain under the corral poles and wait for the big Belgians to drop their necks to eat. Then, I'd leap onto a broad, gold back to sit, lie flat, and sometimes fall asleep. I can still smell that oaty musk, sweat and hay and piss rich as ale, and hear the grinding of those teeth vibrating up through the massive spine. Anyone who's lived with horses knows how I feel. The llamas seem not to fit. For now, they're Linda's beasts.

The day holds out a shifting, somber light. We cross a rocky spine and small moraines, then follow a rock-bound swale toward the lake, which opens ahead, a stony, chilly green. Fall circulation stirs up the nutrients and the plankton, churns the finest sediment and diffuses it, and shifts the lake's color from summer blue to solemn green. Reflections of the shoreline's leafy red and gold suffuse the edges, along with silver from the cliffs, softly framing the dark center.

We stand on the edge and I put my hand in. The water's colder, not so clear. Up close, we see the tiny specks of green, the ancestors of all plants, and the kickers and wigglers, the last bloom before the ice.

We met no one on the trail, and there are no camps in sight around the lake. A few climbers may be through, coming or going from the Divide peaks, but they seldom camp here. My sixth sense tells me there is no one else within a mile or so, maybe farther. We pick an easy camp, pocketed in rocks above the shore, and unload, eating lunch as we do. Linda has brought a newspaper and opens it, and the wind lifts an inside page and carries it into a scraggly pine: a strange sound, here, the rattle of blowing paper.

Jim and I load up with snow collector parts and hike off for the high site, five miles farther on. Bella Linda gets up and heaves the panniers around in a show of industry that will dissolve, as soon as we get out of sight, into flyfishing. She promises to have the tent up when we get back. She will, but first things first.

We take a lonesome shortcut, through a narrow gorge, over windy, silver domes, and then walk the long, deserted trail along Seneca Lake: no campsites, not a single tent this late. The lake is a darker green; it fills a canyon carved by ice, then drowned, the deepest of these high lakes. Around it the grass and sedge are sober gold, while the rocky heath is russet, plum, and saddle brown.

Among the boulders grow laurel, wintergreen, dwarf blueberry, grayleaf willow, planeleaf willow, drummond willow, and arctic willow, all giving up their complex harmony of greens for the low plainchant that calls winter down.

We leave the trail and then take the talus pitches, up along the base of cliffs that shear the wind up above our heads. The flower-garden gully has lost all bloom, except a few small, purple asters tossing in the gusts. We top out on the world and look around, drop our packs, and take the snow-filled funnels of the rain collectors down. Watching the Divide appear and fade in rolling cloud, we split the weight and cap the bottles tight. Then we scramble back down to the sheltered bench, which hangs over a lake to the south.

It takes an hour to get the snow collector up and get the cables right. Torn clouds begin to swallow afternoon. I stand a moment, just to say goodbye to the place and give it thanks, and Jim looks puzzled but I don't explain. Then we go, reversing the turns and traverses that brought us up.

Back at camp, Linda has the tent up and some trout as well. We drop our packs and she hugs me, my nose touching her neck below the ear, her good smell rising up. The night comes faster now. The no-fire rule has ended for the season, and we build a little fire with a big reflector stone behind. She splits the trout and fills them with flecks of butter and herbs from a plastic bag. Then she wraps them in foil and rakes hot ash and coals to cover them as I set pots to boil rice and water for tea.

In summer, I don't fish here because I hate to cook trout on a backpacking stove, chopped into small pieces, in a small pot. I only catch what I can eat, so I don't catch many: two or three, and then I leave them alone. I decide to go for a dip in the lake, walking down to a flat rock, piling my clean longjohns, then sliding into the green darkness. I swim out a few strokes, dropping my head under, then gasping and scrambling out, to shiver and dry myself with my dirty shirt.

We eat in the dark and pass a little plastic jug of rum around. The clouds come in low and the wind slacks off. I can hear the llamas stepping softly in the needles, crunching oats and twigs, then bedding down.

Yesterday afternoon, we pulled into the guard station at Elkhart under cold clouds. As we tied the llamas, it began to snow lightly and the wind huffed out of the northwest, an omen at this time of year. Summer storms charge up from the southwest. As summer wanes, the jet stream dips, and the first heavy snows come out of the northwest, riding arctic air. The temperature can drop twenty degrees in less than an hour. In late September and October, I play chess with the weather. Some years, a big September storm can shut the mountains down to travel, putting two feet of snow on the passes. The last few years, we've had this long autumnal grace, light snowstorms to dust the range briefly, and the dawn gleaming white.

I like to wait on our last set of samples until the lakes are mixed, and that requires cold and wind. Wait too long and the big one might blow in, dooming us to either misery or failure. Before the snowpack freezes to the ground, high, sloping granite slabs, like those below Deep Lake, are not good footing. Neither is it rewarding, except as a survival test, to climb from snowbanks into a boat on a big, windswept lake near the freezing point.

The waiting tunes my nerves. Are the lakes cold enough? Is this next big front the shutdown storm? On the last solitary foot trips, I carry a thermometer and dangle it in lakes. I try to catch the chords of the sky, that low tympanic pulse, turning to a minor key. I try to scent that first unmistakable drift of arctic air. In October, in the tent, I wake up at each rising of the wind or when it changes track. The shifts of pressure and humidity are palpable, like the gusts of mood that pass through theater crowds. A snowflake touching down on the fabric of the tent rings like a struck anvil in my sleep.

If I did the job alone, it wouldn't matter: I could keep my pack ready and leave at midnight on a windshift. In some ways, that's what I'd prefer: fast and light and secret. Instead, I have to schedule trucks and get overtime authorized and arrange for pack animals. I have to work around dentist appointments and Columbus Day and mandatory training and Jim's heartthrobs. I have to assemble the right people, the right beasts, and the right stuff, get us poised at the trailhead, and make a fast dash under the weather, hoping the gods don't loose that arctic blast and chase us all back out again.

But I like it. There's something fine and immemorial about

tuning your senses to the heavens, letting the weather flick you like a taut bowstring. It doesn't come overnight, nor easily, but it comes. The hills still ring with shots, but the high peaks have emptied out. In a way, with all these years of being here, they have become part of my mind. There's no mystery in the bond: it just happens, imperceptibly, the way married people come to know each other's thoughts.

The cold is coming and I feel relieved. It smells of letting go and gathering up, of curling into warmth before the nightly surrender. In winter, in sleep, we are our deeper selves. We let our cones fall and our fields nod golden under the long winds. The squirrels complete their caches and grow quiet. The eagles circle while the last red brook trout spawn and then draft south. We let our leaves die into red and fall, and we wait, calm opening in us like a cool, transparent bloom.

Yesterday afternoon, my bones were wired to the wind. We got to the trailhead too late to start out, really. I chose not to head into a potential blizzard and arrive at our ten-thousand-foot lake to make camp in the snowy dark, which I have done before. Instead, I suggested that we snug into the cabin and leave early in the morning. The wind was chill, but it didn't have that arctic edge.

After stoking the woodstove and lighting a lamp, we boiled red potatoes from our garden, grilled rib steaks over coals, and drank a bottle of red wine to celebrate the final lake trip of the season. Jim and Linda talked about Elizabeth, who worked on the same ranger district as Linda. Elizabeth, Yale biologist, Peace Corps alum, pretty as an aspen leaf, had managed to engage the yearning of about half the male population of the Greater Yellowstone Ecosystem. I thought the trampling of the maddened herd would confound Jim's basic aw-shucks baseball-guy shyness, but I misjudged them both. The spark caught and flared, and now they were becoming a couple, forging their first loyalty.

Jim had an odd, unhappy look. "She has a blood disease," he said. "She got it in Africa when she was in the Peace Corps. She caught a lot of things there, but this one hung on. If it goes on, she'll go blind. There's only a few doses of the medicine in the United States. She says she'll have to go to Washington, D.C., for treatment." He lapsed into a glum examination of the fire behind the stove's heatproof window. "I want to go, but then I won't have enough left to make it through my last semester. I lost my scholarship, since with my knee wrecked I can't play ball."

Linda and I looked at each other and started to speak, both at once. I paused and she urged him to go. "If you care about her, then you should go."

I joined her. "The money's not the crux. We'll loan you some, if you need it." She nodded agreement.

He shrugged. "I'll be okay. I . . . wool . . . I just don't know. I've never done anything like this before. I have to think about it." He didn't want to drag it out further. We talked about the coming fall and winter, talked about what seemed like an impending war against Iraq. Like most high-altitude parties, it ended early. I shut the valve on the gas lamp. Jim crept up the ladder to sleep in the loft while Linda and I cuddled in the big bed lit by the flames.

To be married is a fine thing. Reading Thoreau, I always wish that he'll look out of his open door toward the pond and see a village girl raising her skirts over her head and stepping carefully down to bathe. That she'll be a beauty, high breasts shimmering in the reflected light, long muscles in her thighs tensing as she feels the water rise up on her skin. That he'll watch and never make a sound, not find a single word to recollect the hugeness pounding in his chest. That afterward, he'll run, bent low, boots hurrying through the leaves, to intersect the path and come upon her there, just as if he'd never seen what went before. His loneliness is great, and though he partly fills it with his art, it still resounds, a hollow under the roots.

I hoped that I'd meet my love in some such way. I even knew her look. I carved a girl I saw once in a dream, sitting with arms wrapped around her knees, a long, black braid hung down her back. I thought I'd know her name. But Linda was a waitress in a smoky bar, and I played in the band. She stood me drinks and then, after weeks, came to my cabin in the woods. On the rough bench in front of a fire, she pulled up her legs and sat, just as in my dream. But she wasn't my creation. Her hair was bronze, not black, and her name was not the one I thought I knew.

She's all her own, small and stubborn and fierce, and doesn't easily share her thoughts. God's lioness. When I asked her to marry me, I let the dark girl go.

The night is close. No stars. We sit on rocks and tell tales in the firelight, and I try to fix these faces, wife and friend. Out here I never feel like a created thing, an image from any hand. I feel the air around my face, the pull of gravity. There's a stolen grace to these last nights, under the threat of storm, before the snow begins to build. The pleasures, fire and food and drink, also taste of grief: life's short, the season ends. A mouthful of rum burns; you take the bottle from your lips and pass it on. In the aftertaste, you can feel the turning of the earth, the cooling of the hemisphere. Such thoughts come calling in the dark, when the smallest touch of hand to hand is accurate, profound.

The moment breaks. I yawn, then Linda does, then Jim. We crawl into the tent like yearling bears, fat with the summer's foraging, all yawns. The dome tent will hold three and I'm the tallest, so I take the center spot. "Like Jesus Christ between the thieves," I say, and draw twin groans, twin swats.

The next day, after breakfast, I put on long underwear, a sweater, pile pants and then zip the rubber suit. I've lost one wetsuit glove, the left. The clouds are lower, but the snow holds high. Linda laughs along with Jim as I flop down to the lake in big swimfins, wallowing and cursing over slippery rocks, until I settle in the tube and float away, hearing the rocky echoes of their laughter fade.

At the lake's center, I lower cables and call out the temperatures: 7, 7, 7, 7. Then a 6.5. The lake is nearly mixed, cooling. I cast a red and white reflection in the gold-veined gleam. The heath along the shore is mottled like a trout, corn yellow, scarlet, and dark red. The reflection of the shore swims out toward me.

Jim fishes and Linda makes notes in the book. When I finish the temperatures, she watches with a worried air and takes photographs. My left hand hurts, then stops, then goes numb. I feel like the suit is leaking, but it's just the cold boring in where the suit presses tight. I dip water and catch plankton in a net and try to disregard the chill. I have to watch my ungloved hand and consciously renew my grip. From the pines above, the llamas watch me, mystified. They talk it over with their ears.

I plunk my sample bottles in a bag of net. The plankton bottle and the formalin zip inside a pocket, with the plankton net. The

Van Dorn bottle, cursed thing, hangs like a cannon shell to bump my knees. And then there's nothing left to do. I look straight up and check the clouds. The sky is whale-covered, swimming with rounded bellies of cloud, each one lighter at its margin. There's a soft circulation that means the air is below freezing, that the clouds are ice. Snow's coming, but we'll make it out. Hearing laughter, I head back toward the rocky shore.

19

The sky bends over us, responsible,
as our poem bends over the sadness of mankind . . .

Yannis Ritsos, "Protection"

*T*hursday, the moon in her last quarter, wet snow at night and then a daily melt. In Big Sandy Opening we see a tawny landscape, lower aspens half in yellow leaf, upper aspens bare, bone white. Lodgepole forest is the only green, a heavy, formal green beneath the clouds. There's snow in the woods. The two-track road to the Little Lost House is slick. Even with the weight of the cast-iron stove, the tires spin, then catch, then spin again.

We gain the top, back up to the brick-red board shack, prop the screen back, and unlock the white frame door. The cabin smells mousy inside. We pull the old stove out, the damned skinny, narrow-boxed coal burner, ill suited to the splits of pine this country gives. It was probably hauled up from Rock Springs, a coal-mining town back then. The cabin needs cleaning. We scrub the floor, scour the cupboards, and take apart the propane stove, wire-brushing out forty years of grime.

Then, we work on putting in the stove we hauled up. First, the chimney pipe comes down. I clamber up the old green shingles and saw the rivets off, grunting, perched on a mossy slant, crotch hooked round the shaky roofjack to leave both hands for work. Jim worries,

302

then laughs as I begin to sweat and curse, kicking showers of needles off the roof. I wrench the stovepipe free of the jack and toss it to the snow. Whong. Getting off the roof is worse than getting up. We go inside and pull the lower stovepipe out. It's oxidized and gapped open at a joint, a miracle the place hadn't burnt, those dark December nights when John and I stoked up the stove to bursting and watched heatwaves rippling off the pipe.

The maintenance man, who dislikes me, said there's no money in the budget to fix this place. He wants to burn it down, since it lacks running water, a flush toilet, a shower, the "necessary facilities." Out of the truck I take insulated chimney, polished, bright, donated from my stock of idle parts. It fit the old cabin, Rattlesnake Dick's, where I used to live. In it my face is reflected, long and strange, around the chrome radius. When I open my mouth to ask Jim to get the other section, a dark void stretches out. We join the sections, wrestle it up through the roofjack, get it plumb, and drive the screws in tight. I give the shaky ladder one more chance to break, climbing up to cap and guy the top. The ladder creaks, but it holds.

Snow drops in clumps from limbs, spacking on rocks and shingles. Between patches of snow, the ground is wet, the exposures of earth slick, the beds of duff and twigs quiet under our boots. We look out on the broad, sandy meadow below as we work. Since we arrived, no one's passed on the road, no chugging trucks or rattly horse trailers. In the northwest, where this storm came from, the clouds begin to part.

We hunch the new stove out of the truck and lug it inside. It has a long firebox on short legs, made to heat with pine. It looks like a monument, wire-brushed and freshly blacked, but it's not new. It used to heat the log bunkhouse in town that got burnt down by a sad, transient trailer-kid, from a family of oil boomers. Salvaged, the stove sat on an open dock under a brittle sheet of canvas from a worn-out tent, all pieces solid, red with rust, for nearly ten years.

We scrub the steel heatshield, which has a screened-on design, vaguely Egyptian, that you don't see anymore except in junk shops. We can't get all the fossilized soot off. On it, we center the stove and then plug the new black stovepipe into the silver chimney.

Work done, we drag our packs out of the truck and haul the

foodbox inside. It's almost dark, the air chilling fast, a cloud building over us, small flakes coming down. Outside, the old stove sits forlorn, and I lay a piece of gray plywood on top so that it won't get wet. Then I go in.

I heap dry kindling over a crumpled page of the *Rocket-Miner*, light it, and hear the draft roar up the pipe. *Yá' át' ééh.* I say it four times.

Jim nods and shakes my grimy hand. From me he's used to words he doesn't understand. He looks satisfied. I slide in two fat bolts of pine and do a little jig around the stove. "No more ass-freezing. In December, I'd get up at four in the morning to start that lousy coalstove and keep it burning until seven, and the air in here would still be below freezing." I crack two beers and pass one to Jim, basking in the sudden heat.

It's dark. In the black-iron pan, fat sausages surface and dive, bubbling in red sauce, as spaghetti coils in a silvery pot. We're each on a second beer: thin stuff. I miss my usual ale, but Jim likes domestic, so that's what I got. None of that dark, outlandish brew. After the meal, he washes the pots while I lounge on the lower bunk, enjoying the warm womb room, the den compleat.

He hangs the lantern from a hook and climbs onto the top bunk, drawing creaks from the steel frame and muffled booms from the hollow wall.

"Wool . . . I'm going," he stammers. "I got the ticket to Washington on my last days off. She said her parents probably won't come, so she'd be alone."

"She'll appreciate it. You'll probably starve this winter, but . . ."

"I know. But I don't want to be in Colorado, worrying about her."

"You're doing the right thing. But you won't be her boyfriend anymore. You'll be her man. I hope the treatment works."

He doesn't reply, but I hear him sniff. I know the sound, when you hold back. I let it rest. I hear him open a book.

I'm trying to read *Walden.* I wore out my first copy, carrying it in saddlebags and packs, but have never read it from beginning to end. I can't read more than a page or two at a time. I can't charge up to it face on and read straight through. I always examine the cover for a while, then circle downwind. I open it at random, read a page, then let it fall closed again. I've seen more of the end than of the beginning.

"I don't think I'll be back next summer," Jim says.

"I'll miss you."

"Wool . . . thanks. Elizabeth wants to get a master's. She's got an offer from Colorado State, a full ride. She'll be working on global warming and waterfowl."

"Counting up the losses."

"Huh?"

"That sounds like something that needs doing."

"I don't know . . . She wants to get a place together. I'm worried about going broke. She's got plenty from her family. I've dated girls, but I never lived with one. Especially like her."

"How about your mother? Sister?"

"Wool . . . You know . . ."

"Get a job first. Then you won't have to apologize. There won't be anything owing from the start, except what you feel."

"Wool . . . Yeah. That makes sense. I feel like I'm losing . . . wool . . . all this . . . what I learned up here. I'd like to come back, but I don't think I will."

I look at the page where my left thumb rests and read aloud.

I left the woods for as good a reason as I went there. Perhaps it seemed to me that I had several more lives to live, and could not spare any more time for that one.

"Who's that? How do you remember all that stuff?"

"I don't. I'm reading it. It's Thoreau. *Walden*."

"Oh. That makes a lot of sense."

"Let's douse the lamp. We have to get up early to make it into Black Joe and set up the snow collector. It'll be snowy up high. You know the drill." I set the book aside and nestle into my bag. Jim twists the black valve on the gas lamp and the hiss dies out. Night claims the room. We go to sleep.

Wind slams the walls. Hard pellets rattle on the stovepipe's cap. I wake up. 2:14. Another flurry. I sigh and then go back to sleep, breathing myself into the dark. No thoughts. Morning will be soon enough.

We rise early, hike up to Black Joe Lake, and set up the snow collector. The clouds are close to our heads, heavy with snow. There are no tracks along the trail, but crossing it are the prints of deer, elk, marten, coyote, fox, and squirrel. We load the funnels and bottles of the rain collector into our wet packs and start back down. The Divide is hidden by streaming cloud, like a reef in a gray channel. Only the lichens are bright, on the wet flanks of snow-capped boulders, soon to freeze. Above the creek, thick bluebells are dying under new snow. The leaves clutch at our boots and leave them wet. The weathered log spanning the creek is wet, with new snow melting on it. In turn, we inch across, the creek dropping away below us, making a hollow thunder in the broken stone.

Time to leave. Jim and I tramp between the cabin and the truck, loading packs and stowing samples, covering them with a tarp. The snow is continuous, hiding the ground.

Outside, Jim stacked firewood, shoving each piece hard against the west wall. When he finished the pile, the top leaned, about to fall, and I said so. I grabbed a chunk to demonstrate and half of the pile came down. "If it falls over, it gets buried in the snow. We have to dig for it." Jim frowned and mumbled. His feelings were hurt. So I apologized.

"It's no big thing," he said.

The wood's restacked, straw-colored endgrain showing bright, the lowest course of bolts three inches from the wall, closing toward the top. The right way to stack wood. I step inside. The squat black stove throws heat into the room, and there's a new clamp around the L-brackets at the ceiling, cinching the insulated chimney against the creep of snow down the roof. Both mattresses are stacked on the top bunk, above mouse-limit. There are two cases of water-jugs, three quarters full, stowed under the lower bunk, waiting to freeze. Two metal cans are stuffed with dry food, just in case a lost soul blunders in, or a big storm traps us here. There are ways of saying goodbye; mine is to put things in order.

Chunks of snow fall from the tops of pines and knock others loose, thumping the shingles, showering to the ground in waves. The sun edges out. Marty mailed a card from the Cascades to say he wants to come back for the winter work. I've already asked John, so I wrote Marty that he'd be the back-up this year. A few days ago he called and acted very hurt. I thought that after taking off to Asia with John's ex-girlfriend he was gone for good. He probably made a deal with John before leaving. He didn't tell me.

So I kept my word to John. Marty will be skid-boy number three, despite pressure from above to give them both the gate—bums, crazies, undependable. I recall the points at which I swore I'd never make another trip with Marty, to suffer his glooms and manias. And then I think of nut-brown ale, of telemarking in the sun. Of the worried tone in his questions about aging, losing love, about never settling down. As if I knew the least.

There's a newspaper cartoon tacked to the white wall, a fat forest ranger in a campaign hat, wobbling on crossed skis. "I'm not very good at this!" he says. Centered above the glass-paned door is a postcard I tacked up ten years ago, two Polynesian girls, bare breasted, holding two flowers, pink with dark red throats, bigger than their faces. I know the message on the other side and the postmark: Hawaii, 1980. *I'm heading back to Wyoming soon, but movin' slow. I ain't been this warm since I left my mammy's tummy. Adios, Mitch.*

Tucked behind the card is the tailfeather of a hawk, a big redtail, picked up sometime, somewhere, on which trail I can't recall. Jim is sitting in the truck. The motor is warm. He's looking toward the house. Before I go, I stand up and say a poem. *Whose woods these are . . .* Water. Sky. Mountains. The strong spine of the world. . . . *I think I know.*

None of this is history. If we stayed in this place all our lives and our children did, and their children, and theirs, then we might begin to know it. Not as wilderness, but as life.

There would be stories, at first of ancestors, then of spirits. In the stories, each of us would change. We would accumulate memory, gather event and misfortune until we had something to teach. Marty would be the warrior, the contrary, always in haste. John would be the ever-hungry Don Coyote. Jim would be the farmer's son, handsome and good hearted, and Elizabeth the king's bright daughter. Cheryl, taking the shape of what she feared, could be the Bear. Bella Linda would be the woman with lion-colored hair, a cup in one hand, in the other a spear. And I could be the fox.

Downed lodgepole makes a good seat, once I sweep off the snow. The bark on top is nearly black with moisture, which streaks the reddish brown sides and drips from the bottom. This is the middle country. October, now, almost winter. On the peaks, the snow is too deep to hike. Here, there's two inches of snow on the forest floor, half-new, more in the meadow I just slopped across under an indecisive sky.

Jim's gone to Colorado, and then will leave for Washington. I'm resting, on my way out. I just set up the Indian Park Bulk Deposition Collector, which is actually in Dead Horse Park. It's late afternoon, quiet, verging on cold. The lodgepoles are like columns in a roofless temple, abandoned to the weather. But it's not a temple. The trees are imperfect, some diseased, burled, marred by knots, galls bulging along their trunks.

There's no center anymore. Not Washington, nor New York, nor San Francisco. Something's broken: a root, a chain, a promise? There's no axis, no heart from which salvation can flow, no common shrine. Believe what you see, prophecy, entropy, chaos, and where you are, and the air you breathe.

Above my head, squirrels chat and skitter. A bird calls. Townsend's solitaire. The wind rises, and clots of snow slide from branches and sound like distant hoofbeats as they strike. The wind exhales and subsides, the pines creak. Squirrels are cutting cones, which racket in the deadfall or pock down in the snowy duff. The new-fallen cones are tea brown; old ones, silvery gray. Each squirrel has a cache dug into the soft ground under the pines, full of cones to be dug up and picked open through the winter. Bears dig out the caches to perfect their winter fat, but lodgepole seeds are not as rich as those of the whitebark pine. So the bears move higher to raid caches; the big thieves rob the little ones, high in the rocky breaks where the whitebarks thrive.

After the frenzy of the summer, this is a natural way to spend late afternoon: not worrying, not planning, not straining to sense the next curve of weather or the next mishap. I'm not dodging the consequences anymore. I have no schedule.

The sky is dimensionless, rolling and shifting. Fugitive breezes track the grove, each gust distinct. A wind passes left, then one to the right, then a big one, dopplering down like a blue train, whooshes around each pine, to slap cold in my face. Snow tumbles

from above to spatter like a dropped washcloth. Around the boles, the snow's melted back. The air may be cold but the ground is still warm, the forest floor strong and saturated, rich with predatory colors, needles rusty, leaves oxidized rose. Broken branches lie stacked and strewn, their wood black, gold, lead, white, blue, bearded with lichen, softer as each snowpack bears down.

In 1973, when I spent my first season up high in the Salt River Range with Mitch, I looked for lessons in the woods: metaphors, haiku, parables. I have notebooks full of them. Now I just look. I want to stay exactly here, inside the truth. The woods have nothing to teach, nothing more than the city or the joining of bodies in the dark: nothing is in vain.

I think about the lone track I saw: a fox? I've seen coyotes too, up high in winter. But the pads were indistinct, guarded by thick hair. I see a fox, but it was acting as no fox should. It struck out across the frozen lake, an opening so wide and bright it frightens me. A fox seeks forest, thicket, hedge, brush, tall grass: shelter from the open sky. But someone else, with notions based on the human mass, knowing nothing of my heart, would never find sense in my track. Years ago I saw a fox up high, running on the wind-scoured snow, away from us, hard up toward a pass where everything was bright, open space, exposed.

Snowflakes spin down the river of air. Saying nothing, looking around, I open like a hand in sleep. In a century, you'll find me quiet, a stranger in the city of trees.

A lone fireweed stands apart, magenta blossoms shorn by the September wind. When flowers go, and the green, the dying leaves take on clearer colors: scarlet and hot gold. Then they slip toward gray, memory folded in their leaves. The forest floor is a grave, live trees standing with the dead, all propped and shattered round their feet, jutting like the broken legs of horses or the spears of fallen men, a grave and a seedbed.

A shot. Far below, to the west. The hunt.

I feel like I'm waiting for someone to catch up. But I'm coming out of the mountains. No one follows. Soon, the wind will rise. The clouds will open like a black bear's eye. First one star, than a handful. The night sky opens on infinity, colder than all imagination.

Silence, then another gust. A raucous cry nearing to the thresh of wings between the trees, again the ragged voice, *Keeee-awwww,* the black swim of pinions, spreading as the raven beats up the wind, a fleeing shadow, dark as a rip in the world, tipping past each heavy trunk to hold a course northwest.

Gone.

There's no one following my tracks. I can sit here as long as I want. I can sit here until I'm too cold to think. I can sit here until the choice is plain. Then I'll take another breath. Then I'll get up and go.

Once more, I'll find the trail back, unlock the truck, drive the muddy road, and join the wet pavement shining in the last light of the west. The sky will grow larger as it darkens, as the earth rolls into its own shadow. There will be no one on the road, so I can leave the headlamps off. Watching the road and the sky, I'll traverse the vast blue loneliness until the glow of town blurs up ahead, heading in toward the huddled light.

After

All of us are still alive, and none of us as simple as this book would have it. John, in an accommodation with Marty, yielded the winter work and became a backcountry ski guide at a lodge in the Absarokas. The guests wanted to ride snowmobiles, so he mostly shoveled snow. He parted with Shana before moving to a job as a forest biologist on the east slope of the Cascades where, among other things, he looks for spotted owls.

Marty and I get along, in our edgy, grouchy way. He still skis like a madman, rails about the ruin of Jackson Hole, and talks always of moving on. He summers now as a wilderness ranger in the Cascades and is trying to get certified as a ski guide in western Canada. In 1990, we got the Forest Service Primitive Skills Award for our low-impact approach to scientific monitoring in wilderness.

Jim got a job with a research institute in Fort Collins, Colorado, studying air and water quality, sticking close to Elizabeth. She finished her master's and has a job offer in Washington, D.C. Jim has applied for a job there with the EPA.

Cheryl is now the hydrologist for the Lincoln National Forest in southern New Mexico, where her husband Lee is an engineer. They have a baby daughter, Jessica. She sent me a *ristra* of fragrant New Mexico chili thick as my leg.

Linda and I still live west of Wind Rivers, in a log ranch house on a dirt road. We work in the mountains, have a big garden, and grow Siberian tomatoes in a ramshackle greenhouse. Last fall, I killed two deer in the rocky hills behind our house. When I went out this morning to split wood, a cottontail watched me from the logpile. There was a great horned owl sleeping in a cottonwood to the north and a cow moose browsing the willows behind the house: our closest neighbors.

The fieldwork goes on. As of January 1992, our field trips have covered over 1,600 miles on skis and another 4,000 miles on foot. This equates to hiking cross-country from San Francisco to New York City, then returning to San Francisco, then heading east again to end up south of Ely, Nevada, on Duckwater Peak at 11,188 feet. Most of our travel is above the 10,000-foot elevation. To date, we've collected around 3,000 lbs. of snow; 600 lbs. of rain; 1,300 lbs. of lake water; and several hundred samples of aquatic insects and plankton from the Bridger Wilderness. The scope of our collections and the integrity of our data have attracted related studies pertaining to questions such as long-term climate and global change.

The events recorded in this book were first set down in pencil, in pocket-size spiral notebooks, at night or during breaks. Early outlines and sketches occupied free weekends and the final draft took shape during two winters. I wrote at a table that I built from a big pine slab found among sawmill scrap. In its center is a rich brown knot the size of my face, which radiates in fine swirls out to join the grain of the trunk. My window looks east to the Wind River Range.

One chapter occurred outside the year I chose to recount. Chapter 16 was written in the summer of 1986, and an early draft was published as "Nightwatch" in *High Country News*, the coyote angel of environmental journals. In 1987 the chapter also appeared in *Western Water Made Simple*, a book from Island Press.

One of my fears—one that kept me for years from acting on my desire to write about the Wind Rivers—is that a book may focus more attention than its locale can stand. Most of the spots named in this book are classified Special Management Areas by the Forest

Service, meaning they are heavily used from mid-July through August. The names and directions are accurate. I thought hard about changing them, but decided—for better or worse—that they are part of the landscape as I know it. As Han Shan said, "Empty names are no damn good."

Since this is a personal work, not an official document, I haven't used our data except in fragments, to convey my impressions. Our collections have been analyzed in detail by the National Atmospheric Deposition Program, the U.S. Geological Survey, the USDA Rocky Mountain Experiment Station, and the Forest Service Aquatic Ecosystems Lab, among others. The reports—with sober detail but few conclusions—are available from the Bridger-Teton National Forest.

In 1991, the snow came heavily into December, then stopped. Marty and I broke the first tracks of the season into Hobbs Lake, climbed in near white-out to the high collector, and skied out in a blizzard. Our sled carved a fourteen-inch groove in the new snow.

In January 1992, when this book was completed, John came back for a last set of trips, and we skied to all the places mentioned in the book. The reconnaissance phase of the project was complete, the data analyzed, and the deposition report in proof. Two of the sites, Hobbs Lake and Black Joe Lake, were to be further monitored while the rest would be shut down.

In January, the sled trail that Marty and I had made in December was still clear. As we skied from our camp into Depression Depression, John and I saw the track of a fox following it. The paw mark was smaller, but this fox, too, had gone at a confident trot, straight in, crossing the wide openings as a fox is not supposed to do. There was no returning set of prints. We followed the fox's track all the way to the frozen expanse of Seneca Lake, where it headed toward the granite highlands, into deeper snow, curving downwind, changing to the trace of a hunt.

Bibliography

Air Quality and Acid Deposition Potential in the Bridger and Fitzpatrick Wildernesses (Assorted papers on geology, limnology, aerometrics, vegetation, fisheries, plankton, etc.). USDA Forest Service, Region 4, Ogden, Utah, 1984.

Arno, Stephen F., and Ramona Hammerly. *Timberline: Mountain and Arctic Forest Frontiers.* Seattle: The Mountaineers, 1986.

Bly, Robert. *Selected Poems.* New York: Harper & Row, 1986.

De Voto, Bernard. *The Year of Decision, 1846.* Boston: Little, Brown and Co., 1943.

————. *The Course of Empire.* Boston: Houghton-Mifflin, 1952.

Dorn, Edward, with photos by Leroy Lucas. *The Shoshoneans: People of the Basin Plateau.* New York: William Morrow & Co., 1966.

Frison, George C. *Prehistoric Hunters of the High Plains.* New York: Academic Press, Harcourt Brace Jovanovich, 1978.

Frost, Robert. *The Poetry of Robert Frost.* New York: Holt, Rinehart and Winston, 1967.

Galbraith, Alan, and Sidney Stuart. *Acid Deposition in the Wind River Mountains: Air Quality Related Values Report #1.* Bridger-Teton National Forest, Jackson, Wyoming, 1985.

Galbraith, Alan, Cheryl Harrelson, and Chip Rawlins. *Acid Deposition in the Wind River Mountains: Air Quality Related Values Report #2.* Bridger-Teton National Forest, Jackson, Wyoming, 1992.

Gates, David M. *Climate.* New York: Harper & Row, 1972.

Haines, John. *Living Off the Country: Essays on Poetry and Place.* Ann Arbor: University of Michigan Press, 1981.

Halfpenny, James C., illustrated by Elizabeth Biesiot. *A Field Guide to Mammal Tracking in North America.* Boulder, Colorado: Johnson Books, 1986.

——— and Roy D. Ozanne. *Winter: An Ecological Handbook.* Boulder, Colorado: Johnson Books, 1989.

Holthaus, Gary. *Circling Back.* Salt Lake City: Peregrine Smith Books, 1984.

Huntford, Roland. *The Amundsen Photographs.* New York: Atlantic Monthly Press, 1987.

Kelsey, Joe. *Climbing and Hiking in the Wind River Mountains.* San Francisco: Sierra Club Books, 1980.

———. *Wyoming's Wind River Range.* Helena, Montana: American Geographic Publishing, 1988.

Limerick, Patricia Nelson. *The Legacy of Conquest: The Unbroken Past of the American West.* New York: W. W. Norton & Co., 1987.

Love, J. D., and Ann Christiansen. *Geologic Map of Wyoming.* U.S. Geological Survey, 1985.

Lovelock, James. *Gaia: A New Look at Life on Earth.* London and New York: Oxford University Press, 1987.

———. *The Ages of Gaia: A Biography of Our Living Earth.* New York: W. W. Norton & Co., 1988.

McNeley, James K. *Holy Wind in Navajo Philosophy.* Tucson: University of Arizona Press, 1981.

Marchand, Peter J. *Life in the Cold: An Introduction to Winter Ecology.* Hanover, New Hampshire: University Press of New England, 1987.

Ponting, Herbert George. *Scott's Last Voyage, Through the Antarctic Camera of Herbert Ponting.* Edited by Ann Savours. New York: Praeger Publishers, 1974.

Potkin, Michele, and Larry Munn. *Subalpine and Alpine Plant Communities in the Bridger Wilderness, Wind River Range, Wyoming.* Dept. of Plant, Soil and Insect Science, University of Wyoming, and Bridger-Teton National Forest, undated circa 1988.

Reader, John. *Man on Earth.* Austin: University of Texas Press, 1988.

Ritsos, Yannis. *The Fourth Dimension: Selected Poems.* Boston: David R. Godine, 1977.

Rogers, Eugene. *Beyond the Barrier: Byrd's First Expedition to the Antarctic.* Annapolis: Naval Institute Press, 1990.

Rosenberg, Robert G. *Wyoming's Last Frontier: Sublette County, Wyoming.* Glendo, Wyoming: High Plains Press, 1990.

Sale, Kirkpatrick. *The Conquest of Paradise.* New York: Alfred A. Knopf, 1990.

Seinfeld, John H. *Atmospheric Chemistry and Physics of Air Pollution.* New York: John Wiley & Sons, 1986.

Skinner, H. L. *Only the River Runs Easy: A Historical Portrait of the Upper Green River Valley.* Boulder, Colorado: Pruitt Publishing, 1985.

Stegner, Wallace. *Beyond the Hundredth Meridian: John Wesley Powell and the Opening of the West.* Boston: Houghton-Mifflin, 1954.

———. *The Gathering of Zion: The Story of the Mormon Trail.* New York: McGraw-Hill, 1964.

——— and Page Stegner. *American Places.* New York: E. P. Dutton, 1981.

Stevens, Wallace. *Collected Poems.* New York: A. A. Knopf, 1957.

Steward, Julian H. "The Great Basin Shoshonean Indians: An Example of a Family Level of Sociocultural Evolution." In *The Theory of Culture Change.* Urbana: University of Illinois Press, 1955.

Thompson, Craig, and Charles M. Love. *Reconnaissance Survey: Trace Metals Concentration in Wind River Glaciers.* Rock Springs: Wyoming Water Research Center, 1988.

Trenholm, Virginia Cole, and Maurine Cowley. *The Shoshonis.* Norman: University of Oklahoma Press, 1964.

Trotter, Patrick C. *Cutthroat: Native Trout of the West.* Boulder: Colorado Associated University Press, 1987.

Wetzel, Robert G. *Limnology.* New York: Saunders College Publishing, Holt, Rinehart and Winston, 1983.

Zwinger, Ann H. *Run, River, Run.* New York: Harper & Row, 1975.

——— and Beatrice E. Willard. *Land Above the Trees: A Guide to the American Alpine Tundra.* Tucson: University of Arizona Press, 1988.

Translations of poems and songs in the text are remembered versions, or are based on the scholarship of D. B. Shimkin or Molly Stenberg (Shoshoni); Lawrence Millman (Greenland Inuit); Arthur Waley, Burton Watson, Gary Snyder, Red Pine, Paul Kahn, Arthur Tobias, James Sanford, J. P. Seaton, and Li Pin (Han Shan); Rae Dalven (Yannis Ritsos); and Sam Hamill, Cid Corman, and Kamaike Susumu (Bashō). The versions in this book have, in many cases, been revised by the author and do not reproduce any single published version.

Index